D0489171

TRUNK MONKEYS

**THE LIFE OF A CONTRACT SOLDIER
IN IRAQ**

TRUNK MONKEYS

THE LIFE OF A CONTRACT SOLDIER IN IRAQ

LEWIS STEINER

FONTHILL

Fonthill Media Limited
Fonthill Media LLC
www.fonthillmedia.com
office@fonthillmedia.com

First published in the United Kingdom
and the United States of America 2014

ISBN 978-1-78155-220-9

Typeset in 10/13 Sabon
Printed in England

Contents

Foreword

This book is a violent warts-and-all account from the entrails of the massive army of unregulated and ill-served western 'mercenaries' who were hired by governments, corporations and conventional armies to do the jobs they couldn't or wouldn't do. This horrid but true account opens a window on a vast element of recent western military intervention that is rarely told.

Jon Snow, April 2014

Introduction

The invasion of Iraq as part of the 'War on Terror' will directly affect and haunt millions of people for many years to come. This was a ruthless, convoluted and calculated plan to get a country's oil at any cost, resulting in the persecution and displacement of so many of its innocent inhabitants, the justification for which was achieved only by lying to the masses.

Saddam Hussein was the face of evil, but have you ever wondered what was really happening behind the scenes? How defence companies secured lucrative contracts from the US Government, supplying services that the military couldn't or often didn't want to supply? Many contracts were so dangerous that only the lure of huge salaries would ever get the manpower needed to fulfil the companies' commitments. The promise of these salaries attracted people from all over the world, and the one thing that we had in common was our military background. Some were professional, while others used the opportunity to get as much trigger time as possible. My own beliefs were tested to the very edge, and all the things that I had lived my life by, such as honour, courage, humanity and decency, would be challenged daily.

Trunk Monkeys: The Life of a Contract Soldier in Iraq is not just another book selling the war in Iraq; nor is it hero-mongering by recounting ambushes and near-death experiences. It is the real and raw uncensored account of what it took to accomplish and secure the ultimate goal of war against terror.

We fought a war that knew no restraint and showed no mercy. Are you ready to read the real story?

Lewis Steiner, April 2014

1

Back to the Sandpit

Fear. I feel uncontrollable terror. Not a feeling that I'm familiar with, but it's there. I'm sure that I'm falling and the noise is unbearable— a penetrating scream that is as much inside me as around me. I'm between sleep and consciousness. After a deep breath, I force my eyes open and the memories flood back. I know where I am, why I'm falling and why it's so bloody noisy.

I'm crammed into a Hercules C-130 J transport aircraft, the workhorse of the RAF. I know it's a C-130 J because the ex-Para train-spotter that I'm travelling with has already told me several times. Also with me are a few dozen assorted contractors, military personnel and government types. I'd dozed off before leaving Kuwait, and judging by the sound of the screaming engines and the feeling that I'm on a roller-coaster, we're now descending into Baghdad in what feels like a controlled crash in a bid to avoid ground fire. I never liked this part, and over the next several years I would never get used to it. All it would take was one person to throw up and, as with all laws of inevitability, we would all be retching into our helmets.

Looking out of the window I can see a sand-coloured world rushing up to meet us. We're not landing at the airport, which is closed, but at a small airstrip within the sprawling military complex that houses BIAP (Baghdad International Airport). This is located at the end of Route Irish, as the Americans named it, a stretch of road only a dozen or so miles long and linking the Green Zone with the airport. Within months, this stretch of road will be labelled as the most dangerous place on earth. Many people, some of whom are friends of mine, speak of it with dread and loathing;

to travel along it will cost many their lives. Even now, looking back on it, I find it hard to believe that it was that dangerous, but facts and figures don't lie.

With a less than healthy sounding thump, the wheels hit the runway and we're slowing down. The aircraft comes to a halt, the engines slow down to a stop and the ramp at the rear of the aircraft opens, allowing the heat and odour of Iraq to pour into the confines of the cargo area, and even though we're quite far from the city centre the smell and the heat are not pleasant. There's that Third World smell associated with certain countries— those who have been there will know what I mean— and those who have not are best advised to imagine a catastrophic sewer explosion in Victorian London and you're almost there. At least the heat is a dry heat and not that bad. All of our baggage is on a pallet at the rear and we have to wait for a large forklift to take it off before we can disembark. I stagger into the midday heat, removing my helmet and loosening my body armour— the RAF does not allow its military passengers to fly without both just in case.

Looking around, we're on a narrow airstrip only big enough for one aircraft at a time. To one side is a car park full of four-wheel drives, a few dozen people waiting, and a large truck container with 'AAFES' on the side. It has two doors, one in and one out. AAFES, or PX, is the US military version of the NAAFI, a shop for the military where you can buy home comforts. In the British Army, that means soap and Mars bars; however, in the US Army, expect to find 50-inch plasma televisions and just about anything else.

I was working as a security contractor for one of the many private military companies or PMCs that had contracts with the US Department of Defense (DOD). Before leaving London, I'd been given $60,000 in hard cash by the head of HR and told to give this to my country manager on arrival. Being new to the private military, and not wanting to appear green, I had agreed, assuming it was quite normal to smuggle large sums of cash into war zones, and that was that. I'd just spent twenty-two years in the British Army and how different could it be? Everyone that I'd be working with was from an ex-military background, so it should all be good, right? We will address this later, as the truth is stranger and a lot more confusing than fiction. Indeed, it would almost destroy my lifelong love for all things military— honour, discipline and loyalty. These would become just words, and money, politics and backstabbing would become the norm.

I retrieved my bag and walked towards the car park to find an almost comical scene of men in cargo pants and short-sleeved shirts standing next to Toyota Land Cruisers holding cardboard signs with the name of the company they represented, such as Armor Group, Control Risks and Britam. The list was and still is pretty endless— companies started by ex-SAS men trading on their fame, or in some cases infamy, and now supplying men and weapons to the highest bidder. I wandered over to the guy holding the correct sign and introduced myself to the representative who stood next to a Mitsubishi Shogun. I couldn't help noticing that it was a petrol version. 'I bet that will go off like a firework when it gets hit,' I muttered to myself. Petrol explodes and diesel burns— important points to remember when driving vehicles that are most likely to be caught by an IED (improvised explosive device). I hoped that I was worrying for no reason; however, that would not prove to be the case. The coming years would be a combination of chaos and negligence brought about by penny-pinching, incompetence and ego on an epic scale.

My rep introduced himself as Dave, an ex-Special Forces signaller who was now one of the many managers making sure that money, equipment and manpower got to the contracts that were in turn making millions of dollars a year for the company. I judged him harshly at the start, purely on the fact that he resembled a ferret. However, in a rare change of character for me (I generally make up my mind pretty quickly on people and hardly ever change my mind) he turned out to be okay and I almost got to like him. Dave opened the back door and I threw my kit inside before climbing into the passenger seat.

'You won't need your body armour,' he said as he got behind the steering wheel.

'Really?' I replied.

'No one wears it. Anyway, the Iraqis love us,' he continued. I did not recall the Iraqis loving us, not in the first Gulf War nor in the latest one. Perhaps I was misremembering, as I heard a psychologist say once.

'Here, take this,' he said, handing me an ancient 9-mm pistol, exactly the same as the then current British Army issue. I nodded as I removed the magazine to check that the weapon was safe and functioning correctly. All of this would be second nature to any infantryman, and it had not gone unnoticed.

'Just left the Army, then?' Dave said, smiling. I nodded. Like I said, I'd already decided that I didn't like him much. 'NSP. We all still do it, although some less than others,' he added.

NSP stands for 'Normal Safety Procedure' and is part of the safe handling procedure for weapons. The first thing that you do when checking a firearm is to make sure that it is safe. Even now, I still do it. You could hand me a spud gun and I would still try to do an NSP on it.

I slid the pistol under my right thigh so that the pistol grip was sticking out, covert but readily available. It was something that I had learned from my time in Northern Ireland, and I look back on those days with something approaching nostalgia. A six-month tour with perhaps one casualty, nothing compared to what we do now. Some people would buy into the whole Catholics against Protestants thing and take sides. We called them plastic spud eaters, some of whom went as far as getting posted to Northern Ireland, usually as a dog handler, so that they could marry some girl and become even more of a loyalist than the head of the Belfast UVF (Ulster Volunteer Force). Personally, I thought it was bullshit. I did not trust a Protestant any more than I trusted a Catholic. And as for dog handlers, I still have not met a normal one.

It took about ten minutes to drive to the gate leading onto Route Irish. We passed dozens of young US military personnel walking around the massive camp carrying greasy pizza boxes and paper bags from Burger King (more about this later). Two Humvees in front of us were turning onto the road leading to Baghdad. Dave overtook them and then floored it. Within seconds we were travelling at close to 100 mph, weaving in and out of lines of very slow moving local vehicles. The road was a dual carriageway consisting of two to three lanes with half a dozen sweeping curves, flyovers and footbridges, mostly flat and featureless and with several built-up areas along the way. I was still trying to act cool as I slowly put my seatbelt on and concentrated on where any possible threat might come from. It was and still is a very fast road.

'It's a bit late so I'll take you straight to the hotel. Everyone else is there,' Dave said, casually lighting a cigarette while driving like a madman.

'Okay,' I replied. I had only had my interview in London three days previously and had been given hardly any information about the contract. I knew it was a US military contract, as most were in those days, and that most of the manpower had already deployed; however, the contracts had not started yet, as I was about to find out. The hotel housed some sixty contractors who were waiting around to start work. In less than fifteen minutes, we were approaching a checkpoint.

'I'm going to go through the Green Zone. It's quicker than going round Baghdad. Get your passport out,' Dave said. He was flicking through a clear plastic wallet with several ID cards, and the one he needed was the Department of Defense ID, or the DOD card as it was known. This was issued by the US military and gave you access to everything from dining facilities to the main palace that was at the heart of the Green Zone. This housed all the various military and civilian departments which controlled the area and was also known as the Coalition Provisional Authority or CPA. Most importantly, however, you would be treated as if you were a member of the US military by the military medical services.

Two armoured personnel carriers (APCs) blocked the road with mounted .50-calibre machine guns pointing at us. We slowed down and showed our ID (in my case, just my passport) to the soldiers at the checkpoint after explaining that I'd just arrived and that I was going to the DOD office to get my passes. After a thorough examination, we were allowed to enter.

'We'll come back tomorrow for your DOD and CPA pass,' Dave informed me.

The first thing that struck me was the lack of Iraqis— everyone here was from the US military, and dozens of Humvees, tanks and APCs were parked along the road. The Green Zone was approximately half the size of Baghdad International Airport and housed many of the Baghdad military units that had taken over from the old Iraqi Army that was now long gone. It consisted of wide roads, former army barracks and military buildings, some of which had been destroyed by Coalition airstrikes during the invasion. The Republican Guard Headquarters, probably the most famous and impressive building, now appeared as if it had been it hit by half a dozen JDAMs (Joint Direct Attack Munitions and a guidance kit that converts unguided bombs into all-weather 'smart' munitions) and Tomahawk missiles.

The zone backed onto the banks of the Tigris and was surrounded by high blast walls and several heavily fortified checkpoints. A battalion of US military personnel was tasked with manning the checkpoints and providing security. The former palace, Saddam Hussein's hangout, was surrounded by more security, and when I was there, several companies of Marines had the fun job of protecting the people who worked there. As we drove towards a checkpoint I started to see Iraqis, as well as a small bazaar and several blocks of flats.

'What's the score with those?' I asked.

'Hajjis who used to work here were given flats. Most of them are still here and now sell rubbish to us lot,' he answered.

Hajji is an honorary title given to a Muslim who has successfully completed a pilgrimage to Mecca, but to us it was a generic term for anyone who was not one of us, and was a possible threat or target. We drove through the Green Zone and out into the local traffic. It was a lot calmer than the airport run and we blended in with everyone else; again, this was something that would soon change, just like the body armour and helmets on the back seat. The drive was uneventful and as we drove over a bridge we passed two buildings that had been hit during the airstrikes. One was badly damaged, but the other only suffered from a collapsed floor— what's known as a surgical strike. We stood out from the locals in our new and shiny four-wheel drive, surrounded by battered old cars and plenty of taxis. The latter, white with their wings painted orange, often picked up several fares at once. We approached a large roundabout that had lots of cars parked around it and vehicles going in every direction. There were two Humvees and a small US patrol standing guard. Many of the locals waved and hooted their horns at the Americans, and several waved at me enthusiastically.

'See, they love us!' Dave grinned.

'That will change,' I said under my breath. I felt highly vulnerable with nothing more than a pistol as protection from the 7,000 civilians who would probably be happy to see me hanging from a streetlight. We fought our way through the roundabout traffic and turned off the main road into a side street. The main roads were quite wide and crammed with all sorts of traffic (think rush hour in Mumbai and you have a good mental picture) and did not feel dangerous. To be fair, it would not start to get that way for a while, as the locals had been given freedom only a few weeks earlier and were still coming to terms with it. All along the street, shops were selling satellite dishes and televisions. I had done my homework and knew that satellite television was illegal under Saddam Hussein's regime. Helicopters would patrol the skyline on the lookout for dishes and if you were unlucky enough to be caught, you and your family were most likely to 'disappear'. Most dictators, such as Kim Jong-un of North Korea, like to keep the population ignorant of the outside world, and Iraq was no different. None the less, there was a growing interest in satellite dishes so that the populace could see what was happening elsewhere, as well as wanting a Big Mac and a Chevrolet. The public were experiencing a crash course in consumerism and were waiting for the Americans to deliver it gift-wrapped to them. Of course, when they realised that this wasn't going to happen, it was time to get the trusty AK-47 Kalashnikov out from under the bed.

Passing more side streets and groups of people standing around with nothing to do, we approached a makeshift barricade at the top of a narrow street that was defended by two locals armed with rifles. Dave didn't appear to be bothered, so I assumed we were safe as they recognised the vehicle and opened the barrier, waving us through. On the left was a two-storey hotel (not the Hilton, but not bad either), with a fleet of shiny new four-wheel drives of all makes and models parked outside.

'This is us,' Dave said as he climbed out of the vehicle. I tucked the pistol into the waist of my trousers and climbed out. Dave was already unloading my kit from the rear and I grabbed the rest.

'Follow me. I'll introduce you to the rest of the gang. Oh, an important point to remember is the local off-licence. Everything is $5. A crate of lager or bottle of spirits, it's all $5,' he said, pointing to a tiny shop directly across the street.

'Don't the locals have a problem with alcohol?' I asked.

'No, this is a Christian area. Besides, even the Hajjis like a drink round here.'

We dragged my stuff into the hotel and Dave spoke to the receptionist, a tall and attractive woman in her early twenties. She gave him a key and seemed as friendly as a pit bull with toothache.

'Leave your bags here; someone will take them up to the room. Here's the key. Don't worry about this place as it's owned by a very well-connected local family. It's very safe and all the staff are related.' Dave then slyly nodded towards the receptionist. 'And don't even try it on with her. She's the eldest daughter and no one has managed to get a smile out of her yet,' he said as he handed me the key.

'What happens now?' I asked.

'Nothing until tomorrow. I'll come back here about ten and take you to the airport to get your passes. We have a villa just outside the Green Zone, and all the management and kit is there. Once I have you badged up, I'll take you over to meet the country manager and get you your kit, but for now, it's off to the bar. That's probably where everyone is.'

We walked around the corner from the reception into another room. Here, we met around twenty blokes who all looked as if they'd hit a North Face sale and were lounging in a bar that would not have been out of place in a working men's club in the North of England. I quickly scanned their faces and recognised one person, but that was all.

'Everyone, this is Lewis,' Dave shouted above the racket of the ex-soldiers boozing and laughing. They all looked up, greeted me casually and then carried on. At the beginning of the week there had been one or two ex-soldiers, and during the last seven days the assembled group had arrived in ones and twos from different regiments and had got to know each other well.

'I'll see you tomorrow,' Dave said as he headed towards the reception. I squeezed my way through the crowd towards the one face that I did know.

'I heard you were on the way out here,' John Forbes, an old friend of mine, said as I sat down.

'I thought I better had. Can't have people like you raping this country for everything that isn't bolted down,' I laughed.

We'd been in training together and ended up in the same battalion. I hadn't seen him for a few years as I'd been posted outside the battalion, and it was good to have someone that I could trust in an otherwise untrustworthy place.

'Which contract are you on?' I asked.

'DOD, but it's all sorted. You and I are on the same contract. The rest of our team are coming in tomorrow. The rest of these are going all over the country, some to Basra and the rest to Mosul. There will be two teams in Baghdad; that's all we know,' he explained. 'It feels as if the plan was written on the back of a fag packet when I left London.'

'What about weapons and vehicles?' I asked.

'Tell me about it; the whole thing is Mickey Mouse! No weapons or vehicles yet. There's an AK-47 behind the reception desk and the guys on the barrier outside. We were supposed to pick up weapons and vehicles today. I've been here a week and it's been "tomorrow" every day so far.'

'Oh well, I still have a pistol that Dave gave me. I didn't think he'd miss it,' I replied.

'He won't. The villa is full of clerks, storemen and a few Ruperts (officers) who run the show. They've got plenty of weapons, vehicles and a few tons of ammo. And with all the dodgy deals that are going on around them, they only think about the money,' he added.

'Fuck it. I have $60,000 in my bug-out bag,' I said as I opened it and showed him the bundles of notes inside that I was supposed to give to the country manager. I thought that I might see him straight away, but obviously not.

'Don't worry, you'll see him tomorrow, and you aren't the first. There must've been more than a quarter of a million brought in already. Don't get me wrong, we're all going to get paid, but this whole thing stinks. It's all about money and oil,' John said venomously. The table in front of us was stacked with cans of Heineken lager. I reached forward and opened two cans, handing one to him.

'Well, old son, it's just us again. Here's to freedom,' I said, holding my can up.

'Freedom!' John replied as he held up his can, responding to my toast.

'What the fuck are we doing here?' he added while laughing, almost emptying the contents of his can onto the floor in one go.

I spent another few hours in the bar. I didn't intend to get drunk as I didn't think it was the safest thing to do in a country that we'd just invaded and been at war with only a few weeks ago. I did, however, have a few too many, made my excuses and went to find my room on the upper floor. The room was typical of European hotels: clean and tidy with a television, a small balcony and a bathroom with clean towels. I stretched out on the bed and turned the television on. After channel hopping for a good five minutes, I realised that there were over 100 Hajji stations, and all were very strange. I eventually found Ricky Gervais on BBC World, the only English-language channel available, and it seemed odd sitting in a Baghdad hotel room watching it, but in all honesty I find him to be as funny as herpes. I couldn't stomach him, even if his show was in English, so I fell asleep watching an Arabic game show that reminded me of Italian television from the 1970s.

The following morning, and feeling a little worse for wear, I first checked that I still had the money and pistol before staggering into the bathroom. The water was hot, and after an invigorating shower I started to feel human once more. I quickly dressed and headed downstairs. It was still early, and I'd gone to bed when most were still drinking in the bar, so I didn't expect to see anyone. I took the stairs as the lift was very small, probably steam powered, and did not fill me with confidence; getting stuck in a lift in Baghdad would be an all-day event. As I walked into the reception area, a pretty young woman behind the front desk looked at me without expression— another of the hotel owner's daughters. No doubt her family had done well under Saddam Hussein's rule and were resentful of the West's interference. Now she was like everyone else and no longer part of the ruling class— still, that was not my problem. I smiled and carried on through the deserted bar that had been cleared of the mountain of cans from the night before. In the rear was the restaurant, again deserted, and I sat at a table and waited. A young male waiter complete with black trousers, white shirt and waistcoat walked out of the kitchen with a pot and poured a cup of fresh coffee for me. I thanked him and he returned from the kitchen with a basket of bread, fruit and yoghurt and pointed towards a buffet hot plate with silver platters. After eating some fruit, I investigated the buffet with its fried, boiled and scrambled eggs, fried tomatoes and frankfurter-style sausages. I had to laugh, as it was the first time I'd seen a traditional full English cooked in Iraq by Iraqis. I was starting to think that this might be a civilised contract when a flushed and panicky-looking Dave rushed into the room.

'Morning, Dave,' I said.

'Coffee,' he shouted at the waiter and sat opposite me.

'What's the matter?' I asked, with a good idea of the answer.

'Did they give you anything in London before you left?' he enquired.

'You mean the $60,000?' I replied, pulling a wad of cash wrapped within a Tesco carrier bag out of my pack and placing it in front of him.

'Oh, thank God for that!' he replied with a huge sigh of relief.

'I forgot all about it. I don't often get given large amounts of money to smuggle across the globe,' I said as the waiter put Dave's coffee on the table.

'Okay, I'm going to run this to the villa and will then return for you. We'll be going to the palace for your CPA pass and then back to the BIAP for your DOD card. You can't do anything without these and if we have time at the villa for your company ID, I'd like you to meet the team.'

With that, he finished his coffee and was gone as fast as he'd arrived. Dave returned in double-quick time and we headed off to the Green Zone. The roads were very quiet and the drive was almost pleasant. Once again, we had to explain to the checkpoint sentries that I had just arrived and was going to the palace for my CPA pass. They checked my passport and Dave's DOD and waved us through. After a few minutes, we parked close to the palace and walked to a small building nearby where a bored-looking corporal who wore a Rolex Daytona watch took copies of my passport. He also took my picture using a webcam for my CPA pass. I asked if the watch was authentic, to which he laughed and said it was a cheap fake. Within half an hour Dave had processed all the supporting paperwork and we then drove to the BIAP. A complete US military administrative set-up had been installed with office equipment and personnel in one of the many former Iraqi military buildings— everything needed to organise an occupying force. The wait here was far longer, involving fingerprints, photographs and paperwork, but by mid-afternoon I had all the identification that I needed to play my part in Iraq's new future. Dave had a spare wallet for my cards (standard issue for contractors) that was hung around my neck so it was in plain view at all times. The only time I made sure that my cards were not visible was in the Red Zone or civilian areas, so that the locals had no idea as to who I was.

We were on a time frame (schedule) and our next stop was the infamous villa where the management ruled us without having any idea about what we did. We returned to the Green Zone via our normal route, but turned off before the checkpoint into a nice-looking suburb with palm trees and large buildings with high iron gates. Our villa was located here and we parked next to an enormous generator the size of a van; the houses in this suburb had many of these generators, with thick cables running into various properties. The villa was well furnished with whiteboards on the walls on which were various lists of names and locations, and several educated locals were sitting in front of PCs. Told to sit, I was informed that the country manager would be with me shortly. A door opened and a short westerner approached me and introduced himself as Johnny. I was later informed that he was very high up in the SAS, feared and respected by all, but I can't say that I was instantly impressed by his presence. In all honesty, like many country managers I met, he was a politician whose sole responsibility was to make sure the job got done, and most importantly, that the client was kept happy. I was very naïve in my early days. I expected an ex-Army company commander to act like one and support his men in the face of adversity; however, it was all about the money and I never came to terms with it. As I moved up the career ladder, I kept to my military ethos, which probably explains why I spent most of my time feeling frustrated and betrayed. That being said, I can't blame the system.

Dave returned with a large bag and dropped it at my feet.

'This is yours. The others were issued with theirs earlier today. Go through it and if you're happy, you can sign your life away,' he said as he went to retrieve some paperwork from a nearby desk.

I opened the bag and inside was a cheap set of body armour that weighed a ton, an even cheaper helmet, a Heckler & Koch MP5 machine pistol, five magazines and several boxes of 9-mm ammunition. At this point, I will give the reader a very brief ballistics lesson. The MP5, while compact and considered sexy, is a 9-mm weapon which means that it uses subsonic pistol ammunition and its effective range is about 150 metres. That's being generous, and you can forget about penetration or punch. The preferred weapon of our enemy is the AK-47, a rifle that fires a supersonic 7.62-mm round that is effective at a range of 500 metres. In the hands of a skilled user, the AK-47 possesses a very impressive penetration. It doesn't take the brains of a rocket scientist to know that if you're in the desert and the enemy has an AK-47, you'll be seriously outranged and outgunned. I tried on the body armour and helmet, making a mental note to buy my own at the earliest opportunity. It was not the fact that it was cheap (it would do its job), but for me, if you're spending all day wearing the gear, pay more and get lighter and more comfortable kit. As a consequence, you'll be able to fight more effectively. I've spent thousands of pounds on such equipment and, like good tools for a mechanic, it's a worthwhile investment.

Dave returned with the paperwork for me to sign. It was a '1033 pad', a military form that a soldier must sign on receipt of equipment. I had to laugh and wondered what else had been lifted from the Army.

'MP5s ... really?' I said.

'It's a good weapon,' Dave answered defensively.

'Yeah, no doubt if you're storming an embassy.' The MP5 was the preferred weapon of the SAS for many years and is the perfect close-quarter battle weapon.

'What's wrong with AKs? There must be millions of them here,' I added.

'We got a really good deal on these MP5s. For now you'll have to put up with it,' he said.

'Alright,' I replied, signing my name for the kit and once again making a mental note to get my hands on an AK at the earliest opportunity.

I loaded the pockets of my assault vest with the MP5 magazines, stripped down the weapon and checked that it at least had a firing pin. I was starting to feel less inclined to trust my superiors, but for now all seemed okay. Stashing the helmet into the bag, I donned my body armour and walked outside to drive back to the hotel. Dave looked at me quizzically.

'You don't need to wear your body armour,' he said.

'It's easier to wear it than carry it,' I lied as I climbed into the vehicle and slotted a magazine into the MP5.

We drove back through the Green Zone and this time I showed my DOD card to the sentry who waved us through. The military knew there were hundreds of us transiting through or visiting every day, and as long as no one had an accident there would be no rules to enforce. Eventually, loading bays would appear by the checkpoints— sandbagged areas where as a team you unloaded your weapons upon entry or loaded before you went. Again, this is standard military procedure and nothing to complain about. I asked Dave about the contracts, where the rest of my team was, who was going to be the team leader, vehicles, training, etc. I was so busy being proud of my operator status that I failed to notice that support personnel, who we disdainfully referred to as war dodgers, were being paid a lot more than we were. They were the clever ones and I was being a misguided idiot.

It was early evening and I walked back to the hotel where I could hear that the bar area was in full swing. I ran up to my room, dumped my kit and hid the MP5 under the bed. After a quick shower, I went downstairs with the pistol hidden under my shirt and headed to the bar populated by around twelve people, but none that I wanted to talk to. Like civvies, I put soldiers into three categories: uneducated, educated and idiots. Most were uneducated, came from mediocre regiments and constantly tried to outdo each other, whereas others were here to pay off their mortgage or escape from a nagging wife. I was never very sociable or fitted in and definitely did not tolerate idiots. I was, however, in an idiot-rich environment. Just when I was considering going back upstairs, John walked in.

'How did it go today?' he asked while ordering a couple of beers.

'Well, I met the country manager, was issued with a completely pointless weapon and nowhere near enough ammo. And, oh, I was finally given my ID,' I replied, flashing my DOD card that was still draped around my neck.

'Ah, one of the "Johnnies" (there were several managers called John). You should feel honoured. We never see Johnny, and word is he's the dodgiest man in cowboy town,' he said. Cowboy town was a nickname that Iraq was rapidly earning. It was not just the British that were sending in personnel security detail (PSD) teams, the Americans were also doing so and, unlike ours, many were law enforcement types. In the early days, it was very easy to be posted to Iraq, and like the Yanks we had our fair share of dangerous fantasists. It's just that the Americans tend to do things louder and bigger, and seem to get a lot more attention as well as making a lasting impression.

'Have you heard anything about the contracts or the teams?' I asked.

'Nothing yet. I know that we're the only ones on our team so far and that they're going by seniority to decide who'll be team leader. Personally, I don't care about that. I'd rather be a shooter and not have the responsibility,' he replied.

'I'd agree with you on that, mate, but from what I've seen so far, I'd rather be calling the shots on the ground than listening to some idiot who was team leader just because he spent a few days longer in the Army than I did. We both know guys who did serious time in the Army because they knew they were shit and wouldn't last five minutes having to think for themselves,' I said.

I was getting quite worried at the distinct possibility of being evaporated by a roadside bomb because some twat who'd been in charge of the officers' mess had no real operational experience. And before you think I'm being paranoid, that's exactly what happened to another team. A sergeant-major from some Irish regiment was made team leader (TL) and hired his retarded mate, who suffered from deep-rooted and serious psychological problems, as his second in command (2ic). Between the two of them, it's surprising that they didn't get their team wiped out due to their incompetence. It became apparent very quickly that neither could read a map and were constantly getting their team lost. And when given their marching orders to Mosul, which was a seriously dangerous place, both jumped ship for another company. Afterwards, it transpired that the man in charge of the officers' mess was little more than a waiter.

We both stared at our beers for a while. We all had our reasons for being here. I knew that John got bored easily and was on wife number three, so earning a lot of easy money and being away from temptation was a good thing. When I left the Army at the height of the recruitment drive for Iraq, I'd said to several people that I had no intention of getting my arse shot off in Iraq. After the interview in London, I'd found myself getting swept along and before I knew it was at Heathrow getting on a flight to Kuwait. I always considered myself a bit of an adventurer and decided that if it didn't suit me, I'd sack it and move on. Unfortunately, with my Army ethos, I felt compelled to stay even when things became suicidal only because I felt a duty to my team. Yes, I agree it was stupid, but it does help me sleep at night.

'Did you get a pistol?' I asked John.

'No, they're in short supply, although we were told that if we could source weapons privately we could. But it was at our expense and we were to register any weapons at the villa.'

'Well, that's something. All we need now are some AKs, some frag grenades and smoke,' I said, meaning every word.

'There's a guy who comes in sometimes. He's on the Basra contract that's been running for a few weeks. They sometimes bring some hard-to-find items, but it looks like we have to make do with the Pakistani knock-off MP5s we've been given.'

'You're fucking kidding me!' was my reply. I knew my weapons, but John was a total weapons geek.

'Afraid not, old son. Those MP5s are definitely not what they seem. I'm sure they work, but are knock-offs for sure. They're good ones but not the real thing, and without a range to test them on, I doubt we'll get a chance to see what they're like.'

'Don't worry, John. I've no doubt that we'll be finding out if they work very soon. I just hope it's not the last thing that I find out.'

'Well, if it helps, the rest of our team will be arriving tomorrow. We're going to get two vehicles, probably petrol Shogun death-traps, and we'll all be accommodated in the Green Zone within six weeks. There's a waiting list apparently,' he added.

'Ah, the land of the big PX,' I replied.

Unlike here, the Green Zone had many advantages, with gyms, PXs and a million dining halls all run by the Americans for the military. And people like me, who had the all-important DOD cards, felt very safe and secure, with only a small chance of being mortared. Also, no Hajjis were allowed on or near the base. Everyone seemed comfortable in the hotel, but I thought it was a massive car or suicide bombing waiting to happen. Everyone knew we were there, and I didn't care how many times the management told us it was safe. I was rapidly losing any faith in what they said, and all the smiley locals were seriously starting to get to me. I made my excuses early and went to my room where I stripped my weapons and magazines and gave them a good clean. I'd taken lots of military stuff with me, including a weapon cleaning kit— I wasn't sure what would be issued to us, and silly little things like this are important.

The following day, Dave came round and gave me the keys to two of the new Shoguns parked outside. I signed for them and was told that I was the TL and that my three other team members would be at the hotel later in the afternoon. He also gave me two laminated A4-sized cards— one was a US flag and the other a Union Jack— and explained that we'd need these to get past US convoys. I told him that John and I would be familiarising ourselves with the Green Zone. The day before, John had bought a mobile SIM card so that we had a number. I asked Dave what places were best to avoid, and after a five-minute briefing over my map (which I'd brought with me as this was another hard-to-find item) I was like a child with a shitload of new toys and ran off to find John.

Both Shoguns were identical and brand new. We gave them a good once-over and, when satisfied that they didn't have anything nasty or explosive attached, we grabbed our weapons and body armour and screamed off towards the Green Zone where we hoped to indulge in some retail therapy of fast food and unnecessary electronic goods. We drove fast but at the same speed as the locals; as time wore on, we would be less courteous and eventually our vehicles would have bull bars and homemade battering devices welded on. We approached the checkpoint, showed our IDs and were waved through. Once inside, we pulled over, removed our body armour, unloaded our weapons and drove around as if cruising on a Friday night with the windows down.

The Green Zone was roughly 10 square kilometres and housed much of the Iraqi Command and Control network, including the main palace, which had now been turned into the CPA headquarters, the location of the US forces and several other government agencies. The place was very impressive and we were determined to try the dining hall within it. We'd been told that Camp Victory (where the BIAP was) had the best PX and chow halls, as the Yanks called them, but we would try that later. We parked next to the other cars, mostly other SUVs, left the body armour in the car, but took our weapons which were concealed in bags. Everyone had a bug-out bag or daysack— a small tactical rucksack for essentials, and easily large enough to hold our MP5s.

Two very young Marines stood at the entrance checking IDs and bags. We still had our British Army IDs, which would get you into as many places as the DOD card, so we wore them inside our wallets with all the others. Some people seemed to have four or five ID cards. I showed them my ID and opened my bag, and they didn't bat an eyelid at our weapons and let us pass. The interior was an open space with corridors branching off from a central area. There were many ornate gold-leaf sofas, obviously left over from the previous tenant, and to the left was a queue of people waiting to get to the hot plate. At the risk of stereotyping the Americans, there was a massive selection of fast, greasy food, including pizzas, burgers and a huge selection of cakes. I'd been attached to the US Army during my military career, so was not surprised; however, John was astounded at the selection compared to what we got in the British Army. But to be fair, we still had the Catering Corps, which is a regiment and therefore runs along military lines. If an Army doctor or lawyer was that good, they'd be working in a private practice, and the same goes for the Army chefs. On the other hand, the Americans paid private companies like KBR (Kellogg Brown and Root) to handle their feeding requirements and they ran it along civilian lines. And in typical American fashion, the food was superb and available in massive quantities. I have to say that the food was really good, and Iraq was one of the few war zones I've been to where I put weight on. In the early days, that is.

We'd sat down at an empty table with far more food that we intended to eat and were slowly chomping our way through our monstrous lunch when I heard a commotion to my left. Looking up the long corridor that stretched off from the main area I could see what looked like a scuffle taking place, with several uniformed and non-uniformed men rolling around the floor. The culprits were a unit from the Australian Special Forces and Paul Bremer's Blackwater CPA team. Bremer, who ran the CPA for the Yanks, had his own team that waited outside his office. On this occasion, they were in the process of clearing the corridor so that Bremer could visit the toilet. Unfortunately for them, four members of an Australian Special Forces unit were walking down the corridor and took offence at having weapons pointed at them and being physically pushed back by civilian CPA operators so that Bremer could have a piss. A fight broke out and, needless to say, Blackwater came off worse and the unrepentant Aussies went back to their lunch. Over the next few years, I had a few run-ins with Blackwater operators, who seemed to have been recruited from the worst elements of American society. While there were many decent US companies and operators, I have to say that people only remember the worst examples.

We finished our lunch and headed off in search of the PX. We looked around the Green Zone for an hour or so, found a gym and a couple of smallish PXs, but none satisfied our retail needs. I had seen the one at Fort Benning in Georgia and it was impressive— the holy grail as far as I was concerned.

'Why don't we go to the PX at Camp Victory? We can get a burger for dinner and we won't have to eat at the hotel,' John suggested.

'What about the rest of the team? They might be there by now,' I replied.

'You're the TL,' he said, laughing.

'Fuck it, you're right. If they can't handle being on their own for a few hours, then they shouldn't be out here.'

We went and found our car and, in the spirit of adventure, headed out onto Route Irish. It was still fairly quiet and within a mile or so the traffic had backed up to a slower pace. We weaved our way through and, nearing the front, I could see a US Army Humvee approximately 100 metres ahead. This was followed by a Rhino, an armoured coach that ran between the Green Zone and the BIAP, taking CPA officials to the airport for leave purposes and collecting people coming in. I'd been warned about US convoys, and in the turret of the Humvee was a gunner who operated a .50 machine gun. A sign in English and Arabic clearly warned that those who approached any further would be shot. This was not usually a problem, but the US military adhered to a strict 55 mph speed limit and it could take a long time to get to your objective.

'Shit. Now what?' John said.

'Well, there are these,' I said, pulling the two A4-sized cards out of the glove box. I stuck the US flag against the inside of the windscreen and waved the Union Jack out of the window. We were waved forward and came to a halt 10 metres from the Humvee, the gunner keeping his .50 trained directly at us. I could see him talking on his radio and after a minute or so he waved us on and we slowly overtook the convoy, waving and smiling at the Yanks as we went past. As soon as we were clear, John floored it again. This high-tech solution of printed flags is how we would overtake US convoys. The only problem I encountered, however, was that rear gunners— or trunk monkeys— occasionally failed to recognise the Union Jack, and I was once asked why I was waving the Hawaiian flag. After this incident, I used the US flag only, as it saved a lot of confusion. Most of the time it worked, but when a gunner was jumpy and nervous, he would hold everyone back, including me. Over the next few years, I would also have warning shots fired at me by nervous US gunners.

I was busy covering my side of the vehicle, looking for possible threats and firing points. I never did get used to this road, as it was too long and flat and there were plenty of bombed-out buildings and houses set back on adjacent roads as well as flyovers.

'Look at this twat!' John shouted.

I looked over to where he was pointing on the other side of the carriageway. Heading towards the Americans was a very fast moving saloon car with three men inside. The car hurtled past us with its windows open, and I watched as it approached the patrol we'd just overtaken. Seconds later I heard the noise of small arms fire, closely followed by the heavy sound of the .50 calibre. Instantly, my mouth went dry and I was very aware of the fact that there was a contact behind us. We were heading at breakneck speed towards a jumpy checkpoint that had possibly been in touch with the patrol and might be expecting a secondary attack. John read my mind and slowed down as we approached the checkpoint. Once again, I placed the flags so that they were easily seen and the sentry called us forward. I stuck my head out of the window.

'Your call sign behind us has been hit,' I shouted. The soldier began speaking into his radio and was obviously being told what I'd just said. He looked stunned.

'We just overtook a convoy escorting a coach. There was a vehicle travelling the opposite way and I think it hit them,' I repeated.

'A drive-by on the Rhino?' he queried.

'Yeah. Well, at least I think so,' I replied. I knew what a drive-by was, but up until this point I didn't know that the coach was called the Rhino. Looking back, it makes a lot of sense to do so.

The soldier did not have a headset so I could hear the radio traffic. The Rhino escort was reporting that the coach had taken heavy fire but was still mobile and there were no casualties, which meant that they'd be up our backsides in a minute or less.

'We'd better get out of the way,' I said. The soldier snapped back into action and waved us through.

'Shit, that was interesting! What do you want to do?' John asked.

'Let's get the fuck out of here, find us a parking spot and then it's coffees on me I think.' We rolled through the gate, passed the barriers and the Bradley APC that was now pulling forward onto the road and drove towards the 'holy grail'. We eventually found the PX way over on the other side of the camp—a massive tent-like structure surrounded by fast food concessions such as Pizza Hut and Burger King as well as others such as Popeyes which I was less familiar with. After parking among a sea of SUVs, we showed the sentry our passes and went inside to what can only be described as an air-conditioned nirvana. Set out like a supermarket stocking the usual food and essentials, it also sold all the tactical kit you could shake a stick at, as well as DVDs, laptops and iPods— and all half the price we would pay in the UK. Within the hour, I was $1,000 lighter and had already made my third trip to the car. Later, after our shopping trip, we sat outside on makeshift wooden benches drinking coffee after having pigged out on junk food.

Neither of us had spoken about the contact earlier on. We'd both seen and been involved with a lot worse, but it was our first taste of what was to come and the kind of problems we would face.

'So what's the plan?' John asked.

'Well, I thought we'd finish our drinks and head back.'

'I know that, numpty. I meant with our new team,' he laughed.

'Well, I don't know about the other teams, but I think two vehicles, team leader and driver in the front, possibly with clients if that's how it's going to be, followed by the 2ic in the rear with a driver and a rear gunner. That's the whole team accounted for,' I replied, although I wasn't sure how it was going to work with our clients. Ideally, you had a third vehicle, which would be the client vehicle in the middle. The other two SUVs were armed support, but in our case we only had the two. Neither was ideal as a client vehicle, but there wasn't much we could do.

'I overheard one of the grown-ups talking the other day. Apparently, our clients are US military and will be driving their own vehicles, so they'll slot into our ORBAT (order of battle),' John added.

'Well, if that's the case we should be fine,' I said. 'I'm going to assume that they'll be armed, and that adds a shitload of problems for us. And they'll no doubt have rank, which means they won't want to do what we tell them. Sounds like it's going to be the Baghdad taxi service.'

'Sounds about right,' John replied.

We finished our coffee in silence and headed back to the vehicle. When we got to the gate, we put the body armour on and loaded our weapons. I gave John my pistol, which he cocked and concealed by his thigh. If we ran into trouble, he would be too busy driving to use the MP5, but the pistol on the other hand was better than nothing. We passed the Rhino parked by the front gate. The windscreen was cracked and a mass of bullet holes, but the glass was heavily armoured and had withstood the attack. Our vehicles were soft skins and a single round would go straight through and out of the other side, regardless if it hit a human target.

'Floor it!' I shouted, cocking my MP5. We weren't going to be yet another statistic on Route Irish, as the engine screamed into life and the Mitsubishi propelled forwards into the rapidly failing light.

Initially, weapons had been a problem. We had the Pakistani knock-off MP5s, and some teams had been issued with pistols. I still had my stolen pistol, but I wasn't happy with it and neither was anyone else. It came to a head when one of the Mosul teams was almost wiped out, having been outranged and outgunned by the enemy when returning fire. Our managers told us that if we could source our own weapons, we could buy our own and they'd add them to the company inventory so that they were legal. The only downside was that we had to buy them ourselves. At the time, the AK-47 was going for about $500, so the search was on. I didn't know many people out there, but the Irish did. They had infested the security companies very quickly, many having come from the Royal Ulster Constabulary (RUC). During the Troubles in Northern Ireland, the RUC had developed and practised close protection in a hostile environment, so it therefore made perfect sense for companies to employ them. There were quite a few of them there and most were as dodgy as they come, but John had been chatting to his pals and contacts and told me that we had an invite to a Friday night piss-up being hosted in one of the villas in the Green Zone. It belonged to the sort of people who could help us.

We drove into the Green Zone and after parking inside the grounds of the villa we were shown inside and taken to the armoury. A very suspicious-looking man with a thick Belfast accent stood in a room stacked floor to ceiling with the kind of weaponry that would be on the front cover of *Soldier of Fortune* magazine and give an operator a hard-on.

'So what are you after?' the smarmy armourer enquired.

'All this is your stock?' I asked, sweeping my arm around the room.

'Everything you see here is spare, so anything you see is for sale,' he added, looking bored and wanting to get on with the drinking.

I only wanted a rifle with a decent range but, like a kid in a toyshop, I did a little mental arithmetic and decided I could spend up to $1,500.

'What about this?' I asked, picking up an airborne AK. This was the same issue as a regular AK but designed for paratroopers, so was shorter and more compact. It was also ideal for use in our vehicles.

'Six hundred dollars for that,' he replied. John was drooling as he looked at the weapons with a professional glint in his eye. He was, after all, a complete gun nut.

'Grenades?' I asked.

'I can give you a box of British Army frag grenades for a hundred.'

'Okay, done. And ten magazines for the AK and a thousand rounds for the AK, preferably Eastern Bloc ammo, not Chinese.'

'Alright, let's call it a thousand and, as I like you both, you can come up to the roof for a drink,' he said. John bought the same, so $2,000 lighter, and having no doubt contributed to the cause, we put the weapons in our vehicles and went back inside to find the bar.

'That was a bit strange,' I said as we trudged up the stairs to the roof.

'Well, they must have a really good deal going; it's the only place to buy weapons and I'm pretty sure the company doesn't know what they're up to,' John added.

'Where did you find this lot?' I asked.

'I asked one of the Micks. You know what they're like— thick as thieves. He put me onto them.'

I nodded as we carried on. I'd never bought into this Northern Ireland thing. Essentially it was Protestants who were mostly Army, RUC or Ulster Defence Regiment (UDR), and Catholics who were the IRA. The Protestants also had their own terrorist organisations such as the Ulster Volunteer Force (UVF) and similar, and liked to think of themselves as our allies. I had stopped and searched cars in Belfast where weapons, sometimes still warm, were found, and these sorts of people had honestly expected me to look the other way because, as they saw it, they'd been doing me a favour. As far as I was concerned, my job in Northern Ireland was to keep the peace, not brass up Catholics just because they weren't Protestants. Some Catholics did join the RUC or UDR, but not only were they hated by Protestants because they were the enemy, they were also targeted as traitors by the IRA. There was a lot of hate in Northern Ireland, but I didn't care why and couldn't have given a shit about potato famines. I was just doing a job.

We stepped onto the roof, in the middle of which was what can only be described as a very well-stocked beach hut bar and about thirty people from all different companies as well as a few US and British government types all in various states of drunkenness. I couldn't help but notice the massive Ulster flag behind the bar— a good indicator that we were in the company of staunch Protestants. Don't get me wrong; I'm not for one or the other— I hated them both equally for what I saw as a load of bollocks. But then again, I'm not Irish. I would have felt differently if I was.

'Will you look at that! Here we are, thousands of miles from home, surrounded by Hajjis, and this lot are still fighting each other,' I said disgustedly.

'Sod 'em; let's get a drink,' John the pragmatist said on his way to the bar.

The rest of the evening was spent mixing with a wide variety of different types, among whom were embassy staff from various countries including our own, and managers from all the companies working out there. A selection of western women had been invited because they were women, mostly subscribing to the Baghdad Beautiful philosophy, a phenomenon peculiar to war zones and places where western women are in short supply and the local variety aren't accessible. At the risk of sounding like a chauvinist or generally unpleasant, the fact is that women who would otherwise be considered unattractive, women you wouldn't look twice at in a bar or on the street, suddenly develop into goddesses and become desirable. I'm not saying that these women go to places like Iraq for this reason, but that's what happens, and who am I to deny them this brief moment of adoration? I wasn't in Iraq to get my leg over, but I know plenty who did.

Fortunately I was never in an environment with such predatory females, but as I looked around the roof, the largest and loudest groups of men all had a woman at the centre. John was talking to a weird-looking barefoot South African guy well into his fifties with mad hair and a beard, wearing only shorts and a baggy bush shirt, and with a rather large and evil-looking dog next to him. It was like something out of an Indiana Jones film. I know I saw him, but to this day nobody can tell me who he was. John told me later that he only spoke Afrikaans, and as I know that John doesn't speak the language, I can only imagine what the conversation was like. My next few years would be full of many surreal moments like this.

I was looking at my watch and thinking about leaving when two men wearing black balaclavas stood in front of the Ulster flag and began posing with various weapons while the rest of the Irish contingent photographed them. After nearly choking on my beer and still coughing, I said, a bit too loudly, to John, 'Fuck me, we've just paid for July on the UVF calendar!' The roof went quiet, and a dozen or so angry-looking loyalist Irishmen glared at us with pure venom. 'Ah, there's the Irish I know,' I thought to myself.

'John, we're leaving,' I said loudly, but there was no reply. I looked to where he'd been, but there was just the South African.

'Oi, silly bollocks, what are you waiting for?' I looked left and saw John's back as he ran through the door. He was followed closely by me and several beer cans and wine bottles.

'Get the car started!' I screamed as we burst out of the front doors, chased by a lot of angry people. I jumped into our car and while I was still half hanging out, John floored it out of the compound, almost running over one of the Gurkhas used to guard the villa.

We laughed hysterically as we drove back to our rooms, but I still couldn't fathom the level of hate these sectarian groups felt for each other. As I said earlier, maybe you have to be Irish to understand it. We bumped into three of them at the huge DFAC (dining facility administration center) in Camp Victory a few days later.

'We don't want to see your face again at our villa,' I was told in no uncertain terms.

'Fuck off, Spuddie,' was the reply, which was followed by verbal abuse. I really couldn't be bothered with it all. I thought at the time, and still do, that it was all bollocks.

'Wow, that lot really hold a grudge, don't they?' John said.

'I think that's their main problem,' I replied, in my mind summing up the whole Irish question.

2

Playtime's Over

John Forbes and I returned to the hotel in time for dinner, but as we'd already eaten we weren't going to bother, and I told him that we'd meet up downstairs later to inspect the new guys in the team. I again cleaned my weapons, had a shower and unpacked all the goodies that I'd bought. I put the pistol back in my belt under my shirt and went downstairs. I know that many would have laughed at me, but I've seen a lot of complacency. People mostly get away with it, and I've been guilty of it also, but there was a company up the road from us living in exactly the same situation whose hotel bar was the target of an explosive device. Fortunately nobody was injured, but it could easily have been a lot more serious. As I trotted down the stairs, I saw John arguing with the night-shift manager about missing laundry, but he gave up when he saw me.

'Dirty thieving bastards. I bet there are a few of his relatives wearing North Face T-shirts courtesy of me,' he said venomously.

'Don't worry, mate. At PX prices, I'll buy you a new one. Have you seen the FNGs (fucking new guys) yet?' I said, trying not to laugh at the look of disgust on his face.

'Not yet, I've only just come down. I'm assuming the bar will be a good place to start,' he added.

Round the corner in the bar area there seemed to be quite a few new faces and some groups were starting to form. This was the team dynamic beginning to manifest itself. Team leaders would be stamping their authority on things and trying to get the best from their teams, which was exactly what I intended to do. Luckily I had John with me. He was someone I could trust and was as good as I was. I wanted to make him my second in command, but also wanted him with me in case things went south. But I was being selfish. The sensible thing would be to look at what London had sent us and make an unemotional and informed decision based on the background of the new team members. Fuck that! I was going to do the same as the rest— choose people who I knew, or at least knew of, first.

I said hello to the people there that I'd already met, found a seat and sat down. Looking at the new faces, I didn't recognise anyone and none of them stood out immediately as being impressive.

'What do you think?' I whispered to John.

'No idea. Who's here for Team Two?' he shouted.

We didn't have official team call signs but we were unofficially Team Two, which meant nothing more than we were the second complete team. Team One had already gone to Basra. Three hands shot up. I looked at John and he looked at me as he chuckled into his beer. One looked like he was 10 years old, the other looked 70, and the third just didn't look right at all. I called them all over and we separated ourselves from the main group. It was quiet enough, and John went to get a few more beers as I pulled out my notebook and a pen. I'd only been out of the Army ten minutes and didn't see why I should change from a way of doing things that I was comfortable with and, as far as I was concerned, worked well for me.

'Right, then; I'm Lewis and that's John,' I told them, pointing towards the bar. They all nodded hello and sat there silently, which was a good sign. The gobby ones were the ones to look out for— those who thought they knew everything. They were the ones who got people killed. John sat down next to me and we began.

The older guy was called Tom and was 56 years old. He was ex-Parachute Regiment but had been out a few years and had also worked as a police officer.

'What made you want to come out here?' John asked.

'I went to London for a job as a storeman, then I got to the villa and they told me I was going onto your team until a vacancy came up,' he replied. Obviously he was not a happy bunny.

'Right. Well, having been to the villa, I'm not that surprised,' I said. 'It's pretty obvious to me that they'll have a better war than the rest of us. I have to ask, will you be alright just as a team member?'

'What, do you think I'm too old, you cheeky bastard?' he replied, still not happy.

'No, I meant not being a storeman,' and I did mean that, as I've met plenty of old bastards who are still fantastic operators.

'Aye, I'll be alright as long as one of those trench dodgers at the villa breaks a leg in the jacuzzi or something,' he added, and he wasn't exaggerating about the jacuzzi.

'How's your driving?' I asked. Driving was the least physical job, as when the rest of us were out on the ground, drivers stayed with the vehicle.

'Pretty good. I've done a few driving courses,' he said, looking a bit happier at the thought of sitting on his arse all day.

'Great! You can drive the lead vehicle.' John looked at me. 'John, you're second in command in the rear vehicle,' I said quickly.

'Fuck you very much,' he added, smiling. I knew he would have been happy without any responsibility but, unlike many companies, TLs and 2ics were paid more, so I was doing him a favour and I really needed someone I could trust in the back-up vehicle.

That left the other two. I pointed at the 10 year old.

'What's your story?' I asked.

'My name's Johnny, ex-Jock Guards, just finished five years in, got out last week, and just want to make some money. Oh, and I'm an ex-car thief so my driving's shit hot,' he replied, neatly answering all the questions that I would have asked him.

'Right, that's great; you can be with John in the second vehicle.' I looked at John, who was obviously finding it funny— the thought of being driven round Iraq by a Glaswegian car thief.

That left the third one. He looked the part, but there was something really not right about him.

'My name's Chris. I'm ex-Artillery and ex-SAS,' he answered.

We all looked at each other. I'd met a lot of ex-Regiment (SAS) blokes in the past and he really didn't smell like one, but he must have been vetted in London before he left. However, I still didn't believe it.

'Okay, you can be the rear gunner; very important job.' He looked at me as though I should have made him second in command, but I'd met people like him before and making him rear gunner was dangerous enough. I didn't have to wait long. After a few drinks, Tom, who obviously didn't believe him either, started on him.

'What squadron were you in?' he asked. It stood to reason that he would have known a few blokes in the regiment.

'A Squadron,' he replied, looking sure of himself.

'You must know Paddy Smith,' Tom said.

'I know Paddy. Top bloke. Anyone want a drink?' he asked as he got up. We all gave him our orders and he wandered off to the bar.

'I know a few blokes from A Squadron, and there isn't a Paddy fucking Smith amongst 'em,' Tom said disgustedly.

'I thought as much. Anyone know how old he is?' I asked.

'I think he said 27,' Johnny said.

'That settles it. It's very unlikely he'd have done his time in the gunners and passed selection and ended up here by that age,' I said. 'I'll have a word at the villa, but for now everyone just humour him. As unlikely as it might be, he could be telling the truth.' They all nodded.

The rest of the night was the usual collection of war stories and people trying to outdo each other. Unfortunately super-soldier got more and more pissed and spent most of the night contradicting himself and generally making a fool of himself. I wasn't drinking, as now that the reality of being responsible for a group of men as a civilian had hit home, I wasn't going to get pissed. John, I thought, was thinking the same, especially as he'd have dangerous Chris behind him with a loaded weapon and fuck knows what training.

'You okay with the ORBAT?' I asked.

'Car thief and a Walter Mitty; what's not to like? Just make sure that you square that bastard away tomorrow,' he added.

Walt or Walter Mitty is a common insult used for someone who isn't military or who over-embellishes their career, from *The Secret Life of Walter Mitty*, a film about a fantasist who creates a totally false world for himself. The circuit is a really small world, but they still try to infiltrate from time to time.

I arranged to meet John downstairs in the morning. Knowing that the new boys would be doing the DOD card routine as I'd done gave me time to speak to the country manager to try and get to the bottom of my Walt infestation.

I saw Dave at breakfast, waiting to pick up the new boys.

'Hello, mate; how's things?' he said like an old friend, which immediately put me on my guard.

'Not bad. I do have a problem with one of the team, though.'

'Let me guess— Chris,' he answered.

'There's no way he's ex-Regiment.'

'London vetted him; he must be okay,' he added, unconvincingly.

'Bollocks, and I won't be responsible when the others figure it out and take matters into their own hands,' I said, meaning every word.

'That's probably the only way you'll get rid of him,' he said as they came out of the lift and walked into the lobby. 'Catch you later, mate,' he laughed, walking towards them.

'Thanks for fuck all!' I shouted after him. I wasn't laughing, but I did still have his spare pistol, I thought.

I had some breakfast with John, told him about the conversation and then we left for the villa. After a two-minute conversation in which my country manager, who was in fact ex-SAS, told me that he didn't care and it was all about bums on seats, I was ordered to keep my Walt and if possible try and train him. I was beginning to think that the money I was going to be earning wasn't worth it.

After this rather disappointing start to the day, we drove down to the Arc of Triumph or Crossed Swords, a massive parade ground with two enormous crossed swords at either end, built in the 1980s to commemorate the Iran–Iraq war. It had a grandstand on one side where Uncle Saddam would take the march past of his army, but now that Baghdad was under new management I decided that this massive empty space would be the perfect place to conduct training and vehicle drills. John drove evasively around the square and completed a couple of J-turn manoeuvres, which can be a very effective way of getting out of trouble. If you're driving down a road and suddenly the way ahead is blocked, you throw the car into reverse and floor it backwards; when travelling fast enough you spin the wheel and the car will spin round so that you're facing the other way; while its spinning, engage first gear and you're now driving back the way you've just come. It looks great in the movies, but due to the violence of the manoeuvre it's only really achievable in cars or unarmoured SUVs. I've seen people attempt it in an armoured vehicle but the end result is nearly always the same: the extra weight massively changes the centre of gravity as the vehicle rotates and invariably makes it roll.

Without a doubt, road accidents were one of the biggest killers in Iraq. An SUV is not stable at speed, and after adding a couple of tons of armour it becomes very hard to handle and can easily become a death-trap. Not many of us were trained to drive these vehicles; we were infantry soldiers taking a crash course in being war-zone bodyguards. The SIA (Security Industry Authority) licensing was still a few years away, and the few close protection courses were run by Walts and weirdos. The combination of powerful American SUVs being driven at breakneck speeds on shitty roads surrounded by locals who couldn't drive was just a recipe for disaster.

After the usual PX and chow hall runs we headed back and were approaching the giant roundabout near our hotel when I spotted three fast-moving black SUVs on a parallel road on our right also heading for the roundabout. John also saw them and started to slow down.

'Fucking Blackwater,' he said.

We stopped just short of the junction.

'Watch this,' he said, casually lighting a cigarette.

The traffic was light and there were no visible threats. All the vehicles had their windows down and rifle barrels stuck out of every hole. The lead vehicle screamed onto the traffic straight into the side of a small hatchback, the weight of the SUV and the massive bull bars shunting the small car out of way and blocking the road. The third car overtook the second and stayed on its right as it covered the second vehicle through the roundabout; then the first car tore off and caught up, taking its place at the front and leaving behind chaos and confusion.

'What the fuck was that?' I asked.

'That, my friend, is what passes for vehicle drills at junctions, and don't get me started— they aren't the only ones doing it,' he replied as he drove on through the wrecked cars and dazed drivers.

'Well, they might like us now, but if we keep that shit up, the locals will soon have had enough and do whatever it takes to see the back of us,' I added.

Don't get me wrong. Vehicle drills are vital, and effectively controlling the traffic around you is often necessary. We would soon be operating aggressively, but we wouldn't run people off the road or ram cars when crossing junctions. Threats were dealt with using deadly force, but the Hajji family on their way to the mosque weren't legitimate targets. However, many companies—shamefully, some of them UK-based— behaved this way. The main problem was that we all drove the same vehicles so were frequently mistaken for Blackwater. We often paid for the stupidity of others, and on several occasions it cost the life of friends of mine— but that's another Blackwater story.

Later that night I went down to the bar. I avoided Chris the Walt, and was quickly cornered by Tom and Johnny. I didn't enjoy telling them that we were stuck with our fantasist, but I told them something that I'd end up repeating many times, and hated myself for saying it.

'The reality is this: each of us made up our own minds to come here, for many different reasons, but we are stuck with things the way they are. Our bosses are crooks and incompetents; they only care about the bottom line. People will die and mistakes will be made, but ultimately it's us as individuals that will stay or go. I won't think less of any man who decides that this life isn't for him, and I'll do what I can for those who stay, but if you don't like it you should go because stamping your feet will get you replaced.'

And that was the reality. None of us were so important that we couldn't be replaced. It happened all the time; people rocked the boat and when they went on leave they got the shove when they were at home, never to be seen again, except for one occasion when an operator had done something wrong and was called into the boss's office for a dressing down. While he was in tapping the boards in front of the project manager, his mates packed his bags and he literally tripped over them as he came out. He and his bags were straight on a transport and away to the airport.

They didn't like it, but they knew I was right, so were grateful that at least I was honest with them. I was already starting to get an unpleasant taste in my mouth about the whole thing— and it was about to get a whole lot worse.

'Hello, mate.' I recognised the voice of the rat from the villa.

'Hello, Dave,' I replied, turning around.

'Listen, mate, we have a problem. We had a new bloke fly in today but his flight was diverted to a US air base just north of Tikrit, and yours is the only complete team here. The country manager wants you to go and get him.'

'Okay, give me the details,' I replied very casually. I had been dealing with mongs most of my adult life and knew when to argue and when to shut up. Plus I was more than capable of putting a plan together, and if my new team couldn't handle a taxi run like this I might as well go home there and then.

'Oh, okay; here's all the details. We managed to get a message to him so he's expecting you, and by the way, it's a fucking big place. There's a little tent village near the airstrip where people crash during transit; that's probably your best bet,' he added.

'Right, leave it with me.' The extra info was useful at least.

'Brilliant. I'll organise a room for him here and I'll see you tomorrow evening,' he said, walking off towards the reception and the sour-faced pit bull behind the desk.

I caught John's eye and called him over.

'What was all that about?' he asked.

'We've got a job, old son. Briefing in my room, thirty minutes.'

'Outstanding; and about time,' he replied and walked off towards the bar.

I was bored and John had been twiddling his thumbs even longer than I had, so it would be good to stretch our legs and also raid another PX. I ran up to my room to quickly check my maps and look at the details that Dave had given me, which was just a name and last known location and a UK mobile which wouldn't work anyway. I opened the map and laid it out on the floor and was just looking at the route when John knocked on the door. I let him in and he sat on the edge of the bed, looking at me expectantly.

'Sorry, mate, it's just a taxi run. One of the FNGs was diverted to Tikrit and we've got to get him and bring him back. On the upside though, it's at least 100 miles away.' The reality was that it was closer to 130 miles.

'Better than nothing,' he said.

We quickly marked up the map. Ideally you want at least three routes, but with the terrain and distance we only managed two, plus the fact that we wouldn't know what obstacles we'd face until we hit the road. The rest of the team squeezed themselves into my room, and Chris the Walt got down onto one knee and pulled out his notebook. I could feel that there was a bit of tension forming already.

'Okay, tomorrow we have a job; I wouldn't call it a mission. We leave here tomorrow morning at ten hundred in our standard ORBAT; our destination is Speicher, a US air base north of Tikrit, approximately 120 miles north of our location.' I rattled on for about twenty minutes, covering the route and actions if we encountered problems. Chris was scribbling furiously in his notebook the whole time, which was very strange. Most of us only ever make a note of the key points, not every single word.

'Any questions?' I said, finishing my brief.

'Isn't ten hundred a bit late? Shouldn't we leave at first light? We can be back early afternoon then,' Chris said. Everyone looked at him, then at me.

'There have been quite a few roadside bombs in the area north of Baghdad, especially around Samarra which is very dodgy, so any IEDs that are being set are being done in the middle of the night. Do you want to be the first one up that road, effectively clearing it? And bring a toothbrush. If we're held up, we'll have to overnight there and return in the morning. Also, drivers can check their vehicles in the morning. We'll have plenty of time before we leave. Any other questions?'

They all shook their heads, and Chris, feeling suitably stupid, was the first one to leave. The others stayed back for a bit and made a few notes about the route, which made me feel a lot more confident.

'Everyone happy?' I asked.

'Well, you know what the problem is,' Tom answered.

'Look, we're stuck with him until we can rotate him out. John'll keep an eye on him and if necessary take the required action.'

What I actually meant was take his weapon off him. I found out later that Tom had thought that I meant frag him. Fragging was an Americanism that we'd picked up. During the Vietnam War, unpopular officers would be killed by their own soldiers, usually with a fragmentation grenade, hence the term 'frag' or 'fragging'. I spent the rest of the night checking my kit and weapons, and then got my head down.

The following morning after breakfast I went outside where the drivers were checking the vehicles. This usually consisted of mechanical checks, radios, spare tyres and breakdown kit. I was confident with the route and the maps, but I did have my own GPS as a back-up. I always carried one if only to double-check myself if I wasn't sure of our position on the map, which could happen. I'm the first to admit that I'm no Christopher Columbus. I went over the route one more time with John and then let him get back to his crew, and was just putting on my body armour and trying to load my weapon without drawing too much attention to myself when Tom called me over.

'Have you seen the Walt?' he asked.

'No, can't say that I have,' I replied, not too keen on starting about our Walt infestation again, when Chris burst forth from the hotel looking like something out of *Special Forces Monthly*. Sporting an assault vest, all sorts of utility pouches, knives and all manner of equipment, he came bounding over towards us. He was even wearing a black turtleneck under his vest. Within a few months we'd all be wearing this kind of equipment, but at the beginning it was all very low key. I nodded towards him as I climbed into my vehicle. I wasn't that bothered that he looked a bit of a wannabe, but better over-equipped than under. Tom was already in the driver's seat with the engine running.

'I see what you mean,' I said, as I turned on my personal radio. The second vehicle had already pulled in behind us, and I gave a radio check. When everyone in the team had replied, I gave Tom the nod to move out. I had my window open. Some people kept theirs shut in case a local managed to get a grenade in, but in all the years I operated in Iraq I never heard of such a thing— as if a standard car window would stop a grenade anyway. I thought being able to hear what was going on around me was more valuable. Sometimes on the open road you'd be travelling so fast that you'd drive through a contact and not even realise it. Obviously that only happened if the shooter missed!

That's how it started for me. We completed the mission without incident and did nothing for the next six weeks. Our clients weren't ready for us, we'd been deployed early, so the next six weeks entailed shopping at the various PXs and sunning ourselves by the pool at Saddam's old palace, or using the gym. Many of us intended to go on our first leave looking like well-paid, bronzed man-gods.

After seven weeks I was told to move my team and equipment *en masse* to the Green Zone, where after some paperwork we were given our new accommodation. By now, things were getting a bit twitchy with the locals. The hotel bar where Armor Group were accommodated had been blown up. Fortunately nobody was killed, but it sent a strong message. We had two double rooms joined in the middle by a bathroom, and each room had two beds, a television, a fridge and air conditioning. The rooms were trailers of the US variety, and our area resembled a clean and very well organised trailer park surrounded by sandbags. We were approximately 200 metres from the palace and the same distance from the gym. I never allowed myself to fall under the illusion that all I'd be doing was sunbathing and shopping, but it was nice while it lasted. However, I was being paid over $100,000 a year, so I knew that someone would want their money's worth, but as I was later to find out, the security companies were charging over $1,000 a day per man to the US Government, so the money being spent was enormous. One thing war is guaranteed to do is boost the economy. After all, these bullets and missiles are made in the US and Europe, governments buy them and the funds go straight back into their own economies. Even so, I wasn't complaining, and neither were the several hundred contractors like myself already in country or the thousands queuing up to get in.

3

New Beginnings

After a boring and uneventful first rotation and squeezing in two weeks' leave, I returned with a lot of uncertainty. I knew things were going to change— I just didn't know how or in which direction and how much. My team all went on leave, which made a lot of sense to me. As contracts became bigger and bigger, things wouldn't be so simple, but for now they were.

Everyone had returned with the exception of the Walt, and as time progressed it became more apparent that he had blagged his way in and that he wasn't SAS. It transpired that he hadn't even been in the Army. Even now, I don't know how he managed to get past the recruitment process. When I joined, which was at the same time that he did, I'd been asked to produce a ton of paperwork from the Army proving my service. I put it down to one of life's great mysteries, but people did and still do slip through the cracks, and a dedicated and professional Walt can easily obtain documents and doctor them to suit. I've met a few medics who bought their qualifications on the internet, and until someone dies they remain undetected. I found one out after he self-medicated with the contents of the med kit. It was a miracle he survived his self-inflicted cocktail of ketamine and morphine. I found him dribbling like someone who had been recently lobotomised with a dessert spoon and spent five minutes watching him trying to climb inside his helmet. As funny as it was, I had to stop him and get him evacuated, after which he was never seen again.

On our way out on leave we all sat down at the departure lounge in Kuwait after flying military from Baghdad and clued him in. I left him under no illusion that if he returned he would probably be having an accident along the lines of a safety failing in one of the hand grenades that he was carrying. He pointed out that he didn't carry grenades (mostly because I didn't trust him with any) and I added that this was a mere technicality; history being written by the victor, I would be the one drafting the incident report of his tragic and untimely death. As harsh as it sounds, my concern was with the rest of my team, and he was an accident waiting to happen. In addition, I didn't doubt that eventually somebody would end up taking the initiative and getting rid of him. I'd heard the phrase 'dirt nap in the desert' used more than once and it wasn't just my team that hated him; the whole contract pretty much had it in for him. I found out later that Armor Group employed him after he left us, but he was rumbled again and this time fired. Believe it or not, he ended up as a project manager with another large and respected UK-based defence company. However, management being mostly administration is probably a lot easier to blag than being operational, but never underestimate the power of Walting. Personally, I believe that, like rats, for every one you see there are a dozen skulking in the shadows.

So suddenly there I was back in the sandpit, minus a rear gunner. You'd think this would be a problem but apparently not, and I was told to carry on until a replacement could be sent out. I had a couple of days before we were going live and we spent these on the Crossed Swords conducting vehicle drills. In these early days of unarmoured vehicles, or soft skins as they are referred to, we practised getting out of the killing area as quickly as possible, but no plan survives first contact with the enemy. Driving in convoy, the front vehicle is Vehicle 'A' and the second is Vehicle 'B'. If 'A' drives into an ambush, 'B' stops short and while 'A' is taking fire from the side, 'B' drives in and stops on the non-contact side. While this is happening, the crew in 'A' have exited their vehicle on the non-contact side and are putting down fire on the enemy from behind 'A'. From here they can jump into 'B', which then reverses out of the contact and returns the way it has come, or the shooters from 'B' can debus and put down fire while the crew from 'A' get into 'B' and then blah blah blah … This is all textbook stuff and looks great on paper or in a PowerPoint demonstration, but the reality is often different. An important point to note is that a soft skin vehicle offers no protection from bullets, and even less from an IED followed by bullets. Most of the ambushes I had the misfortune to encounter were initiated by an IED, and during the chaos and confusion were followed up by a small arms ambush. In these circumstances, the first thing to do is get out of the vehicle— a crippled car becomes a bullet magnet— and if you have to take cover behind a car, the only part that offers any protection is the engine block, and this is limited to the size of the block. A large American SUV isn't so bad; a Nissan Micra isn't so good. Keep all of this in mind.

'John, built-up area ahead; looks quiet,' I said into my radio. John was in the vehicle behind me and we were travelling at 90 mph, heading north near Taji. 'I don't like this,' I said to Tom.

The area should have been busy. What we call a combat indicator is when things aren't how they should be, and there were no people on the street, signifying that they'd been warned that something was up. We weren't carrying clients and I had a rule that if we were bumped we would fight through the ambush. I didn't intend to be a target while we fucked around with disabled vehicles or moved all the kit from one vehicle to the other (known as cross-decking) while Hajji took pot shots at us. Unlike the Afghans, Iraqis didn't like a fight and were rubbish shots; they would get better as non-Iraqis with greater insurgency experience began appearing in order to help out.

'White vehicle, parallel left,' I said into my radio.

If there was an IED out there it would have to be triggered by someone who had line of sight of us. The device could be triggered several ways, one being a wire, which was instant but impractical because it could be seen and easily damaged. Trigger men liked to be as far away as possible, and in the open you could still see your target a couple of kilometres away. More commonly a mobile phone was used, an artillery shell often being attached to the device to act as a detonator. All the trigger man had to do was call it and it was game over. The upside for us was there was a certain amount of guesswork involved, the timing had to be perfect, and the delay in making a call could easily mean we were well past it when the device went off. Thankfully during 2004 things were basic, and later far more complicated tactics and devices would start to appear.

At this point I was looking for a marker. The potential trigger man was 700 metres away, and obviously he wouldn't be able to see the device because it was hidden, maybe dug in next to the road, secreted in rubbish. We avoided obvious hiding points so burying was often best, and a marker was something that the trigger man could see clearly, such as a telegraph pole. As soon as we were level with it we were in the killing area. I was also looking for parked cars, a brightly painted door on a shop, anything that would make an easy aiming point for someone a few hundred metres away. I should have turned around and gone back the way we'd come. We'd already cleared it by driving down it, but if we stopped we'd become a slow or stationary target, so I decided to push on. I might have been wrong, as we were nearly through the small collection of shops that constituted the built-up area, and really it was just a feeling— nothing more. I glanced at my driver, who was concentrating on the road, and checked my mirror. I could see my second vehicle a couple of hundred metres back. We kept an eye on the spacing, especially on the open road, as it would be stupid to lose two vehicles to an IED because they were too close to each other. Still no signs of life outside— even a dog taking a dump would have made me feel better. I tightened the straps on my helmet, then everything went loud, there was an enormous thump and I could feel the air being sucked in around me. Gravity shifted as the rear of my vehicle was picked up by the blast and the fireball that erupted just behind us. I quickly looked at Tom; he was steady and kept the vehicle moving. I waited for follow-up small arms, but nothing. I scanned for targets, still nothing. I swivelled round in my seat and looked behind us just as my second vehicle emerged from the dissipating fire and smoke.

'John, are you okay back there?' I shouted into my radio.

'Fuck that. What about you two? You caught that blast pretty full on,' he replied quickly.

'No, we're fine; it was behind us. We're going to push on and reorg at the next safe location,' I replied.

'Better make it quick; your arse is on fire.'

I looked back but couldn't see anything.

'It's the rear tyres, and I'm fine, thanks for asking,' Tom added sarcastically from the driver's seat.

'Sorry, mate. Better pull over up ahead, there,' I said, pointing to a quiet spot ahead. By now we'd put a couple of kilometres between us and the site of the IED and there hadn't been any follow-up. Better to stop than risk the vehicle becoming useless.

'John, we're going to stop and put out the fire,' I said into my radio. I quickly climbed into the rear and grabbed the fire extinguisher as Tom pulled in. I fell out of the back door and could see the tyres still burning and rapidly melting, but it wasn't the tyres so much as the fuel tank I was worried about. I pulled the pin and sprayed the tyres as John's vehicle pulled in behind. John got out and ran over to me.

'Fuck, that was close!' he said, looking at the scorched rear of the vehicle.

The tyres were fucked but we were using run flats so we could carry on, albeit at a slower pace. I intended to get to the next US base, pull in and change the wheels and reassess from there, so I got back inside my vehicle and we carried on to the next safe location. I told the guys guarding the gate what had happened and we pulled in and parked up.

'Tom, check the vehicle; and good driving,' I said, getting out. John was looking over his vehicle and Johnny was underneath.

'I don't think we caught anything,' John said.

'Good; I had a feeling,' I replied, shaking my head.

'Well, I think you called it with the white vehicle. He definitely had something to do with it. He was watching your vehicle as you went by and was straight on the phone, sneaky bastard,' John added.

At this point in the game these tactics were new to us. We'd all done tours in Northern Ireland, but general tactics used there by terrorists were more complex and this kind of insurgency was not what we were used to, although I was going to be learning quickly. As Hajji changed his tactics, so would we. I called our base and let them know what was happening and that we'd return as soon as we were satisfied that the vehicles were roadworthy.

'Fine underneath,' Johnny said as he crawled out from under his vehicle.

'Ours looks fine, too. We just need to change those two back wheels and we should be okay,' Tom said as he walked over to us.

'Fine, alright. Well, that was our first enemy action and I doubt it'll be the last. We were very lucky. For whatever reason, the IED went off between us, and judging by the lack of shrapnel it was either dug in too deeply or was mostly fuel. Either way, it looked impressive but did little damage. You all did really well. Next time it might be more serious so we can't think for one minute that we'll be this lucky every time,' I said.

I couldn't think of anything else to add. I knew it was blind luck that had got us through and I didn't want them to let their guard down. I also knew that driving round the country undermanned in vehicles that mothers use to drop their kids off at school wasn't the way forward. We changed the wheels and carried on.

We were still operating from the Green Zone and our missions were pretty mind-numbing. We would collect clients who worked for the US Government and were mostly military; they would drive themselves, slotting their vehicle between ours, and we would then escort them to reconstruction projects so they could assess where the US taxpayers' money was being spent— mostly rebuilding schools, hospitals and police stations. Unfortunately the reality was that local contractors would take the millions of dollars to build a new police station, but every time we would go to that location it had progressed no further. There was always an excuse— insurgents, kidnap and murder being the favourite ones. It may have been true, but the main reason was corruption. Companies took the money and kept it; they had no intention of building some of these projects unless it really suited them. One police station in north Baghdad remained in the same state for over a year. I went past that location four years later and it was still an abandoned building site, long forgotten by the Department of Defense even though it had been bought and paid for by the US taxpayer.

This level of corruption was played out all over Iraq. The money that was spent there is mostly a matter of public record now, but I'd like to know how much of that was just wasted. Obviously some reconstruction projects were successful, but I saw more waste and theft than good during my four years in Iraq. Unfortunately it seemed common practice to just throw money at a problem, and there was a lot of money being thrown around. Whether it was because we as an occupying force felt guilty or just needed to be seen spending huge sums of money in a post-conflict environment I don't know, but between 2003 and 2010, Brown University estimated the cost to be around $1 trillion, although other economists have estimated it to be as high as $3 trillion if you factor in lost equipment etc. Either way, it wasn't cheap, but war never is, and that's often the point.

Don't get me wrong, I'm not a conspiracy theorist and freely admit that I've been at the coal face for a lot of this and have had my hand out with the rest, but I'm a realist and don't for one minute believe that we invaded Iraq for the right reasons unless that reason was to get paid. However, having said that, it would have happened regardless, so I never stood there on my soapbox shouting about freedom for the Iraqi people. I met a lot who did, but in many ways I think it's how people dealt with it. Ask an infantry officer who lost men during the invasion, and lost even more afterwards during the occupation. He wants to believe that he was there for a good reason and that his men died for something, and he deserves that peace of mind. I don't know many men who could accept as a reason for being at the arse end of nowhere facing death every day that it was to make rich people back home richer; men (and I use the term loosely) who would never risk themselves or their children's lives but are happy to sacrifice the youth of their country for their bank balance. Sorry, I forgot weapons of mass destruction. Well, they must have been really well hidden, that's all I can say.

During the next four years I'd be asked to run missions of almost certain death. Mayhem and destruction would be commonplace, but I would stick it out, not for the money but because I stupidly believed that my skills and experienced made the difference to my team. I still had my Army head on, you fight for the man to your left, and in those days companies didn't tolerate dissent. If you complained, you were replaced very quickly before you could poison the contract. I felt that my place was with my team, that it was better that someone with experience was with them, and that's why I stuck it out for so long. And the really annoying thing is that I still do it. I won't allow myself to believe that it's all bullshit, even though I know deep down that it is. I've cut my leave short or even volunteered to stay longer, sometimes sacrificing a leave completely and doing two rotations back to back. I even refused to be medevaced when injured and soldiered on, all because I felt that my team needed me, not in a megalomaniacal way but because we had been through the wringer. Men had died, my team was undermanned and my second in command was in worse shape than me. For these reasons I carried on, and as much as the company shows you no loyalty or even cares, I'd like to think that my team-mates appreciated it, plus it helps me sleep at night, and that's the truth of the matter. We all had our reasons. Initially I was curious, and the money was a real attraction, but it soon became something else entirely.

I'd recently heard on the grapevine that things were changing for the worse. No more smiling and waving from the locals; there was a definite change in their feeling towards us— a lot of it further north towards Tikrit and Mosul. Baghdad was still all hustle and bustle and there had been several contacts, but I still felt safer there because I'm a city person and have always felt more vulnerable in the sticks. As soon as you left the city, especially as it usually involved fighting through traffic in the suburbs with a ton of chokepoints and places where an enemy could hide, not to mention overpasses and bridges, it would become a real problem. As you approached, quite often you couldn't see what was hiding up there, and the enemy had the advantage of height and surprise as you came out. I used to treat each one like a possible ambush point. Drivers would change lanes while underneath and out of sight if the bridge or flyover was wide enough, and our rear gunner was our only defence, but the gunner's weapon was little more than noise. Imagine sitting facing backwards in a truck travelling at up to 100 mph, swerving erratically in an attempt to avoid incoming fire and accurately engaging an enemy, possibly in cover, who is rapidly getting further and further away. This was compounded by the gunner not being strapped in and at real danger of being thrown out of the vehicle if the driver became a bit too aggressive, not forgetting that the road would be full of other vehicles getting in the way as well.

I was at week eight, and we all had one week left before going on leave. Our contract had ended and another company had taken over, which wasn't uncommon as contracts changed regularly. In this instance it was Aegis, a company made infamous in the early days by a video clip posted on the internet showing a rear gunner engaging civilian vehicles for apparently no reason, and having a man in charge with a slightly chequered past involving mercenaries in Africa. Aegis had appeared overnight and had starting taking contracts at an alarming rate. In fact I'd been in the Green Zone café once when the company's founder was going from table to table blatantly poaching guys by offering more money than they were already on. Many did jump ship almost immediately, although I, with my stupid loyalty, did not, and that was the reason this loyalty thing afflicts me so.

As a team at large we were being used to fill in here and there, and as there were always new contracts on the horizon, we were kept together just in case we were needed. One particular day just didn't feel right. We'd picked up a couple of missions, starting with an airport run taking our country manger to the BIAP so he could go on leave. He was okay with me, and I like to give people the opportunity to annoy me in person before I make a judgement. One thing that I have learnt is that you can be a good operator and move on to management, but I honestly believe you cannot continue to be popular with the teams, the client and the company. The wishes of the client will always conflict with common sense and the safety of the teams, the company will always give the client what they want, no matter how stupid, and the manager will have the unenviable task of getting the job done regardless, because ultimately he is as easy to replace as a rear gunner and there will be no shortage of backstabbing snakes all coveting his job. So suddenly that team leader who you used to have a lot of respect for is asking you to take on a mission that you both know is a bad idea.

However, I discovered that some managers only had their jobs because somebody important owed them a favour; they were incompetent and poorly equipped and most had never been on the ground as a PSD operator. Most of the managers with whom I came into contact had left the Army in a senior position and had walked straight into a management job. Although the Army gives you great training, in those days it didn't give you experience in PSD operations or dealing with clients like ours. You may say I'm being cynical, and there may be great managers out there who can balance the needs of the client and manage risk and all those other buzzwords people like to throw around, but I haven't met many, and they don't last because they get as disillusioned as the rest of us and tend to throw their hand in. I know because I've done exactly that. Later on, when I became a manager, I lasted five minutes. I couldn't find it in me to ask people to do things that I felt didn't matter, and on more than one occasion, when the mission was going ahead regardless, I went along myself, in a display of solidarity that only got me noticed by my superiors for all the wrong reasons.

We'd picked up the country manager, who was in the second vehicle, and had just started our run on Route Irish. We were running two soft skins and, as far as I was concerned, the country manager wasn't a client, he was an extra gun if we needed it. My logic was that if we got into trouble, the second vehicle could bug out the way we'd come as we'd just cleared that way and knew what was behind us. But in the end, it doesn't really matter what you do. It's just as common for the second vehicle to be targeted as the front. It all depends on what Hajji has planned on that particular day.

Tom started to slow down as we saw the vehicles ahead, a three-vehicle PSD team. We didn't show any identifying marks in those days and we all drove the same vehicles, so we rarely knew which companies we encountered unless their tactics gave them away, like our friends in Blackwater. We were approximately 200 metres behind.

'Friendly call sign ahead,' I said into my radio. John replied with two clicks on his talk switch. I swear that I looked in my side mirror to check on the spacing of my second vehicle for a second, two at the most, and when I looked back, the rear vehicle of the call sign in front of us was engulfed in flames and swerving violently to the side of the road and the two other vehicles were firing wildly to the side. I couldn't see an enemy, and people did often just shoot wildly— not something I ever did, but I was definitely in the minority on that one.

We were approaching a large flyover and I decided it was best to stop there and quickly reassess. We had cover from above and the sides, and I'd already decided that going back was probably the safest option. I certainly didn't want to get involved in somebody else's contact or become another victim of it.

'Tom, stop there under the flyover. Did you see what happened?' I asked.

'Fucked if I know. There was a flash from the right side, then the rear vehicle went up; must be petrol not diesel. I heard it go off though, but it didn't sound like an IED,' he replied, slowing down and pulling over.

'John, we're going firm under the bridge and we'll reorg from there.'

I received the customary two clicks and as soon as we stopped I jumped out. As we were in soft skins, we were safer on foot away from the vehicles anyway. The other call sign had carried on rolling and we had matched their speed, so we still had about 200 metres between us. I took my binoculars out and scanned ahead. It looked like carnage. The first two vehicles had stopped and several guys were out in the open trying to get the crew out of the burning vehicle. Fortunately there wasn't any enemy small arms fire. John had walked over and I gave him the binos. He looked on in silence while I was debating whether to help.

'Army's coming,' John said flatly. I looked round and could see a couple of Humvees approaching from beyond the burning vehicle.

'Okay, fuck this, we're going on; follow us,' I said as I got back into my vehicle. When I saw that John was back in the second vehicle, we set off again. 'Tom, take us over to the other carriageway and carry on. As soon as we've passed, cross back over. The Yanks have just cleared the route.'

He nodded and carried on. As we drove past, I could see the devastation. The third vehicle looked like someone had punched a hole right through it. I could see at least one body without a head, but there was still a lot of smoke and I didn't want to see it. I quickly looked ahead and we crossed back and floored it to the airport. After dropping off the country manager we went for coffee, none of us feeling particularly chatty, but we needed to reorg and carry on.

'The country manager says it was an EFP,' John said matter-of-factly.

'Shit, that's not good,' I replied.

'What's an EFP?' Tom asked.

'Fucking bad news! It's a tube packed with explosives, and capped with a copper disc. The explosives detonate and the copper turns to a molten mass and cuts through up to 10 centimetres of armour. EFP stands for explosively formed penetrator or projectile, is easy to make in a workshop and can be as small as a Pringles tube,' John replied.

'I heard about those. The Yanks had an M1 tank fucked up by one near Taji; nearly took the turret off,' Johnny added, looking very worried.

And that was my first experience of the EFP, a simple yet highly effective weapon that a child could make, and within a short space of time would be used widely in ever more complex attacks on military and PSD units. It didn't matter how fast you were going, you couldn't outrun it; your only chance was if another vehicle in your team got the good news. I've only ever known of one person surviving an EFP attack and he didn't exactly walk away unscathed. The rest of his team weren't so lucky.

Initially the devices were homemade, but more and more Iranian military spec ones would be deployed, and friends of mine working in Basra would on more than one occasion capture Iranian Special Forces disguised as Iraqi civilians in possession of Iranian military issue ordnance of this nature. But unless you were working out there you wouldn't really hear about it. I'm sure our government gave them the five-star treatment before shipping them back to Iran in some underhand deal. Can you imagine the fate of NATO Special Forces being captured in Iran? I've no doubt it would have been very public and very hard to watch, but that's what we're good at— putting our enemies first.

I had a strong urge to forget the rest of the day, but we had one more mission, a trip to Balad, a large US camp called Anaconda between Baghdad and Tikrit, not a million miles from Samarra, one of the more unpleasant parts of Iraq. Anaconda was about thirty minutes off the MSR (main supply route). There were two roads and it didn't really matter which way you went. Common sense dictated that you went in one way and out the other, but they were both dangerous. One of our guys had been flying in and had been diverted north of Tikrit. From there he'd jumped on a Blackhawk helicopter that had also been diverted to Anaconda due to bad weather, and that's where he'd been for a couple of days. We were to go and get him and bring him back to Baghdad. The alarm bells had started, and after the EFP incident that morning I wasn't happy. However, I couldn't refuse a mission just because I didn't have a good feeling about it.

We left the BIAP and headed back towards Baghdad. As we passed the earlier ambush site there was nothing left other than some burn marks, glass, and what looked like blood. I had no doubt about the seriousness of it and never liked to see it. It so easily could have been you. I hadn't even started to think that if we'd overtaken that call sign or left five minutes earlier it would have been us, as I always tried to push these thoughts from my mind. You couldn't waste time worrying about what might have been, especially when you were out on the road. I was more alert than usual; I knew something was going to happen but I didn't think for one minute that the earlier incident was it. That had been someone else's destiny; ours was yet to come. Traffic was unnaturally light and we made good time— on any other day it would have almost been enjoyable. My rifle was across my lap, my hand on the pistol grip, thumb on the safety. By now I'd managed to acquire some better weapons and I carried a US M4. Some preferred the larger-calibre AK-47, but it was old and cheaply made. Although the M4 had a smaller round, it was more accurate and the ammo weighed a lot less, therefore you could carry a lot more ammunition. I valued hitting the target over a bigger bullet.

'What's the matter?' Tom asked.

'Is it that obvious? I don't know; I feel like there's something out there, something big and hairy with our name on it.' I hadn't wanted to say anything, as fear is infectious and can undermine the best team.

'Thanks. Sorry I asked,' he replied sarcastically.

'Everything alright back there?' I said into my radio.

'All good,' John replied.

We'd gone past Camp Cooke at Taji about forty minutes earlier, where we'd previously been hit by an IED. The road was long and a dual carriageway for the most part, with the occasional built-up area of a few shops and small gatherings of people. It was getting close to lunchtime and there were fewer people as it was the hottest part of the day. I looked at my GPS— I'd been this way before and had marked the turn. I still carried maps, but it was easy to mark the turn as a waypoint and the GPS would tell me how far ahead it was. Mine also told me our speed. It was more time management than navigation; I knew where we were going and unless we had to make a diversion to avoid something, the map would stay folded up and stuffed into my body armour.

'Ten clicks,' I shouted to Tom above the wind and road noise coming in through my open window.

He nodded. He knew this part was the most dangerous leg of our route, approaching Samarra, an insurgent HQ where nobody went and was permanently out of bounds. Insurgent teams operated from there all along this stretch of road and the Samarra bypass, a long sweeping road and bridge that avoided the town completely but was still dangerously close. I'd read an intelligence report the previous week that a melon seller by the side of the road had given an Iraqi patrol poisoned melons, and many had died within minutes. When those unaffected had gone back to arrest the man he had disappeared, but his stall was still there, containing enough explosives to take care of those the melons hadn't killed. When they arrived, he detonated it from a hidden position. I had to respect the melon seller. That might have been nasty, but it showed guts and tactical awareness. I immediately guessed he probably wasn't an Iraqi— they tended not to be that switched on— but was probably a jihadist on a religious holiday. After all, Mosul had a gang of Chechens running around creating mayhem and giving the US military and several of the companies up there a hard time, and from what I'd heard had managed to kill several people in very effective small arms ambushes with almost no fear or regard for their own safety.

It's hard to defeat an enemy who wants to die. In the end, it's your skills and awareness of the situation that might give you the edge, but how do you defend against someone carrying a shitload of explosives either on their person or in a car? They don't even have to get that close to you, and it's all over in an instant, quicker than your brain can register. I never got over that feeling, flying along at warp speed trying to identify every threat and knowing that in less time than it takes a nerve impulse to travel to your brain you might not exist any more. Even now, thinking about it sends a shiver up my spine, and getting into my vehicle every day knowing that was the hardest thing for me. As a friend of mine used to say when he got on the flight from the UK to Kuwait on his way back from leave, he considered himself dead already; that's how he dealt with it. Sadly he was killed in an accident when the armoured vehicle he was driving rolled several times and he was thrown out, landing on his head in the road.

I looked at my GPS again— 6 kilometres to the turn. I could see a US military call sign of several Humvees ahead, and we decelerated and approached slowly.

'Army ahead,' I said into my radio. I pulled my US flag out and pressed it against the inside of the windscreen. The rear gunner kept us back for a few minutes while he radioed the rest of his convoy and then waved us past. As we overtook slowly, several of the US crew waved at us, using the common hang loose sign, clenching a fist and extending the little finger and thumb. We got past the convoy and Tom accelerated hard to put distance between us and them. They were probably a bigger target than us, so not being near a massive ambush magnet was always a good idea.

'Rear vehicle clear,' John said into his radio to confirm that our call sign was now complete.

There was no traffic in either direction as we approached the turn. Ordinarily our second vehicle would block as we made the turn.

'No need to block; there isn't any traffic. Just follow us through,' I said into my radio as we began slowing down for the turning. By now I was trying to look in every direction at once. I felt a thump similar to when someone slams a door in a building and you feel the vibration, although a lot more so, and looked in my side mirror but couldn't see the road— just the fields that had been on our left. I looked at my driver, who seemed fine, and then I looked back through the windscreen. At that point I knew something was very wrong. The horizon was at about forty-five degrees, and looking out the side window all I could see was the road. I braced myself, dropped my rifle and pushed my hands as hard as I could into the area around the sun visor. All this happened in probably less than a few seconds, and those last few micro-seconds, during which my vehicle was now travelling sideways and in the early stages of a rollover, were strangely calm. My mind hadn't yet fully grasped what was happening, and definitely not why it was happening, but the peace was short-lived and my side of the vehicle crashed into the tarmac with the most violent and sickening thud. The one thing I do remember was the windscreen flying out and spinning off into the distance like some kind of transparent Frisbee as the vehicle continued to roll like an out-of-control washing machine stuck on a spin cycle. I was being thrown around and was by now gripping the window frame where the windscreen had been. My head was spinning, and in the initial rollover the foresight of my rifle had smacked me on the side of the head, breaking one of my molars, or maybe I had bitten down. Either way, it was enough to disorient me.

The whole event seemed to last forever and my next conscious recollection was of the vehicle sliding along the road on its side, with an almost unbearable screeching of steel against the road. Eventually it came to a standstill and smoke filled the cabin (probably dust from the road as there wasn't any fire). I shook my head and looked around. I was alone. I couldn't see Tom. I was still in my seat and was still gripping the window frame like a man hanging onto a ledge as if his life depended on it. I took a deep breath and quickly checked myself. My head was spinning and my right leg had a rapidly expanding bloodstain near the knee. My ribs hurt when I took a deep breath, but I seemed alright. My rifle was in the back and I reached for it, pulling it towards me, and began crawling through the gap left by the windscreen. I fell onto the road where I could see the second vehicle, engine screaming, coming towards me. Shakily I got to my feet and leant against my smashed vehicle. The pain around my ribs was agonising. John was running towards me, and beyond him Johnny was now out of his vehicle and was leaning across the bonnet putting down fire. I felt the rounds pass me— the displacement of air as a piece of lead goes supersonic causes a shock wave. We were obviously being shot at, but the danger didn't register. I looked in the direction in which Johnny was firing but couldn't see anyone. John was next to me now and was pulling me to the ground. I could hear the shooting but it was like I was underwater and completely disconnected from it— my ears were ringing but my senses were returning slowly.

'Are you alright, Lew?' John was shouting. I focused on him and managed to nod.

'Where's Tom?' I asked.

John scrambled round to the front of the vehicle and climbed inside. I scanned our flanks but still couldn't identify any incoming fire. My hearing had levelled out and I decided that if I didn't act, I could easily find myself succumbing to shock and then I wouldn't be of any use to anyone. I got up on one knee and, using the vehicle as cover, watched where Johnny was shooting. I could see a car on a parallel road near a ditch and some shrubs.

'Johnny, where's the enemy?' I shouted between shots.

He looked back and using a chopping open-handed gesture, often referred to as the Brecon Indication, he pointed towards the vehicle. Sure that I'd seen a muzzle flash from the bushes, I took aim and emptied a magazine at the vehicle. I wanted these bastards to have no escape route. I reloaded and started to lay down deliberate, aimed shots around the bushes. I was in agony and it felt like my whole body was screaming, but the massive amount of adrenaline had definitely taken the edge off the pain and was allowing me to focus and react rather than collapse in a shitty heap. I was sure that would come later when I had time to stop and think. I considered using grenades but the suspected enemy were at least 200 metres away. John came back, looking bewildered.

'I can't find him,' he said.

I was weighing up the options. We couldn't reorg until we'd destroyed the enemy, so the only real choice was to attack. We couldn't outflank, and there was at least 200 metres of open and very uneven ground between us and them. I was only good as fire support and that only left me with two shooters, hardly enough to mount an effective attack against an unknown enemy. We couldn't begin to look for Tom until we controlled the ground. He'd obviously been thrown out of the vehicle and was probably dead or worse underneath the vehicle.

I remembered the Yanks we'd passed on the road. If I was right and they were from Anaconda, they would soon be along.

'We'll wait for five minutes. The call sign we passed should come this way; keep laying down fire until then. Let Johnny know what's going on, okay?' I ordered.

John nodded and while I emptied another magazine towards the enemy, he ran across the short gap between the vehicles to let Johnny know what was happening. I could see a car approaching from the opposite carriageway and began firing warning shots as I didn't want any unfriendly elements at our rear or flanks. However, the car continued on, oblivious of our little drama, so I took careful aim and put two rounds into the engine compartment. That seemed to do the trick, and the car, a red Caprice, came to a screeching halt. I watched with satisfaction as the occupants ran unhurt from the vehicle. I swung back and saw the US call sign trundling up the road towards us. As soon as they got close enough, the .50-calibre gunner in the turret began to let rip at our hidden enemy, laying down a vicious amount of fire. The Humvees stopped and, after debussing, the soldiers began to clear towards the enemy, but not until they'd flattened the area with a mixture of rapid-fire grenades from the Mk 19 and other assorted heavy weapons. In less than five minutes there was silence. No return fire and no sign of the enemy. While John was talking to the US commander, a medic ran over to me. My leg was bleeding heavily and I sat down thankfully. He asked if I was alright, a silly question, and I just said that my leg needed a field dressing, so rather than waste one of mine I let him use his med pack to patch me up. I thanked him quickly and made my way over to where John was.

'Right. We need to find Tom; and what the fuck happened?' I said.

'Well, the Yanks were looking, and you were hit by an IED, old son; turned you sideways and then you flipped. I counted at least five rotations before you stopped. You're lucky to be alive.' That explained the thump I'd felt; it must have been small. The Yanks were waving frantically from where the enemy vehicle was, but I was still a man short and the rest of the soldiers were looking through the undergrowth, John having told their commander that we had a missing man.

'Did you see Tom get ejected from the vehicle?' I asked.

'No, didn't see a thing,' John replied. I then remembered the windscreen coming out, and began walking, or more accurately shuffling, up the road in front of us. I had a horrible feeling that he might have gone through the windscreen, and my fears were confirmed about 20 metres further on when we found him just off the road.

'John, get the medic!' I shouted as I got down next to the bloodied and unmoving body. I checked for a pulse and quickly looked him over; he was alive, but unconscious. He had a lot of abrasions and cuts but nothing that looked life-threatening, and I was hoping he had no more than a bad case of gravel rash and would be okay. The medic ran over, dumped his bag and immediately started working on him. I stood up and watched—there wasn't much else I could do. We had no communications with our operations manager, my satellite phone had been destroyed, and mobile phones didn't work out in the boonies where we were.

'Hey man, you okay?' the US commander asked as he walked over.

'Yeah, I'm fine. Just a bit banged up. I'm glad you showed up,' I replied.

'Our guys found three bodies over by the car, all armed. I guess they thought they had an easy target,' he added.

While all this was going on, Johnny had run up to us and was helping the medic with Tom. It was all I could do to stay upright, and I was rapidly starting to feel the pain and light-headedness as the adrenalin began to wear off.

'We'll have to strip the vehicle and frag it. Can you push it off the road and get a medevac for Tom and escort us into Anaconda?' I asked. I needed to focus on the admin points otherwise I would have drifted off.

'Sure, no problem. A chopper's on its way,' he replied, and as if prompted by his words, two Blackhawks came in hard and fast, the second one providing cover.

'Johnny, go with Tom and stay at the hospital; we'll be there shortly.'

Johnny nodded and ran back to his vehicle, grabbed his kit and helped the medic get Tom onto the Blackhawk. John had transferred any sensitive equipment from the stricken vehicle into the other one. Using a Humvee, the Yanks pushed the wrecked vehicle off the road and dropped a thermite grenade into it to deny the enemy our equipment. I climbed inside our good vehicle and John got into the driving seat, the Yanks pulled away and we slotted into their convoy.

'You should have got on the Blackhawk,' John said to me.

'I know, but did you see Johnny? He was hanging out,' I replied. But he was right; I should have. I was in no condition to do my job, especially if we had another contact, but I'd seen Johnny's face when he saw Tom. I was hoping it looked worse than it actually was, but it looked really bad and I suspected that Johnny hadn't been exposed to that kind of thing before. We followed the military call sign into Anaconda and they took us to their medical centre. Anaconda was another of those sprawling camps, so large that it had a bus service to get you around if you didn't have your own vehicle.

I fell out of my vehicle and tried unsuccessfully to remove my body armour; it was just too painful. I thanked the soldiers for their help and we went inside. My priority was my team, then getting in touch with our operations manager, and then the person we were there to collect. I was quickly seen by a doctor, who insisted that I was treated. Managing to get my body armour off with some help, I had my leg stitched up. There was a nasty gash just below my knee, but it was a clean cut and not that deep, just long and bleeding quite heavily. The medic had a look at my ribs and said they were probably cracked and that my tooth would have to wait until I got back to my dentist. He gave me some strong painkillers and told me that Tom would probably be okay; they hadn't found anything serious but he was still unconscious, which was a worry, and he was about to be X-rayed. The biggest concern was a skull fracture, and although well-equipped, the medical centre had its limits and an MRI machine and brain surgery would be off the menu. I'd asked John to get in touch with our Ops room and get clarification on what to do next; we were down to one vehicle and, whatever happened, Tom would have to be evacuated back to the UK and we would need some form of support, although we did have another operator waiting for us there to be collected, so technically we were up to strength.

'Can I have a word?' Johnny said, sticking his head round the cubicle curtain.

'Sure, how are you doing?' I asked.

'That's what I wanted to talk to you about. I can't do this. I'm going to quit as soon as we get back. When I saw your vehicle getting smashed to pieces I thought, "That could be me." I can't stop thinking about it.'

I knew he'd made his mind up, and I also knew that it wasn't easy for him to say. None of us wanted people to think we were cowards.

'I understand, really I do. As soon as I get in touch with one of the grown-ups I'll let them know, but don't worry; this isn't for everyone.'

'Thanks. It's not that I'm scared. It's my family. I don't want my kids growing up without me. The money is great, but it's not worth it. Nothing is worth dying in this shit hole,' he added.

'Okay, mate, I'll take care of it,' I said.

Even if he was terrified, who could blame him? Only an idiot isn't scared at times like this. Bravery is nothing more than controlling your fear and making yourself function when all you want to do is disappear up your own arse.

All I wanted was coffee, almost an addiction of mine. I drink far too much of it. I stood up and limped outside to ask if there was any, and one of the medics sent me to their office. I helped myself and sat down, still replaying the events in my mind. I didn't want to forget as I was sure that I'd be writing statements later. John walked past and through the open doorway.

'John, over here,' I said loudly enough for him to hear. He turned and came over, also making a beeline for the coffee.

'What is it with Americans and this non-dairy creamer shit? It's full of palm oil; it'll kill you,' he said, disgusted by the lack of real milk. All US locations seemed to use only powdered milk of the Coffee-mate variety; they even had flavoured ones like hazelnut that you could buy in the PX, but it made sense as it's lighter to transport and doesn't go off.

'What's the latest?' I asked.

'Well, Tom is still being X-rayed and I've spoken to Ops. They're going to send another team up, but not until tomorrow. We're running out of daylight after all, and this coffee isn't all that bad,' he said, taking a sip.

'Johnny's just quit,' I added.

'I thought he might. He didn't seem to enjoy today at all. He might have the right idea, of course,' he stated flatly.

'What about you?' I asked.

'You must be fucking kidding. I'm on rock star wages. Just think of all the shiny things I can buy now that I'm single again.'

'You won't be single for long. I know you. People like you should stick to prostitutes or sex tourism. Five minutes back in the world with all your wages and you'll have some life-sucking gold-digger hanging off you, spending your money and shagging your mates as soon as you come back out here,' I said, laughing.

'Ah, you know me so well!'

'Do me a favour. See if you can find the bloke we're here to collect, and we'll need some accommodations for at least tonight.'

'Sure, no probs. Beds I've already sorted. There are transit rooms for people passing through. I'll head there now. Chances are our boy is there waiting for us.'

'Thanks, mate, and maybe take Johnny with you. Keep his mind off things until we can get him home,' I added as John left.

As I was starting to drift off, no doubt a lot to do with the lack of adrenaline racing through my system, the doctor came in and gave me an update on Tom's condition. He had intracranial swelling, which basically meant that during the incident he'd hit his head with sufficient force to cause swelling inside the cranium— which was quite common. The rest of him was fine; a few stitches here and there, but they would monitor the swelling and hopefully it would subside, but it meant that he wouldn't be travelling anywhere until he was back to normal. I was also ordered to get my head down for a few hours, and after finding a quiet corner did exactly that. I was woken up several hours later by one of the medics, but as I went to sit up I found that I couldn't move. My whole body was racked with pain.

'Fuck!' I hissed as I tried to sit upright.

'That'll be your ribs. Might take a week or so for the pain to go, but you'll be stiff for a while,' he laughed as I struggled to my feet.

I looked at my watch; it was now early evening. There was no further news on Tom, so I went outside and stood there for quite a while. I had to wait for John. We had no comms and the location was too big to start trying to find people. I knew he'd be back soon. I was trying not to think about things too much when I saw our only working vehicle approaching. It stopped next to me and John got out along with one other.

'Enjoy your sleep? I came round earlier but didn't want to wake you. Found our missing guy, though,' John said, pointing at the passenger.

'Why not?' I thought. It was that kind of day. The passenger, who I immediately named Rat Boy because he had the furtive look of a shit house rodent, smiled at me with rotten teeth and introduced himself. I could see John trying not to laugh. His name was Kevin, he lived in Northern Ireland but was English, and he was a dog handler.

'What a fucking surprise!' I thought again.

I can't even remember which regiment he'd started out in. Most dog handlers start as an infantry soldier of some description, and when it's discovered they're rubbish or weird, usually transfer to become a dog handler. If you're a dog handler and aren't one of the strange ones, I apologise, but if you are then you know that I'm not wrong on this point. As for other countries' dog handlers, I can't comment; I only have experience of British Army dog handlers prior to 2004, and I'm not talking about the Special Forces dogs we use these days.

I won't even waste space on this. In the end, he quit before we even left Anaconda. He was under the delusion that the locals didn't use the road, and the following morning when we were getting ready to return to Baghdad he asked about the route back. When I told him that we'd be driving back and that it would take a few hours depending on traffic and IED threats etc, he looked at me open mouthed— which wasn't pretty— and said he couldn't possibly go out on the road. What if something happened? I reminded him about the IED we'd just driven through, with one of the team still unconscious in hospital, and that was that.

'Send me home,' he said. 'I'm not leaving here.'

'Fine with me,' I said and telephoned our Ops manager. A flight was arranged for him and he packed up his stuff and hitched a ride on a chopper with the Yanks a few days later.

I'd been assured by the doctors that Tom would be fine— the swelling was going down and all the arrangements would be made to medically evacuate him back home. That was down to the company and the Department of Defense to sort out. Another team was on its way up to meet us and we'd be heading straight back down. I was feeling even worse after a night's sleep; my whole body ached, and it felt like I'd taken a good beating off several lumberjacks. Before we left we quickly looked in on Tom, who was conscious but a bit out of it. I put Johnny in with us and we slotted in, travelling back as a three-vehicle call sign. True to my word, we went straight to the villa, where Johnny handed in his notice and I started filling in a mountain of paperwork and statements. Then there were two. We were officially combat-ineffective. One vehicle and two men do not a PSD team make.

4

Thanksgiving, You Say

I found myself filling in on a US commercial contract, as the previous TL had been injured and medevaced home so I was now based at a small army camp south of Tikrit. We operated nine-man teams, all a mixture of Europeans and Kiwis, decent blokes, and again the project managers were the usual collection of people determined to get us all killed. This time we also had the clients' own security manager to deal with— a huge bear of a man called Jimmy who was ex-US Special Forces. Judging by his age, he'd probably left a while ago, but he was the poster boy for Frontier Spirit. I liked him instantly, and for all his tobacco-chewing, southern stereotype, he was a straight and honest man. The clients were employed by an explosives disposal company with the contract for getting rid of the Iraqi stockpiles of bombs, bullets and rockets. It would all be shipped up to disposal sites located in remote areas where another company would undertake the actual destruction. Our job was simple: the clients had offices all over Iraq and we took them to meetings or to the remote sites to oversee the progress of the ordnance disposal. The manager on the clients' side was another matter altogether. He was a fiercely religious southern Baptist who many, including me, found to be as fundamental as many of the Hajjis happily blowing themselves up. I've always tried to respect people who believe in anything strongly enough that they'll defend it with their lives, but there's a line between that and being a zealot of dangerous proportions.

'Hey Johnny, don't forget to ask for pumpkin pie when you get there,' our site manager said as I staggered past him on my way to my vehicle, carrying the world's allocation of ammunition, radio batteries and a medical kit, not forgetting my rifle, a pistol and, just in case, a belt-fed machine gun. For the sake of ease, we were all 'Johnny', even the Kiwis and the South Africans, as far as the Yanks were concerned. I looked at my rear gunner and he returned the look.

'Americans!' I muttered as I dumped all my kit into the vehicle and tightened the straps on my body armour and assault vest. That is how it started. We didn't want cowboys for clients, and they didn't want a bunch of tight-assed Limeys protecting them— their words, not mine.

This mission, like most, was to drop some clients off at a US Army camp and leave them there, an unusually simple task and very short, but my spider sense was already starting to tingle. All missions started with a tailgate brief, the team and clients gathering in a circle around the team commander while I ran through the mission— typically the route, what we could expect in the way of support, and what to do in case of a contact. This was solely for the clients' benefit. For instance, I'd explain that should the client vehicle become disabled, they should stay in it and do exactly as the vehicle commander said, not jump out of the vehicle screaming 'We're all gonna die' and then run towards the people shooting at them. Believe me, I've seen this. People of all nationalities do the weirdest things when they're terrified, none more so than civilians.

After the usual round of stupid questions, I put the clients in the only armoured vehicle that we had and I got in the front vehicle. Every team had their own way of doing things with regard to the positioning of personnel. I always stuck my second in command in the rear vehicle with all the firepower, with me in the front and a shooter in with the clients. If it went loud, the client vehicle's only job was to get out of the ambush, and if either the front or rear vehicle was taken out then that was our lookout. Going back to base with a dead client would not look good on your résumé, but a dead team was acceptable as long as the clients were okay and you didn't leave any bodies behind. Again, I'm speaking from experience— not mine, thankfully, but a dead driver who was left in a vehicle from another company.

We weren't travelling far. Our destination was Camp Cooke, which is in Taji, half an hour north of Baghdad. The main problem was the traffic. Like anywhere else, Baghdad has a rush hour, and this, coupled with military patrols blocking lanes and suspect packages by the side of the road, can make a thirty-minute journey last a day. But this was a good day. Three fast-moving vehicles that look like they're doing a practice lap at Monaco meant that we got to our destination very quickly. While the locals were on autopilot, we were definitely not. We were all trained to do each other's job, but we had dedicated drivers and they knew what they were doing. Reading the road makes all the difference, which is something lacking on the roads in the real world. Next time you're driving, try looking three cars ahead for brake lights, cars creeping out of side turnings, obstructions ahead. Most traffic jams and accidents could be avoided if people paid attention.

We dropped our clients at their Camp Cooke office. Also with us was Jimmy, the clients' security manager, who because of his status could carry weapons and be used as a shooter during missions. I began to smell a rat and quickly found out why.

'Johnny, it's Thanksgiving this weekend,' Jimmy tried to mention in a casual way.

'Isn't that when you butchered all the Indians?' I replied.

'No, it's when the Indians fed the starving Pilgrims, to be precise,' he quickly replied.

'We don't celebrate Thanksgiving,' I added, and had an idea what was coming, especially after the pumpkin pie comment earlier.

'Well, we do, and the site manager really wants to put on a big spread for everybody, to improve morale, that kind of thing. As we're here anyway, I wanna try and scrounge some supplies from the Army,' he added unnecessarily.

'Pumpkin pie?'

'You got it, buddy. I knew you Brits would get into the spirit of things,' he shouted as he walked off, leaving me the task of trying to explain to twelve Europeans that they were about to risk their lives for turkeys.

As you can imagine, the news didn't go down too well. To be honest, we took too many risks as it was, and this was just asking for trouble. Things tended to go wrong when you were least expecting it; we seemed to take casualties on low-risk missions whereas the high-risk ones that we all thought we were going to get spammed on seemed to go off really well. So this was one of those 'it's all going to go horribly wrong' moments. Even more infuriatingly, our project manager, who was supposed to be on our side, was a total yes-man and if we'd refused, which we'd have been within our rights to do, he'd have fucked us all for it and probably had us replaced before you could say 'cranberry sauce'. I only needed to point this fact out to my kids for them to realise the futility of argument. Things were rarely ideal, and I always said to the team that each man as an individual had to evaluate the risk and make up his own mind to stay and risk it or bug out and not look back. Some had done just that, but most remained and some of those had paid the price.

Once the PX had been hit and everybody had bought a Whopper, we loaded up and drove over to the other side of the camp to try and talk the Army out of its precious supply of streamers and chocolate logs. However, it soon became apparent that we weren't the only ones on this kind of mission, and an argument quickly ensued between our Jimmy and the Army about the importance of morale at our location and how the only thing that would avoid a mass suicide would be the donation of several boxes of frozen turkeys. After a mixture of bribery and arse-kissing, we were soon loading the rear of the gun truck with more turkeys than we actually needed. My rear gunner pointed out that we could always throw them at the enemy if we got bumped on the way back.

We weren't done yet, though. Helpfully the soldier guarding the turkeys suggested that we go to the Green Zone because he was sure that they had cranberry sauce and pumpkin pies. This of course appealed to Jim, and we were soon screaming out of Camp Cooke heading to the other side of Baghdad at breakneck speed. It was obvious that nobody apart from the Europeans found this almost suicidal obsession with Thanksgiving strange. We finally fought our way through the traffic, narrowly avoiding several nasty collisions, and boxed around one suspect IED in the road that the Army were poking with a stick. New camp, new PX, so again we stocked up on beef jerky and Gatorade before hitting the supply store. After more begging and bribery we were soon loading the client vehicle with pumpkin pies and cranberry sauce. But still we weren't finished. The supply sergeant said, almost in hushed tones, that he'd heard that somewhere in Camp Victory there was a supply of stuffing. This was obviously the holy grail of all things Thanksgiving, and the only thing separating us from nirvana was the BIAP road.

My previous contract was in the Green Zone and we'd run that road all the time. I'd lost count of the amount of times we'd weaved our way through burning vehicles that had been hit only minutes earlier. Usually the enemy had withdrawn, leaving only the carnage they'd caused and us bearing witness to this surreal sight. I'd also been shot to shit several times myself but had been lucky. Most of my team weren't familiar with this area, so I gave it to them straight. I told them it was fifteen minutes of straight road with a million possible firing points, overpasses and flyovers that insurgents had used in the past to fire from, plus countless spots to hide IEDs. I also mentioned that my vehicle would be travelling at over 100 mph and they had better keep up.

We drove slowly through the staggered blast barriers at the front gate, and as soon as the last vehicle was clear we floored it. I have to admit to a certain amount of exhilaration, travelling so fast in hostile terrain, ready for an ambush but still prepared to do the job, knowing that the men you're working with will die if they have to, yet not in the fanatical way of our enemy but to protect the whole. It's hard to describe. Obviously you have to be there to fully appreciate the complexities of the situation. At that moment our biggest concern was a car full of explosives just looking for a nice fat PSD team to evaporate. The rear gunner kept everything back and we sacrificed tactics for speed and aggression. Technically we didn't have any real clients and Jimmy was as expendable as we were as we rapidly approached the first army checkpoint of Victory. Unfortunately the Army had repositioned their blast walls and tank traps, and we almost caused World War Three as the soldiers on the checkpoint, which was now a lot closer than it was the previous week, almost opened fire on us. We weren't the only ones worried about suicide bombers, and fast-moving vehicles tended to encourage only one response from the Army; it usually involved several hundred rounds of armour-piercing, which to be fair was a reasonable reaction.

Fortunately the whole team was well spread out and I managed to warn the other vehicles to slow down. I apologised to the soldiers on the checkpoint and we drove into Victory, but I was determined to make this the last stop, as I had visions of us going further and further and ending up in Najaf or somewhere equally Coalition-friendly.

We were back on track for the stuffing quest. The good thing about Victory was the amount of military there, so if we were going to find stuffing anywhere it was there, and it wasn't a total waste of time from our perspective as I sent two vehicles to steal and scrounge as much medical equipment and anything else that we might need. An hour later, and about to run out of daylight, we all met up at the main PX. Jim was beside himself because not only had they managed to get stuffing, they'd also got several cases of alcohol-free Budweiser, or near-beer as they called it. The US Army was fanatical about not drinking, and it was almost a shooting offence to get caught doing so, even though a case of Heineken was only $5 and the British Army in the south was allowed to drink without any problems. They also had some party decorations, which really made risking our lives worth it. I said that we were going back before it got dark as we really didn't want to get caught out after nightfall. There was no argument and we headed back into the evening rush hour.

That weekend we all gathered in the dining facility. There before us were the fruits of our labours— turkeys, pumpkin pies and a million other items of a Thanksgiving nature. The site manager recited the story of Thanksgiving, making it far more religious than I remember, but I was right that they took the Indians' hospitality and wasted them later when they were well fed. None of us felt warm or fuzzy, and most of the clients thought the food had magically appeared, but it was an amazing spread. As much as Thanksgiving as a holiday means nothing to me, I could see that the clients appreciated it and that it meant a lot to them, so as foolhardy as it was, at least we had made a difference, no matter how small. John, who had been on leave throughout all of this, refused to believe that such a thing had happened. The injured TL returned, and John and I headed back to the Green Zone. A new team would be arriving the next week and we were needed back online.

We'd only been back a day when our company lost two men in Mosul. That was where John and I were going next— replacements for two fatalities. Mosul was rapidly turning into a meat grinder and several companies had lost men, in some cases an entire team taken out with a mixture of dead and wounded. Armor Group lost more than most, but none of us came away unscathed from there. Rumours of Chechens on religious holiday had been leaked by the military, but whatever was waiting for us, they were fearless and effective. Originally we weren't down to go, but the team that had been ordered up there had quit to a man rather than go to Mosul, and we were the only ones available.

We took two soft skin Pajeros, loaded our kit and drove from Baghdad to Mosul in one go, just the two of us. Again, a really stupid and almost suicidal thing to do, but that was what the project manager and country manager had decided. We were totally on our own, no support, and with us both driving, not very tactical either. I've spoken to many people since, some of whom I respect as exceptional operators, and not one has said they'd have agreed to those conditions, and to this day I can't say why I agreed, but I did. It was nothing gung-ho, just blind obedience and, dare I say it, lunacy.

I'd recently found myself developing a disdain for everything and everyone. I hated the locals and everything they believed in, seeing them as prehistoric fools following an archaic religion that made no sense, and as much as they hated me for my beliefs, I hated them more. My peers who voiced their concerns and caused trouble because they felt things were too dangerous I called cowards and said they had no business being there. I was beginning to hate everything and everybody. I knew I was being unreasonable, regardless of what George Bernard Shaw had said about progress being dependent on the unreasonable man. I'd started to take everything personally, and something had to give. John had already warned me about my attitude, especially with our management, who I'd begun to consider cowardly yes-men. Very few had been on the ground, most having walked in as managers because they knew the right people. I was also quite fond of letting them know what I thought of them and their idiotic ideas, but even so I would still undertake any mission given, in an almost 'fuck you' kind of way. Looking back on it, I'm surprised, as I'm usually very level-headed and sensible, but I'd gone there straight from the Army and the invasions of Iraq and Afghanistan, so was a prime candidate for post-traumatic stress, and I'm sure I wasn't the only one. I did see a few people completely unravel. You can go through the worst experiences again and again, then just come apart over nothing.

The drive up was long and uneventful, which in my experience is typical. As I've said, when you expect trouble nothing happens, but when you're on a so-called easy mission that's when it all goes to rat shit. We were met by the project manager, another bureaucrat, as I was about to find out.

'Hi! Good drive up?' he asked.

'Yes, pretty quiet. Not ideal travelling like this,' I added, not sure which direction the conversation was going to take.

'Well, you can get rid of those assault vests. We don't operate like that here, and also we don't go out made ready either,' he said.

By now we were all wearing assault vests over our body armour, a heavy nylon mesh vest with magazine and utility pouches attached. This meant that all your ammunition and, equally importantly, your personal medical kit was on you, making it accessible. Being made ready meant putting your magazine on your weapon and loading a round into the chamber so that all you had to do was flick the safety off and pull the trigger.

'You're not made ready, and where do you keep all your magazines and med kits if they aren't on you?' I could feel myself losing my grip, and suddenly I was about to snap.

'You carry a backpack with everything inside and wear your body armour under your shirts. We're low key here,' he added.

'You know what? Fuck that and fuck you!' I ranted. 'If your guys had been operating like we do in Baghdad, I suspect that you might have had fewer casualties. I'm not working for a clueless twat like you,' I screamed, getting right into his face.

I'm embarrassed to say that I lost it completely. In my mind these stupid rules and cowardly operating procedures were getting us killed. The clients weren't making us do this. We had the same clients in Baghdad and they let us get on with it— that's what they paid us for— but some project managers had decided that they wanted things a certain way and they were getting us killed. It only takes a few to ruin things, and right now I wanted this little prick to know it.

'You can't talk to me like that!' he screamed, turning purple.

'Really? And what are you going to do about it? Report me? People have died here, and looks like you're the reason,' I said, getting ready to start swinging. Again, this isn't like me at all, but I just snapped. Men had died, and as far as I was concerned, bad tactics and stupid rules had allowed that and I'd just had enough.

'Stop, both of you!' John said, pushing his way between us.

'Fuck him, fucking amateur!' I said with as much disgust as I could manage, and walked out.

I stood outside, shaking with anger. I wanted to go back inside and tear this office boy to shreds. I'd never been this angry before, but the casualties that we'd been taking and the fatalities had all been mounting up, and it was nearly always avoidable. Bad judgement, pointless missions, rules like being low key— three identical off-road vehicles being driven and crewed by white faces is not low key, and even a moron knows a PSD team when he sees one.

'What the fuck's got into you?' John shouted as he came outside.

'I can't follow these ridiculous orders any more. Too many of us are getting killed through negligence, and it's all down to idiots who don't know what they're doing.'

'You can't threaten the project manager,' he said flatly.

'You don't get it, John. There aren't any rules here. We own this country, and as for that twat, I'll frag him and make it look like an accident. I mean it!' I said, walking off to find a PX and coffee, and I did mean it.

I'd got to that point, and what was worse, I knew I could get away with it. What I didn't realise was just how frazzled I'd become, and as always in this sort of situation, you're the last to know. However, I stand by what I said to the project manager. Maybe I shouldn't have been so in his face about it, but I'd got the point across and that left him with a massive problem: what to do with me. I wasn't in the Army any more and I was only just starting to realise it. Nobody could make me do anything, and I wasn't going to back down. I caught up with John later, and went to the accommodation. The following morning I decided I was going to find another job, and, as often happens, Armor Group who operated along the same lines, laughably covert, had an entire team taken out by a drive-by, with one fatality and several wounded. Having spoken to one of the Armor guys who came up from Baghdad to fill in, their project management was even more determined to get everyone killed. Mosul seemed to be a problem. I spoke with several operators from many companies and they all did the same— magazines in grab bags and not made ready. I never understood it, but the Armor Group incident had made my mind up for me.

I quit and was glad that I'd done so. I then had to wait for HR to organise a flight on the big metal freedom bird from Kuwait. I'd been doing my best to avoid the project manager because I was sure that another encounter would escalate into something very unpleasant, and although there wouldn't be much of a comeback on me, it was not as though I would get arrested there. I was enough of a professional to not want that kind of label. After all, I intended to return as soon as I could. I was moping around a small coffee place inside the MWR (morale, welfare, recreation), a building for US service personnel that usually had games and televisions, computers as in an internet café, and sometimes a gym— basically whatever the people who ran them could get hold of. I'd been in some that were enormous, but this was a bit smaller. We all appreciated the effort that these people had made to make it as comfortable as possible, and often it was the only point of contact with the outside world. The internet wasn't fast enough for webcams— it was only dial-up speeds— but email is better than nothing, and I needed to put my feelers out for another job. John came in and sat down next to me.

'So that's it then; you're leaving,' he said, looking a bit pissed off.

'I can't work like this,' I said. 'God knows, I'm not scared of danger, but I'd feel pretty stupid bleeding to death in a burning vehicle because I went on a pointless mission.'

'I know, but I can't leave. I need the money,' he said.

'John, it's not worth it. I know most of the blokes out here are being fucked around by idiots, but I can't believe that there aren't any companies that have higher standards than the usual suspects. There's got to be a project out there, where the security contractors are allowed to do their jobs properly and the clients listen to us. We're employed to manage the risk, after all. If we're just going to do what the clients want, regardless of the risk, what's the point in employing us?'

I was still yet to see the full picture, which was that clients were there to make money, and if we stopped them from doing so they wouldn't listen to us. We were also there because an insurance company had insisted that security should be in place, and the people in charge of the invasion were all carving the country up and giving bits to different security companies. This is a simplistic way of looking at it, but ultimately it came down to money, as most things generally do. I was still stuck in a soldier's mindset—

honour and all the things that I believed in while serving my country— but none of this is transferable and I needed to get my head round that, otherwise I'd implode. The sad fact was that all the major players in Iraq operated along the same lines: clients' wishes first, companies' wishes second and ours last; it was just business.

I came to believe that this period in my life was confused. Looking back, I think I did everything in reverse. I should have left the Army, sorted out my life, put things in perspective, gone on a massive holiday (probably involving vast amounts of alcohol and debauchery) and re-evaluated everything before deciding on a career, but had in fact done the opposite. I was technically still in the Army when I'd deployed as a contractor, not serving but on my terminal leave, and hadn't even handed my kit in, something that I was intending to get around to but never did. I was quite lucky and hadn't really broken any major rules, but I hadn't given myself any downtime. I'd gone from regular soldier to private soldier in a flash and I think that had an impact on my well-being. It had certainly unbalanced me a bit, fortunately not in the 'let's kill everything' way but more in a lack of tolerance and short-tempered kind of way. I worked this out for myself, and felt that speaking to a professional would not be a bad thing. There's no dishonour in seeking help. I was lucky, and armed with that epiphany, I did just that. I went on the massive holiday, sorted my personal life out and spoke to someone and, several weeks later and feeling a lot better in myself, I decided to go back. I'd looked around in the UK and elsewhere for gainful employment, but nothing came close to the level of income and freedom that working in the sandpit offered. And whether I liked it or not, I'd got a taste for it and wanted another bite of the cherry, but this time I had the benefit of experience and knew what I wanted and, most importantly, what the realities of the job entailed.

Fortunately for me I still had some influential friends, and one thing I'd learnt was that who you knew was far more important than what you knew, and that protection from on high was far more useful than being good at your job. A good friend of mine, also in Mosul but working for a rival company, told me the chilling story of a project manager who was ex-Foreign Legion. There were quite a few ex-legionnaires in Iraq, and like everybody else, you had good and bad. No doubt a good unit, but more famous for fighting to the last man and following orders regardless of the outcome, even if that meant certain death rather than actually winning wars. This kind of indoctrination breeds a certain type of soldier, and in this case a manager, who, even though now a civilian, expected the men on his contract to do whatever he felt was necessary. The unfortunate outcome was the wounding and death of several people, and him being moved to another contract where he did exactly the same. When it was becoming apparent that the men of his contract were about to take matters into their own hands, he was promoted and sent to Africa, and all because someone higher up the food chain had his back.

It may sound as though I'm going overboard about management and how rubbish they were, but in the early days, between 2004 and 2007, there was virtually no oversight. Contractors couldn't be arrested, and the only people we had to watch out for were the military with whom we lived and ate. An operator could literally spend all day shooting at people, and as long as a military call sign wasn't involved and none of his own reported him, he would get away with it. Our vehicles had no identifying markings and we all drove the same kind of vehicles, and the Iraqi Police had no jurisdiction over us. With the bad guys stealing police uniforms as disguises, we would light them up as much as the next target. Many of us operators and management did our jobs with as much professionalism and restraint as we could, but unfortunately this environment did attract some people who wanted to get as much trigger time as possible or make as much money as possible by misappropriation of funds and matériel. There was a lot of cash floating around, and a lot of weapons that could be sold or smuggled by unscrupulous people, and operators constantly jumped between companies. In the end, we were all in it to make as much as possible for ourselves.

A friend of mine gave me an introduction to a small US outfit that was about to start operating in Iraq and had already picked up a few lucrative and well-organised contracts. The owner, an ex-Delta Force guy who'd left the military and been working within the State Department and no doubt a few other shady organisations, was looking for 'a few good men' as he put it, Iraq experience essential. I flew to the US and met him in Maryland, and after hitting it off straight away and having a few beers, he offered me a job as a PSD team leader on a Department of Defense contract, protecting US officials whose job it was to see where the US taxpayers' money was going. It all sounded much of a muchness, as that's what a lot of companies were already doing. The job was again based in the Green Zone and the offices were in the palace— all good. The pay wasn't astronomical but was still good, US companies tending to pay less as they employed mostly US nationals and $100,000 goes a lot further in America than it does in Britain, especially after you exchange your currency. The leave wasn't great, as most UK companies were doing a nine weeks in and three weeks home rotation, but because the Yanks usually employed their own, and their tax laws are much stricter than ours, they needed to spend longer out of the country to be non-resident for tax. As a result, most US contracts had a twelve weeks in and two weeks home rotation, and this one was no different. However, I was willing to do it for the money on offer and the decent working conditions. We were only paid when we were in country, so a longer rotation meant more money. Before I left the US my new ID was sorted out and issued by the DOD, which was a good sign as this meant that the company had some pull. It wasn't unheard of for DOD cards to be issued in the US, but for them to be issued to Europeans was unusual.

I flew back to the UK to sort out my admin and was then on a plane back to Kuwait. After twenty-four hours at Ali Al Salem, a massive air base 20 miles from the Iraqi border in Kuwait, I was on a transport plane to Baghdad, same as before— the unforgettable roller-coaster into the BIAP and the searing heat when the back doors opened to let the smell of Iraq into the confines of the aircraft.

Staggering out into the sun and the heat, I collected my bag and then made my way over to the pick-up point. This time I was met by a PSD team and was driven as a client to the Green Zone. I spent the short trip observing the drills and expertise of the team and, equally importantly, the equipment. This was already looking like a no-expense-spared operation; the vehicles and weapons were all high quality and the team seemed to operate very cohesively. By the time we reached the Green Zone, I was already feeling very hopeful.

The TL showed me to my accommodation, the standard well-equipped trailers, although this time I wasn't sharing, and I unpacked and squared myself away. I met with the project manager and was issued with all of my personal kit. The team was already up and running, and I was taking over from the previous TL. However, this would present its own problems, as I'd have to fit into a team that was already operating. I'd therefore be an outsider, and it was possible that someone on the team might think that they should be the TL, especially if the second in command had been filling in. That does sometimes happen, a 2ic moving up, but equally it's not unusual for a company to bring in an outsider— either a new person or someone from another contract because they're better qualified. Either way, the person who's been filling in nearly always feels as though they're being overlooked. I guess I would too.

My team was to provide protection to a small Department of Defense group who were supplying expertise to the new Iraqi Police and Army. We'd therefore be covering a lot of ground and, as we were the only team,

I'd be going all over the country, which meant many miles of danger. My second in command, an American called Geoff, an ex-Ranger with quite a lot of military experience but not so much PSD, commanded the rear vehicle with Patrick and Travis. George, a Kiwi, was my driver, and Paul, a Canadian, travelled in the client vehicle with Karl, an ex-Recon Marine. I was impressed with them all and we got to know each other quickly, doing the necessary training, and I was more than satisfied that they all knew what they were doing. It's always hard initially with a new team; you don't want to appear too friendly, as this can often be seen as weakness, and being too distant can make you look like an arse, but if you have a good team it all works out fine on its own. Some people didn't like mixed nationality teams, but personally I always thought and still do think that they're a good thing, giving you a mix of skill sets and different attitudes towards things. I never liked the blinkered approach, and so many of my species tried to get all their mates and people they'd served with on the same gigs as them. I'm not saying that's a bad thing; just that I liked to think outside the box and something different wasn't necessarily bad. We had an armoured Excursion as our client vehicle, but our front and rear vehicles were semi-armoured F350 Pickups. The front screen was armoured, there was a steel tub in the rear for the rear gunner, and the doors had armoured panels mounted to the inside as well as shielding for the engine but not the side windows or the roof. It wasn't ideal, but was a lot better than I was used to.

We were on our way to Mosul again, this time taking clients to the dam, from Baghdad. Mosul is 400 kilometres give or take, and it's a brutal trip even when nothing happens. Generally we didn't move at night, but as a trip there could easily take all day, I decided to leave in the middle of the night. After all, it was unexpected, which was always good, and Hajji likes his sleep. I got all the intelligence I could and we picked up the clients, and at zero three hundred we had a final check and rolled out into the darkness. Baghdad was still well lit but the roads were quiet and in no time we were on Tampa flying past Taji and heading north. I was keeping my GPS on grids so I could quickly check it against the map if we should have to deviate from our route, and if I saw something, I could mark it on my GPS so that when it came to passing on information or writing a contact report I'd have an exact location. Most of us bought GPS units from the PX, and for many it was the first time using them. The Army didn't issue Gucci bits of kit like that, and many, myself included, used to look on them with disdain, describing them as kit for the lazy. You can't overlook skills like map-reading and using a compass, but having a GPS is a life-saver. Most used MGRS (Military Grid Reference System) which knows which map sheet you're using as long as it's a military map. Setting it to grids on my unit showed speed, travel time, sunrise and sunset and also the current grid reference, so if I wanted to check our progress or had turned off the road in a hurry, let's say to avoid an IED or a contact, and was suddenly off the normal route, I just had to find the current grid reference on the map in order to know exactly where we were. This was easier than finding reference points on the ground, orientating the map and trying to find said points on the map, so not lazy but sensible, and I still do it today, although from time to time I hear people saying it's lazy.

Unlike my last contract, we had a dedicated Ops room manned by a watch keeper. Whenever we had a call sign on the ground, and all the vehicles were fitted with a tracking system that was monitored back at Ops, the watch keeper could see our progress in real time, including speed. We also had a panic button that when pressed informed the watch keeper with an audible and visual alarm. As for communications, we had the Codan Radio system, best described as somewhere between a mobile phone and a radio, which gave us comms over a greater distance than normal radios, as well as satellite phones, which, although slow, nearly always worked. Things had come a long way in a short space of time as PSD operations became more mainstream and less Mickey Mouse. Although all this kit was available, it was ultimately down to whether the company could afford it. If the contract didn't stipulate it, it was unlikely that you'd have it, and all these things were massively expensive. We were lucky that the DOD insisted on these measures, as they protected their personnel better, and the fitting of this and similar equipment was written into the contract. Obviously the company charged more so they didn't lose out on the cost, and it also meant that they could then go after other contracts and use these little things to make them look better than the competition when bidding on the many lucrative opportunities that were out there.

Just past Camp Cooke the surroundings become more desolate, more open in nature and with fewer buildings, so that movement stood out. I could see something ahead by the side of the road—a bit like a rabbit in the headlights, a Hajji was squatting with a shovel, and the look on his face was comical. Obviously PSD teams didn't normally travel at night, so he wasn't expecting any traffic. I didn't see any weapons, but he was obviously digging something into the side of the road. I marked the location on my GPS, later handing the location over to the military so they could check the area for any unwelcome presents for any call signs, and radioed along my convoy telling everyone to be on the lookout for similar things. Speaking to the military later, they told me that sometimes one guy with a shovel comes along, digs a hole and wanders off. If he gets stopped he only has a shovel— no weapons, no IED— so he's clear. His friend then comes along with the IED, drops it in the hole and wanders off. Then someone else wires it up and finally he comes back and camouflages the whole thing— very neat.

I still think about it and wonder what I'd have done if we hadn't had clients. The golden rule when travelling with clients was that you got them to wherever they were going with minimal fuss, didn't look for trouble and didn't engage the enemy unless you had to, and even if you were ambushed, you drove through and out and kept going or went back, whichever was the tactically sensible thing to do. You didn't stop and fight. However, if you didn't have clients, it was really down to you. I personally always fought and if possible destroyed the enemy. If you didn't, they'd be back the next day with more weapons and manpower. So would I have brassed up the guy digging by the side of the road at three in the morning? He certainly wasn't gardening, so I think that I probably would have.

'One, this is Rear Gunner, radio check, over,' Travis said from the bucket, an armoured tub in the flat bed of the rear pickup. It was welded in and had a seat fitted with a mount for the M240 Bravo, a belt-fed machine gun. The rear gunner was there to watch our rear and not let any vehicles pass. He was authorised to use deadly force as per the rules of engagement issued to us by the Coalition, and while every company had its own way of doing things, we'd try to wave the oncoming car off; if it kept coming, we'd fire warning shots either side of the vehicle and if this didn't work, aimed shots into the engine; if that yielded no result, we'd brass up the occupants. With the speeds we travelled at, we very rarely had locals trying to overtake us. When moving at slow speeds, which wasn't often, or when static, we'd keep a distance between us and any potential threats, the biggest being a car bomb— a real threat to us— and if it was big enough, they didn't have to get that close. On the open road it was easier to defend against, but in a built-up area like Baghdad it wasn't so easy. There were certain times when you were vulnerable, especially when queuing up to get into a military base. For instance, in 2004, a truck bomb weighing half a ton exploded outside Assassins' Gate at the Green Zone, killing over twenty and wounding a hundred, including an American PSD team. A device that size wouldn't have to be that close to you to ruin your day. I didn't intend to get taken out like that, and gave my rear gunner explicit instructions to open up if he felt the threat was real and that we'd worry about the fallout afterwards.

'You're okay, over,' I replied.

'I can see two vehicles, maybe 200 metres behind us. They don't have their lights on but they've been with us for a couple of clicks.'

'Roger; keep an eye on them and let me know if they try to get closer.'

I looked in my side mirror but couldn't see anything. Our rear gunner had a very good set of binoculars and, although the light wasn't great, we did pass through small lit-up areas where the available light could be used to get a better view.

'One, this is Rear Gunner. These two are definitely suspicious; they keep falling back and pulling forward and I think are together. They keep pulling up next to each other and communicating,' Travis reported several minutes later.

'Roger; sounds odd. If they try to get close, engage them. Everybody, understood?'

'Roger,' Travis replied, followed by several double clicks from the rest of the team.

It was rare that you got to prepare for a potential threat. Usually it just happened and you reacted. I knew that the rear vehicle would be getting ready to ruin the suspicious vehicles' day if they got close, and that the rest of the team would be getting ready also.

'One, this is Three. Something's definitely wrong here. We're going to drop back a bit and take care of it,' Geoff said.

'Roger that,' I replied.

On the open road like this a three-vehicle call sign could easily be spread out over a kilometre or more, as being bunched up just increased the chances of losing more than one vehicle in an IED. It also gave the other vehicles more time to react if, for instance, the front vehicle was hit. And importantly, if we could prevent the clients from knowing what was going on, so much the better. We all wore earpieces, so the guys in the client vehicle who had stayed silent throughout wouldn't have alerted the clients to any potential problem. The last thing we needed was panicky civilians or, even worse, clients trying to tell us how to do our job.

'Firing now,' I heard from the rear gunner.

There were several bursts from the rear, but even with my windows down, at the speed and distance apart we were travelling, the sound was faint, so the clients, possibly asleep in their fully armoured vehicle, wouldn't have heard anything. I marked a waypoint on my GPS for the grid, just in case.

'One, this is Rear Gunner, over.'

'Send,' I replied.

'All good. They were side by side and began accelerating toward us. I let them get within 100 metres and lit them up.'

'Roger that. You all okay back there? I asked.

'All good,' came the reply.

'Roger; out to you. Vehicle Two, give me two clicks if all that went unnoticed at your end.'

I quickly received two clicks and was satisfied that the clients knew nothing. This wasn't an unusual occurrence, and it wouldn't be reported. Why leave yourself open to any potential problems? Not because we'd done something wrong— we were within the rules to engage targets under these circumstances— but by making it official you could easily get blamed for something that a Mickey Mouse outfit had done in the same area. Besides, many PSD call signs fired a hundred warning shots a day. Sadly the Iraqi people were slow in learning to keep away from PSD vehicles, and I don't doubt that many innocent civilians met the rough end of a rear gunner, but I tried to do the job properly and we opened fire only if we had to. We left the cowboy antics to the likes of Blackwater and the many other less than reputable companies operating there.

We carried on into the night. By zero five hundred we were approaching the Samarra bypass that would take us on to Tikrit and then Baiji, places where I never felt comfortable. There were a lot of tribal problems up there, which meant people with no shortage of guns and experience shooting at each other, and there's nothing like a common enemy to bring out the worst in people. We passed two more suspicious-looking types by the side of the road, both close to the bypass, and again I marked the location onto my GPS. Although we had enough fuel to reach our destination, I intended to stop at Camp Speicher, just north of Tikrit, to rest the team and maybe get breakfast. We were going to overnight in Mosul anyway, but I'd already decided that a return trip at night was definitely the way forward and was going to chance coming back same time tomorrow, as long as the team were up to it. It would be a long trip, and the drivers would be hanging out. We could always swap, but even sitting in the passenger seat watching your arse and being ready for anything took its toll and was very tiring. With mile after mile of nothing, it was easy to drift off; staying alert was the hard part.

Streaks of light started to penetrate the blackness as we approached Tikrit, always a bad area. The Al-Tikriti were Saddam Hussein's tribe and big players in the place of his birth, and this meant that those operating there didn't get left alone much. Incidentally, it was near there that Saddam was found and captured, and there was no shortage of hostility to all Coalition personnel, be it military or PSD, the daily intelligence reports nearly always featuring bombings and shootings in the area. And if they weren't trying to kill us, they were quite happy to have a go at each other. We bypassed the town and carried on, and by the time we reached Speicher, a sprawling US air base, we were ready for a break. The sun was beginning to invade the sky and I could already feel the temperature rising. It got very cold at night, and the heat of the day was welcome. After a breakfast that would have killed a camel (KBR might be a shady bunch but they do a good breakfast) we stocked up on everything that we could liberate from the dining facility— drinks, namely Red Bull and Gatorade, and snacks, which were always available— before checking the vehicles and refuelling. I informed our Ops room of our location and passed on the grids I'd collected earlier. I didn't mention the contact, and finally we let the clients hit the PX. Speicher was great; you could buy almost anything, eat almost anything, and you could even get a massage from a group of oriental women who'd set up shop there. They had a full-on beauty salon offering manicures and facials, everything completely legit, no extras (several of my colleagues had tried and failed). The services were cheap, about $20 for a massage if I remember rightly, but we didn't have time that day. It was the kind of place that was hard to leave, purely because it was safe and well stocked.

While the clients were busy in the PX we waited by the vehicles, drinking our Iraqi version of a frappuccino from the Green Bean coffee company, one of the concessions that had sprung up along with Burger King and Pizza Hut. It looked like a Starbucks and had a similar menu, but it wasn't. I preferred it, and it didn't feel like I was giving my money to a bunch of left-wing tree-huggers every time I paid for coffee. One of my team had decided to write to large companies like Starbucks to try and score some freebies but received a reply from them saying that they couldn't possibly condone the invasion of Iraq by giving us free bags of ground coffee. Needless to say, that left a rather bitter taste— a bit like their coffee really. Most companies were more than happy to send us stuff, and we were soon tripping over boxes of energy bars and Pringles that had been sent to us.

'Travis, what happened with the car that you lit up?' I asked.

'Bastards must've thought I just fell out a banana boat. They kept pulling forward within maybe 200 metres, having a look and dropping back, then they'd drive side by side. Looked like they were talking to each other. They kept this up for about twenty minutes,' he replied.

'Could you see anything— make of vehicle, that kind of thing?' I asked.

'One was a Caprice, and the other looked like an Opel, but I saw them in the light as we drove past a bunch of shops and I'm sure they were wearing shemaghs,' he added.

'Sounds wrong,' I said, to murmurings of agreement.

'Anyway, you did the right thing; and the clients didn't hear anything?'

'Not a thing. They were sleeping, anyway,' Karl added.

'All good, then,' I said, satisfied that we'd avoided any incidents.

'We were all surprised that you called it so quick. Thought you Brits were a bit slow off the mark opening fire,' Geoff said.

One of the problems we had when working with Americans was that they always assumed that we don't like shooting people, whereas we always assumed that they're cowboys who shoot at anything.

'Only at each other,' I said with a smile.

We also liked to dig at the Yanks about the amount of friendly-fire incidents they seemed to have. It was a constant source of banter between us and them, the whole cowboys versus tight-assed Limeys thing, but it was just that— banter— and I had a lot of respect for these guys, regardless of nationality. There are good and bad in all nations.

'Maybe on the way back we can see if there are any abandoned cars. I marked the grid so we can have a quick look as we drive through.' The clients came out of the PX, weighed down with bags, and we loaded the vehicles and headed out on the remainder of the journey.

As you enter northern Iraq the landscape changes quite dramatically. It becomes more mountainous, and snow and extreme temperatures aren't unusual in winter. It was almost pleasant to look at. The further north you go, the closer you get to Kurdistan, an autonomous region within Iraq and quite a picturesque place. The Kurds, who were another group that Saddam Hussein liked to upset on a regular basis, occupy an area spanning northern Iraq, southern Turkey and parts of Syria and Iran, and there's very little love lost between them and the Iraqis. Kurdistan was then considered a safe place to go, the capital, Erbil, being quite famous for hotels and restaurants and, dare I say it, a nice place to go on the piss if you have the time.

We arrived in Mosul after lunch at some building project that looked like it had only started a few days ago but in fact had been running for months. As was the norm, a local company was paid millions to build something, such as a police station or a hospital (children's hospitals being a favourite as they were more likely to get money for that). We paid and they built, and periodically we visited and had a look at the progress. Quite often, as in our case, the clients were engineers and knew what they were looking at. Without exception, the work was never as far along as it should have been and would invariably need more money thrown at it, a favourite excuse being that workers weren't coming in because of a kidnap threat, or that more money was needed to pay a ransom, or Abdul had run off with all the money and was now living in Kurdistan where they couldn't touch him. We'd given the Iraqis a crash course in capitalism and consumerism, and they'd learnt quickly. We probably felt a little bit bad for bombing them, so we were quick to put our hands in our pockets to try and improve their lives, and for them it was an opportunity. They'd got by without a hospital or police station for years, and if it didn't get built, they'd manage and a lot of people would get richer. That was not always the case, but I saw enough projects abandoned because eventually even the people paying for them had to admit that they'd been taken for a ride. The money had gone and another unfinished building sat there. We visited locations like this all the time. Initially I was outraged, but as time wore on I became more of a realist. Seeing the amount of money being spent, or wasted, in a place like Iraq, it had been easy to be overwhelmed by it all, but by now it was just another mission; it wasn't my problem and I didn't really care. All we had to do was escort the clients while on site, my second in command keeping the vehicles moving around the site as we moved in order to provide cover and an escape should there be a problem, and when we'd finished we left. I frequently wondered how quickly after we'd left these sites that the workforce also left. It was often blindingly obvious that they'd all arrived just for the day of our visit, as they'd had prior warning that we were coming, but that wasn't my problem, infuriating though it was.

We drove to the nearest army base, where I received a phone call informing me that the grids I'd sent in had been checked and that two IEDs had been found. I must admit that for once I actually felt like I'd made a difference, and it did give me a real lift to think that fewer of us had died or been injured because of something as simple as passing on the grid of some Hajji doing a bit of moonlight gardening. I told the rest of the team over coffee, and for once we all sat there outside the Green Bean café with stupid satisfied looks on our faces.

5

Greasy Bandits

At Camp Cooke near Taji we had a location where we took our vehicles for servicing and general logistics. Our accommodation at Camp Cooke, another large army base with all the usual luxuries, was an old two-storey building that seemed to have more camel spiders and things with more than two legs than I'd ever seen before. It wasn't my favourite place—fortunately we rarely overnighted there— and backed onto part of the perimeter fence beyond which was a no man's land roughly 100 metres wide that was a debris field and had a large amount of unexploded ordnance. There were several places like this in Iraq. As Coalition forces moved through the country during the invasion, if it wasn't feasible to hold the ground before moving on, Iraqi ammo sites were blown to deny the enemy. It sounds great, but ultimately it left huge debris fields of stuff that the locals wanted to steal in order to turn into IEDs and similar unpleasant things. But hindsight is a wonderful thing, and sometimes shit happens. Even more strangely, the watch towers at this part of the perimeter were manned by Ukrainian snipers who were under orders to shoot to kill anyone caught in the debris field, and, being Ukrainian, appeared to have had a fair bit of practice before they arrived. They also seemed devoid of a sense of humour, but orders are orders and they did a good job.

Having come up early one morning to get our vehicles serviced, we were standing at the back of the building engaging in gossip with the military when we saw three very dishevelled Iraqis being led out of no man's land; two were covered in blood and looked in shock, and the third was holding his right forearm in his left hand, literally, while above us in the tower a

Ukrainian sniper shouted abuse at them. To this day, with the exception of the naked Iraqi I saw in Baghdad, it was one of the most surreal things I've ever seen, made even more strange by the Iraqis trying to apologise for getting shot.

'What the fuck happened there?' Geoff asked.

'Three guys in the debris field; the sniper clipped one, took his arm right off and the others stood up and surrendered.'

'Wow, it's not like that lot to take prisoners. Normally he'd have slotted all three,' I said, 'and it wouldn't be the first time either.'

'You're right, but our captain saw it and ordered them to cease fire. Doesn't look like they're too happy about it,' he added.

'Bastards. Do they get paid per kill or something?' I asked.

'Knowing this lot, I wouldn't be surprised,' he replied.

While I was having this conversation, the three Iraqis were sitting on the ground waiting for a Humvee to take them away to be processed. We wandered over as Paul was putting a field dressing on the one-armed man and had a quick look at him. Regardless of what I thought about the enemy, it was the decent thing to do, even though if it had been me who'd been taken prisoner I'd probably have got arse-raped to death.

'They see us with special weapon,' one of the intact Iraqis said, while mimicking someone looking through binoculars. I assumed he meant a night sight or possibly a thermal sight, something I knew that the Ukrainians had.

'Yeah, that's right,' I said.

'You have to be naked, man,' George said. We all looked at him; then kneeling down next to the Iraqis, he said really quietly. 'The special weapon can't see you if you're naked.'

'Really?' the intact Iraq replied.

We all nodded. He rattled on in Arabic to his friends, and then they all made an 'aah' sound as if they were saying, 'Of course it didn't work; we weren't naked!'

'Also, it's even better if you cover yourself in oil,' Karl added, keeping a straight face.

'Oil?'

'Yeah, you know, cooking oil. It reflects the light, confuses the weapon,' he added. Again the 'aah' sound and more whispered Arabic.

'Thank you, my friend,' the intact Iraqi said.

'Any time, Bro.'

We stood there for a few minutes, fighting to keep a straight face while the Army guys looked at us strangely.

It ended up with us having to spend the night in Taji, but we weren't that bothered as it meant more PX time, and while we were there we wouldn't be on any missions. However, in the middle of the night an irate army captain dragged us out of our vehicles, which we'd decided to sleep in rather than risk being eaten alive by the unmentionables living in the Taji accommodation.

'I hope you guys are proud of yourselves,' he said angrily.

'I'm sorry but you'll have to be a bit more specific than that,' I said, struggling to gain full consciousness.

'Follow me!' he shouted, storming off.

We followed him to one of the guardrooms, and inside were three naked and greasy Iraqis sitting on the floor with cable ties around their wrists. We all immediately started laughing.

'We caught these three trying to get into the camp.'

'They say they're invisible,' a US Army interpreter said.

'See, this is your doing,' the captain added.

'They don't understand why you can see them,' the interpreter added.

While all of this was going on, the Iraqis were babbling in Arabic to the interpreter, who to be honest was just making it worse, and I was finding it really difficult to hold it together.

'How am I supposed to explain this?' the captain said.

'Well, to be honest, I didn't think you would let the ones you caught this morning go so quickly,' I said.

'We just passed them to the Military Police. I don't know what they did with them.'

George was talking to the interpreter. 'It's the flip-flops,' George said.

'What?'

'They're wearing flip-flops; that's what gave them away.'

The interpreter translated this for the Iraqis, who all started arguing amongst themselves.

'One of them's saying that he told them the flip-flops would give them away,' the interpreter added.

'Get out, for fuck's sake!' the captain screamed, and we all left the room like naughty schoolboys and spent the rest of the night laughing about it.

Sometimes it was the little things like that that kept you sane when things got bad. As brutal as Iraq often was, it did have its light-hearted moments, although many would say that it wasn't light-hearted for the Iraqis. However, a soldier's sense of humour is vastly different from most people's, so for us it was hysterical. I'll let you make up your own mind.

We had a week of BIAP runs, but none of us particularly liked the 'fiery road of death' as we'd blithely nicknamed it. Everything we did was like playing Russian roulette, so it was chance and numbers whether you got hit or not, but numbers don't lie and the statistics for enemy action on Route Irish backed up the claim that it was the most dangerous road on the planet. Occasionally, however, other factors made it even more hazardous, and if it wasn't companies like Cochise or Custer Battles then it would inevitably be our nemesis, Blackwater.

Founded in 1997 by Erik Prince, Blackwater won many very lucrative US Government contracts and had been linked to CIA operations and all sorts of cloak and dagger stuff. After several high-profile incidents, the company rebranded to Xe and was eventually bought by a group of private investors; it's now called Academi and has no link to Prince. Now, for me, Blackwater had all the potential to be the best and most respected company out there. Prince came from a successful family and had a brief career as a Navy Seal. His mother sold the family business for over $1 billion, which no doubt helped in the formation of a training academy that started Blackwater. Having seen the need for private security and training facilities to work alongside military and government units, Prince pretty much moulded the way in which private military companies would operate. He was no doubt a very clever and driven man, so I still don't understand why every single time I came across Blackwater operators I was less than impressed. I'm sure they did have good personnel but can only speak of my own experiences of them.

When a good friend of mine was desperate to get out to Iraq, but due to his civilian background couldn't get his foot in the door, I suggested that the best way to go would be for him to join the Army Reserves and get a tour in Afghanistan or Iraq, but he felt he didn't have the time to do that, being convinced that the whole 'War on Terror' and associated employment would dry up and we would all be home by Christmas. Against my advice, he contacted Blackwater who offered to train him and employ him. The list of courses that he'd need to complete would cost him over $20,000, and they assured him that when it was all over he'd be as good as any ex-military operator. This is an interesting concept, but while he might be as well trained, he'd still lack actual combat experience. But it could work. The right person with the right training could make a first-rate operator. When I spoke to him during the training he described a boot camp experience and said he was enjoying it, and at the end of the training they deployed him to Iraq, as promised, where he was the only non-US person on a contract and was treated like a leper. I'd warned him that because he wasn't ex-military he could expect a bit of shit, and he informed me that many of the operators weren't ex-military either but law enforcement or correctional officers, and to make matters worse, he was getting paid less than everyone else. He stuck it for one rotation and then resigned. Unfortunately, because he'd done a Blackwater course and finished only one rotation, none of the UK defence companies would touch him, and eventually he did join the Reserves and completed an Afghan tour and now works in Kabul on some embassy contract. If only he'd listened, he would no doubt be twenty grand better off— but what doesn't kill us makes us stronger.

Another friend of mine, who was on an ammo disposal site near Tikrit, took over from a Blackwater team that had been supplying the PSD services and for whatever reason had lost the contract. It could have been down to cost; it wasn't necessarily because they were rubbish. My friend and his team arrived to a very frosty reception. Being professional, they'd turned up a day early to complete a proper handover. All the weapons and vehicles were supplied by the US Army, which was normal considering it was an Army contract, and all of this had to be checked, accounted for and handed over to the new company. The next morning they discovered that the Blackwater lot had bugged out in the middle of the night, taking everything— vehicles, weapons, ammunition, even the gym— and had literally left the front gate open on their way out. The military were informed but nothing was ever done about it. The Army produced new equipment and life carried on, for some anyway. Over the next year that contract suffered several fatalities purely because the previous team had pissed off the locals so much by shooting at them for no reason. Because the new operators were using the same kind of vehicles, they were mistaken for Blackwater and ambushed relentlessly. This info came from a captured insurgent who told the military that they wanted to kill all the Blackwater guys, but the locals had no idea that the Blackwater operators had left months before.

We were doing our usual super-fast speeds along Irish. In front of us was a PSD call sign, and I flashed our US flag at the rear gunner. He waved us off, indicating to get back. The unwritten rule was that PSD teams looked out for each other, and as long as you looked like a PSD team you let each other overtake, the rear gunner usually looking you over and telling the rest of the convoy that he was letting a team past, and that was that. But not this time. He was waving frantically.

'Pulling back. The rear gunner is a bit panicky,' I said into my radio. 'George, pull over to the other carriageway and get past them. I don't know what their problem is.' George nodded. 'Crossing over the median,' I added.

There was another thing we did if there was an obstruction and we couldn't wait, or sometimes with the military, who for reasons unknown to me were only allowed to travel at a maximum speed of 55 mph, no doubt some kind of health and safety thing. It meant that whenever you tried to overtake a military convoy, and they were nervous and didn't want to let you past (which was very rare), if you were travelling on a dual carriageway, like we were then, you'd cross over the divide into oncoming traffic and push past. It sounds dangerous but wasn't actually that bad, and this was also one of the unwritten givens. George waited for a break in the median and pushed over onto the other carriageway.

'Call sign complete,' Geoff said into his radio, letting me know that the last vehicle was across and we were all together.

'Roger; overtaking,' I said as we began to pass them, bearing in mind that we were almost 100 metres on their flank now. We were level with their vehicles when from the side window of their rear vehicle one of the crew began firing at us, not wildly but aiming shots at my vehicle. George slammed on the brakes. At least if we stopped, only our front vehicle would get the good news, which is exactly what happened. Now out of the firing line from the side, we were back in the firing line of the rear gunner, who gave us a couple of bursts for good measure. Fortunately for us, our front screen, which was hit three times, was armoured. Had it not been, I wouldn't be here as the rounds all hit my side of the screen and would have no doubt killed me.

'Everyone okay?' I asked, and everybody answered up. 'George, get after these pricks. They have to be going to the same place as us.'

What followed next is one of the few times I'm ashamed to say that I lost my temper. We caught up with them at the checkpoint for Victory, where even they wouldn't be stupid enough to open fire because the Army would have lit them up. George, who wasn't small, had jumped out of the vehicle while it was still moving— which wasn't good as he was driving— and was pulling the rear gunner out through the back window. They had SUVs, so the rear gunner was sitting in the trunk area with the rear window open. The rest of my team had also jumped out and, following George's lead, were running for the other team's vehicles. Realising what was going on, they were debussing and trying to help their rear gunner, and the whole thing turned into a brawl in which the Army had to intervene. What was even more infuriating was that they were totally unrepentant.

'I don't care who you are. If you come near us again, I'll light you up like a rodeo,' the team leader said as we were leaving.

I was amazed. I had no idea that rodeos were so well illuminated. But we had no recourse. It wasn't as if we could have got them into trouble;

we still didn't have any rules. And yes, you've guessed it, it was Blackwater again. We weren't the only ones. As well as the incident with the Australian Special Forces mentioned in Chapter 1, I also witnessed the Blackwater guys ordering a military PSD team and the Australian Ambassador to leave a restaurant so that their client could have the place to himself.

'I'll shoot!' the operator had said.

I can still see him standing there with his hand on his pistol getting very jittery while an Aussie Army CP team watched in disbelief. That also turned ugly, so personally I can't say anything good about them, and over the next few years I would be shot at by them on four separate occasions and twice by the military. The Army I can understand— young, overworked kids, terrified and inexperienced, can easily get spooked and accidents happen— but PSD guys are supposed to have done all the military stuff, be experienced and switched on. There are no excuses for those kinds of mistakes, and if you work in Iraq now, you have to sign a declaration that you've never worked for Blackwater; if you have, you won't get a visa. I apologise if you worked for them and aren't like this, but if it looks like a duck, walks like a duck and smells like a duck, it's a duck.

I wrote a report for that, but only because my boss would want to know why one of our vehicles now had holes in it and ultimately somebody would have to pay, and it sure as hell wasn't going to be me. There had been a lot of vehicle accidents lately. Overloaded and heavy off-road vehicles travelling at warp speeds all over the country, often driven by people with no formal high-speed training, had meant a string of written-off vehicles and fatalities across all the companies. I always felt that it was unforgivable for people to do such a dangerous job as we did and be killed in an accident that could easily have been avoided. Almost invariably a high-speed accident in an armoured vehicle involved a fatality, as a high-sided vehicle like an Excursion or Land Cruiser always rolls, and usually with catastrophic effects. As a result, we had two armoured vehicle instructors who were doing the rounds of the contract and running small courses for everyone, and new employees also had to go through a training package in the US before deploying. This was a two-week course involving small arms, medical and driving, and we all thought it was a very good idea. For a start, it prevented some of the idiots slipping through the cracks. It was also now an instant dismissal if you rolled a vehicle due to negligence. Another contract had rolled three when doing vehicle training at relatively low speeds. As I've said, you can J-turn an ordinary SUV, but you can't J-turn an armoured SUV without it flipping— an important point to note. One TL, who was very popular and good at what he did, had been given the option of paying for the damage to keep his job; he was told that $70,000 would be deducted from his wages for as long as he worked for the company. We all thought it was quite fair; he's probably still paying it now. Apparently we invited Blackwater to pay for the damage but they declined, saying that if such an incident did occur, and they wouldn't admit that it had, it was no doubt our fault and therefore our responsibility— a polite way of saying 'Fuck off'.

As there was no regulation as such and each company decided on the requirements of the personnel it employed, this meant that anyone who could pass company vetting procedures could end up carrying a weapon in Iraq. Most of the UK companies relied on proof of military service, supporting documentation and a medical, but as the size of operations increased, it became apparent that there weren't enough qualified people who could be deployed quickly, especially if a company picked up a large contract suddenly. They would need the manpower for it and, as it was expensive to keep people on standby, a delicate balancing act was needed to keep people waiting at home for these contracts, not being paid, and usually deployed in a day. The starting point was that a large defence company would have a briefing day, and if you fitted the bill for employment and were already on file, CV submitted etc., you'd get a call. This would usually involve going to London and sitting in a room full of men like yourself who all wanted to get to the sandpit and make a lot of money. Many knew each other, and in the early days the recruiters were all ex-military, so also knew many of the blokes who were applying for the jobs. Obviously this helped a lot, and the regimental system which has served our country well for hundreds of years was very much enforced. After all, if I was recruiting hundreds of blokes for a contract I'd probably employ as many men who I'd served with. You know them, good or bad, and can make a decent judgement about their suitability. Not many people can say that they were interviewed by someone who actually knew what the job involved or even had the necessary skills themselves to do it. In fact, many of the recruiters ended up as operators, because the money was a lot better than being some HR bod in central London. But the thing I've never understood is that we were always short of people, yet we all knew good guys sitting at home waiting for a deployment date.

These days there are problems with visas. The Iraqis, who are now totally in charge of everything, like to fuck us around and make as much money as they can in the process by introducing as much costly bureaucracy as possible. In the early days there wasn't any. Once you'd attended the briefing, which would usually conclude with everyone being interviewed and all relevant paperwork and applications completed, you were told to wait for a call while the company vetted you. Now some did more than others. Obviously if you recalled a PSD operator going on a murderous rampage in Baghdad and the ensuing witch hunt regarding vetting or lack of it, if a contract needed filling, then corners were cut, I'm sure.

The Security Industry Authority was formed in 2003 in an effort to license the security industry in the UK. You'll often see doormen at nightclubs and security personnel wearing a blue credit-card-sized badge, which means that they meet the requirements of the SIA and are able to work in their chosen field. There are several types, from door supervisor to close protection (CP). To qualify for a CP licence you have to attend a course approved by the SIA, involving 150 hours of classroom and practical tuition and a final exam. Mine was nearly four weeks long and cost over £5,000, but the amount and quality of the courses vary. However, as long as the course is on the SIA list it's acceptable. You also have to undergo a criminal records check and pay £200 to the SIA as an application fee. It wasn't until 2006 that security companies began making it a rule that all of us, even those already employed, needed to have a CP licence. I thought it wasn't a bad idea, as if you're a serious professional then you should be willing to make an effort. The hardest part wasn't the cost but using up valuable leave to do a course instead of going on the piss in Thailand.

Companies like Armor Group and Control Risk started their own courses or, in Armor's case, bought an existing training company, and if you worked for Armor you got a discount and they'd let you do the course over two leaves so that at least you got some time at home. Initially this wasn't fully enforced, as technically if the client wasn't British and you were working in Iraq, you didn't really need to have one, but as time went on it became more and more set in stone, and today you won't even get an interview if you haven't got a CP licence. Even non-British personnel have to do a course and get licensed, which for them can take a long time because the SIA has to contact the police in their own country. Many people felt it was a con and another way for the government to make money, which was no doubt true, but I feel that it adds rather than detracts, and that extra vetting is not a bad thing. It also means from an employer's standpoint that if you have a licence at least you aren't a criminal and you've been trained, hopefully by a good company and not above a pub by some ex-doorman. Obviously the licensing requirements differ, a course for a doorman costing £100 and lasting a day or thereabouts. Many of my peers felt it was an outrage that they should have to do a course and spend all that time and money when they were already doing the job, and I know quite a few who point-blank refused to do it, jumping from contract to contract trying to avoid the inevitable, but ultimately we all had to do it or not work.

I always hated Basra. To me it was like a backwater shit hole of a backwater shit hole. It's at the southern end of the country, close to the border with Kuwait, and as well as being hot, miserable and windswept, during the summer it's like standing under a giant hair dryer. Anywhere else on the planet the wind is a welcome thing on a hot day, but not there. It just makes a hot day even hotter. The area was flat and featureless, and the city itself was a heaving, sweaty, unpleasant place full of the worst of humanity, and they'd probably be the first to admit it. There are parts of southern Iraq where the houses have three walls and no roof— I'm sure you get the picture by now. We'd been sent down south to cover for one of our teams that was understrength, and considering that most of my team were from the US, and the US Army wasn't really in Basra, they didn't have much of a clue about it. I, on the other hand, had had the pleasure of invading Iraq twice and knew Basra better than I wanted to. I tried to tell them what to expect, but they just looked at me like I was some kind of maniacal Basra hater, which of course was and still is true. I was there recently, and it's still awful.

At the time, Basra could be as dangerous as the rest of the country. The British Army generally has a better record for keeping order in post-conflict environments, and that was usually down to foot patrols. We conducted a lot of foot patrols, whereas the US military employed more mobile patrols using vehicles, which were easier to spot and hide from than a foot patrol. To prove my point, when the war ended, the commanding officer of the US Airborne unit in Mosul, an old-school warrior, introduced foot patrols, as he felt strongly that the British way worked. Although more dangerous, it's more effective in denying the enemy the ground, and for a while Mosul was called the ideal post-conflict town. However, when the Airborne left and the Striker Brigade took over in their massive slow and noisy armoured vehicles, Hajji had a field day and Mosul went from being the best to the worst almost overnight. So even though the British Army at the time had a firmish grip on Basra, when it turned ugly, it could really turn ugly. Statistically, however, it was a lot safer. I didn't hate it because it was dangerous, I just hated it. To me, it was the equivalent of waking up with a hangover, a sore anus and a man's name tattooed on your behind, and no recollection of the previous forty-eight hours. We were just driving out of Basra city, no clients with us, having been on a wild-goose chase looking for a location that didn't seem to exist, and were conducting a reconnaissance for an upcoming mission. The location was a children's hospital supposedly started a year before, but the grid location we'd been given took us to a deserted piece of waste ground. I'd decided that we'd spent long enough making a target of ourselves so we were heading back to our base location. I later found out that the waste ground was the correct location and that, even though millions of dollars had been paid to local contractors, the site had never got past the drawing board stage. The contractors had disappeared off the face of the earth, either kidnapped or more likely had just run off with the money. By now it was mid-afternoon and the roads were unusually quiet, which was making me a bit nervous. I told everybody to keep it tight and we drove quickly but not recklessly through the outskirts of the city.

'Stop, stop, stop!' Geoff shouted over the radio.

I looked in my mirror and could see the second vehicle but not the third, as we were on a bend. Either side of the two-lane road had a collection of shops and houses but was by no means overpopulated. A crowd was quickly forming as I jumped out of my now stationary vehicle and ran towards the rear vehicle. As I approached I could see straight away that Geoff's truck had hit a kid, who was lying lifeless just behind the rear wheels. The crowd watched as Patrick, our unofficial medic, started to work on the kid. No doubt our efforts to revive him made a difference to the crowd, but all the while I was expecting them to slip into the pack animal mentality and try to rip us to shreds. But they didn't; they just watched. An old man stood there expressionless, closer than the others, and I guessed that he was the father or at least a relative.

'Geoff, what happened?' I asked.

'Fuck, man, I don't know. We came round the bend, we saw these kids, they weren't in the road, but we drove over him, the back wheels ...' he trailed off.

Travis, who'd been driving, was still behind the wheel. Our drills were that drivers should stay in control of the vehicle. If things turned nasty, getting back inside the vehicle was a matter of life and death, and if the driver wasn't there it was all over. If he was ready, all you had to do was dive in or just jump in the rear deck with the gunner and you could get away. But I don't think that was why Travis was still in the truck; I think that he didn't want to see what was lying in the dirt behind his rear wheels. It was obvious that the kid was dead and that no amount of first aid was going to make a difference. A six-ton vehicle driving over you is something that the best medical services in the world can't fix. We could have driven off; we could have decided not to stop in the first place. I don't doubt that many wouldn't have stopped, and if the crowd had turned on us I wouldn't have given a second thought about opening fire on them, but I like to think that most of us operating there were decent people and professionals. We carried cards written in Arabic and English identifying who we were and how to contact us, which were supposed to be used in cases such as this, and obviously there was nothing else we could do. Waiting around would be stupid. Everybody was watching. Patrick retrieved a groundsheet from the back of the vehicle.

'Get back inside,' I said to Geoff, and I said it in a way that meant 'Do it now'. He didn't argue. 'Pat, there's nothing we can do. Get back in the bucket,' I said quietly in his ear.

He stopped, realising the futility, and did exactly that. George had reversed the first vehicle up so it was close, and I put the sheet over the boy and gave the card to the old man. I didn't say anything. What could I say? It was an accident, and we'd done the right thing. Everybody was still looking at the groundsheet as I climbed back inside my vehicle and we drove off. On the way back nobody said anything. I felt bad, but I didn't feel guilt, because shit like this happens, and the Iraqis— well, Muslims in general— have a very different outlook on death. For them, everything is 'Inshallah', meaning the will of God. When you speak to an Arab and say I'll meet you at two o'clock outside he'll say, 'Fine, see you then, Inshallah', and I'm not exaggerating. It's a great system; whatever happens, it's God's will and there's nothing that you can do to prevent it. And with this kid who we'd run over, it was the same thing— it was God's will that our rear vehicle clipped him on that bend, and that's probably why the crowd didn't turn against us. However, had we stayed any longer I don't doubt that they would have. Any crowd from any nationality is a pack animal, and it only takes one person to say something and the whole dynamic will change in a second. Before you can say 'angry mob', you're having your clothes ripped off and camel-faced hags are trying to tear your testicles off. This happened to a cameraman friend of mine in Egypt recently, when one protester pointed at him and shouted 'Jewish spy!' He was lucky to escape, but not before being beaten to a pulp.

I'd made a note of the location on my GPS and told the team upon arrival to sort the kit out for tomorrow, wash the vehicles and fuel them up. I then went over to our Ops room to tell our project manager. Keeping the team occupied was the best thing, as I couldn't have them focusing on the accident. As callous as it sounds, I knew that we hadn't been behaving stupidly and I hadn't been directly involved. I was worrying about the crew of the rear vehicle. Geoff would feel bad because he was the vehicle commander, Travis the driver because he'd actually run the boy over, and Patrick because he'd had a ringside seat sitting in the bucket and had tried to revive the boy. They'd all be living with this for a while, if not for the rest of their lives. The project manager listened to my report, told me that I'd done the right thing and that he'd speak to the Army, and that they'd now be the ones to negotiate with the family.

'Negotiate what?' I asked.

'Payment,' the project manager replied.

'What payment?' I said, starting to feel stupid.

'Compensation. This happens all the time down here. Don't worry; you won't have to get involved. The Army will take over from here. I'll give them your report, and nobody will argue because the Army will do what it always does: pay the family off and that will be that. These bastards breed like flies anyway. They can afford to lose a few,' he said matter-of-factly.

I walked out a little bit stunned. Thirty minutes later I'd transferred the completed report to a memory stick and dropped it back into the office. I might have been used to shooting armed men intent on killing me, and doing it all day long with a smile on my face, but running children over, even by accident, was a new sensation for me and not one that I wanted to repeat, or get flippant about. I knew I hated Basra, but at least in Baghdad they had the sense to get out of the fucking way when they saw us approaching. I told the rest of the team, and they seemed as shocked as I was. It didn't make it any easier on the guys directly involved, but I kept them all busy and kept an eye on them.

The following day the father demanded $1 million for the life of his son. I thought it was a bit excessive myself. The Army, the US Army that is, even though the British Army were resident in Basra due to political reasons way above my pay grade, had decided they were going to pay for this, maybe because we worked for a US-based company. I'd like to think the reasoning was that simple. The Iraqi Police had been nominated to act as intermediaries for the negotiation, which so far sounds sensible, and even though we were not involved, I made it my business to find out what was happening through a mixture of curiosity and wanting to be able to tell my team what the conclusion was. In some small way it might give them a bit of closure. After a week of back and forth, the sum of $20,000 was agreed upon. Later, the jungle telegraph informed me that the father was happy with the $10,000 he'd received. Obviously the police involved had managed to lose $10,000 along the way.

The Iraqi Police under Saddam Hussein had very little power and existed more to settle family disputes than anything else. The Coalition had pumped a lot of money into reforming and training the new police force, and several defence companies had the contracts for training them. Police officers from all over the world came to Iraq to teach at the several new police colleges, and eventually out came the rookies, all shiny with brand new Glock pistols. However, they still had no jurisdiction over us and we were still prone to brassing them up from time to time, but always with good reason. There was one thing that they were useful for. Weapons were never a problem for us. As we were on a US Government contract, we were supplied by the Army, but pistols weren't in our contract and the company had to source them. Like most companies, it was easier to buy ex-Iraqi stock, as it was cheap and already in the country, but unfortunately it was also rubbish, as was the ammunition. We could get US-made ammo and had huge stockpiles of it, thoughtfully supplied by the military, including pistol ammunition.

Personally, I didn't like the Iraqi Police's nice new Glock pistols. Although they're one of the best weapons available, and many police forces and military units use them, I've never liked a weapon where you can't see the hammer. It's just a personal thing of mine. I won't bore you with handgun theory; those of you who know your weapons will know what I mean, and the rest of you can Google it. The fine for Iraqi police officers who lost their pistol was between $400 and $1,000, depending on which part of the country they were in, and no other disciplinary action was taken against them. As a result, they'd offer to sell us the pistols for $1,500, paid the fine and kept the rest. Capitalism at work. So within a very short space of time we all had Glock pistols. I bought four from the same officer. In any other police force such a man would have been investigated and fired, but he was probably promoted for displaying exceptional business acumen. So it was no surprise that $10,000 had gone astray, but everyone was happy, and in those days that sum was rock-star money. I told the team, and it did make them feel a bit better, especially as the family in question had turned their grief into a money-making exercise.

Our time was up in Basra, and not a moment too soon. We were due out on leave in less than a week and we all needed a break, our workload having been quite brutal and tiring due to the nationwide nature of our project. Most PSD teams limited their area of operations to a region at least, but we were all over the country. There was talk of bringing more teams online, which we were praying for, so we could split the country up. Even just north and south would have helped us a lot. It was hard to stay alert and focused when you were exhausted, but the clients probably didn't realise as we had different people all the time.

Our vehicles were now all packed up, and all I wanted was a cold beer and a decent meal at the Chinese restaurant in the Green Zone. We rolled out of the gates and headed north. Problems with the route took us out through Basra itself, something I'd wanted to avoid, and we found ourselves approaching the bend where we'd hit the kid. Ordinarily you don't slow down. Call it instinct, spider sense, anything, but I had a feeling.

'Slow down,' I said to George. He looked at me funny, but did as I asked. I didn't say anything on the net; there wasn't any point. But there on the bend was the father of the dead boy, with the rest of his kids, and he looked ready to push one of them into the road.

'Look at this bastard!' I said into my radio. I really couldn't think of anything else to say.

'I should run him over,' George replied.

Because of the reduced speed we were bunched up a bit. Then I heard the rear gunner open up and watched as the civilians scattered, the father running for cover as the dirt kicked up behind him. George floored it out of the bend and we left Basra behind us, for now at least.

'Feel better, Pat?' I laughed over the radio, knowing that the intention was to scare, not kill. If Patrick had wanted him dead, the first round would've killed him, he was that good a rear gunner.

'Yes, thanks; just zeroing my weapon,' he replied.

'He probably pushed that kid under the rear wheels,' Patrick said.

'Yes, mate, he probably did. He has a lot of kids and that's a good return on his investment. Suddenly I feel a whole lot better. How about you, Vehicle Three?' I added.

'You know something? I do, and the sooner we get back to civilisation for a beer and a massage the better,' Geoff said, sounding a lot better already.

'I hear that, brother,' George added.

In a way, I'm really glad that we had to go through Basra again to see that. We now knew that for that kid it was not because God willed it but because his father was going to push him under a PSD vehicle that day regardless of anything. His fate had been sealed on the day he'd been born into a backwater shit hole with an animal for a father and no future. I never had felt responsible for the kid's death, and I wouldn't have if I'd been driving, not because I didn't care but because you can't allow that shit into your head. Those doubts will make you hesitate, mistakes will be made and people will die. If you don't want to get run over, stay out

1 A surgical strike on an Iraqi Government building in Baghdad in 2004.

2 A surgical strike on an Iraqi Government building in Baghdad, from inside a PSD vehicle in 2004.

3 The remains of a suicide bomber on the front of a Bradley APC.

4 The head of a suicide bomber next to the track of a Bradley APC.

5 The Crossed Swords monument in Baghdad.

6 The base of the Crossed Swords, with Iranian Army helmets from the Iran–Iraq war.

7 The mosaic of Saddam Hussein inside the MWR building in Mosul.

8 The coffee shop inside the MWR building in Mosul.

9 A PSD vehicle in Mosul.

10 Inside the palace in the Green Zone, partly converted into a dining facility for troops.

11 A homemade pressure plate connected to an IED.

12 The aftermath of a contact in which the driver was killed.

13 A blood-spattered flag used when overtaking US military convoys.

14 What I was carrying in 2005.

15 The Burger King outlet at Speicher air base.

16 A truck bomb at Assassins' Gate in 2004, twenty killed.

17 A truck bomb at Assassins' Gate in 2004.

18 A truck bomb at Assassins' Gate in 2004.

19 The PSD vehicle I was in that rolled.

20 Pizza run for clients.

21 Santa in Taji.

22 A toilet in the Iraqi Ministry of Oil.

23 Inside an up-armoured PSD vehicle after an IED.

24 The bucket.

25 A PSD vehicle with identifying numbers in 2013.

26 Run flats without the tyre.

27 Unexploded ordnance found during a site survey.

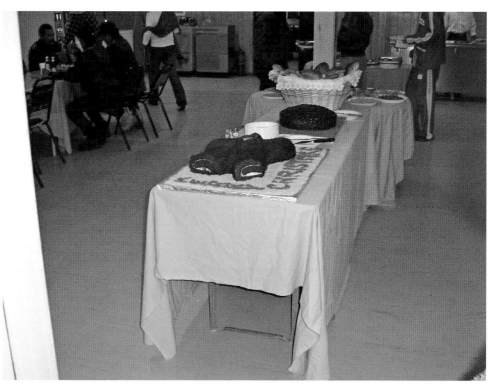

28 Thanksgiving dinner.

29 A rear gunner in an SUV.

30 Debris field clearance.

31 A subway in Camp Danger, Tikrit.

32 A gunner in a bucket with a SAW.

33 A vehicle fragged by a 155-mm shell IED.

34 The transit accommodation at the airstrip in Speicher.

35 A C-130 Freedom Bird with a forklift in the foreground for removing baggage pallets.

of the fucking road. I've never allowed other people's stupidity to make me feel bad for the consequences of their idiocy, or in this case greed and downright wickedness, but with the amount of kids that guy had or could produce with any of his four possible wives, he could make a few hundred thousand dollars, and the police would do well out of him too. It was easy. The Army didn't want to know the family, they'd take the word of the police, they wouldn't even realise that it was the same family, and $20,000 is such a small amount in a place like Iraq that it wouldn't be noticed by anyone holding the purse strings. Those people dealt in the billions not the thousands. I heard two diplomats talking in the Green Zone once. One said that the war had cost a lot financially and that they needed to get that money back from the Iraqis. The reply was simple yet eye-opening. The other diplomat replied that when the country was back to full oil production they could pay us back in a weekend. That's the kind of money we're talking about here. Twenty thousand was nothing, and neither was a boy's life.

6

Belt-fed Mayhem

I felt a thump and the vehicle began to swerve towards the kerb. George quickly corrected and began to slow down and I started to look for the best place to stop.

'Geoff, I think we've had a blowout. We need to pull over and get it changed,' I said into my radio.

We were on the open road and fortunately had just passed a small collection of shops, but Tampa north was just that— a long road, mainly dual carriageway, with small villages or a row of shops but mainly open.

'I can see the problem. Looks like your front left tyre has shredded,' Geoff replied.

He'd got his driver to pull out and could see the problem. All this happened in seconds. At the sorts of speeds we travelled at, a blowout could feel like a contact. If we'd been shot at, having possibly not heard the shots, and the tyre had been hit, stopping would have been stupid, but on the other hand it could easily have been a normal tyre malfunction. The roads were terrible and we drove across all sorts of rough terrain, probably damaging and weakening the tyres constantly, so each vehicle carried two spares and we practised changing wheels all the time. It was something that happened a lot, so reactions like those of a Formula 1 pit crew were needed, and a good team could stop and change a wheel in minutes.

Certain that it wasn't a contact, I stuck my head out of the window and listened. Even with the wind noise I should have been able to hear gunshots, but it sounded clear to me so I decided that we'd have to take a chance. We had run flats, which allowed us to continue at a reasonable speed for quite a distance. Imagine a Polo mint, only a lot bigger, clamped around the wheel inside the tyre. When the tyre deflates, the car continues on the disc, and even after the tyre has shredded completely, the run flat will last a long time. Years ago these were military-only items, but I believe that now you can have them as an option on many commercial cars. They've saved my life many times, so if you get the option you should have them.

Having spotted a decent area, George aimed the lurching vehicle towards it. As we stopped, my second vehicle pulled in front of us and to the left, giving us enough room to change the wheel, and the rear vehicle did the same behind. Both stopped at an angle, creating a wedge formation around the disabled vehicle, and the crews then debussed and took up fire positions. George and I got out and I started to loosen the wheel nuts while he pulled the trolley jack and spare tyre from the rear and began lifting the vehicle. When the nuts were off and the car was jacked up enough, I pulled the damaged wheel off and George gave me the new one. I tightened, George lowered, and we repacked all the kit. It was all done in less than five minutes and we were on our way again. Like I said, we practised this a lot, and one thing you could pretty much guarantee was a few tyre changes a week. In a contact you kept going, hoping that the run flat would stay in place.

'You still haven't beaten my record!' Geoff said from the rear vehicle.

'Next time,' I replied. Geoff held the record and we always tried to beat it either during training or the real thing. I'd got close a few times, but was doubtful that I'd ever manage it. We continued north.

'Bridge ahead,' I said into my radio.

Along most of the routes were overpasses and all manner of bridges, large and small, and many of the smaller footbridges had been blocked so that the locals couldn't use them. For us they were a major threat, as the larger ones, like flyovers, not only provided cover and the ability to engage us from height but also provided a getaway route. Hajji could engage us, jump in his car and bug out on a different road to us. This time we were travelling under a flyover, and all eyes and weapons were on obvious threat areas on the bridge as we approached. The drivers would quickly change lanes as we passed below in order to put off anyone waiting to engage us from the rear after we'd gone under, and all weapons would be on the rear as we drove under and away. As George accelerated hard out and changed lane, the rear window of my truck exploded in a shower of glass and I felt several rounds pass between George and myself. Two hit the inside of the armoured windscreen, sending more glass flying around the inside of the truck, but I always wore a helmet and goggles during missions so didn't have to worry about flying glass. I heard my rear gunner open up. It felt like hours but lasted just seconds. I stuck my head out of the window; there wasn't any point shouting into the radio or trying to direct fire as everyone knew what they had to do. George was driving defensively, which made accurately returning fire difficult. On the overpass to our rear about three or four shooters were pouring fire down onto us, with the advantage of a low wall to hide behind, but fortunately for us they weren't well organised or very accurate. However, three large trucks are an easy target, and all the while that I was returning fire I was aware of strikes on my own vehicle and the feeling of air displacement as high-velocity rounds passed close by. I could see the rear vehicle driving in a straight line. It was a method we'd discussed, and the rear gunner with a belt-fed support weapon was really the only member of the team who could put down accurate and suppressing fire, and to do this he needed a stable platform. It took guts from the whole crew to be a sitting duck, but they could do the most damage to the enemy, and it's hard to sit in the driver's seat in a contact when holes are appearing in the bodywork around you, but the alternative is to swerve madly which doesn't really do anything. A good shooter can easily lead a target, and although it might feel violent to the crew, for the insurgent you're a big white box moving left to right— still an easy target, and, worse, a target that isn't shooting back accurately. I looked at the second vehicle, which seemed okay, and fired back using single shot, again the most accurate way to engage the enemy. I guarantee you that at range of over 50 metres, if you unload at a target on full auto you will miss.

'Fuck, fuck, fuck!' George shouted.

'What is it?' I asked, getting back inside the truck.

'My shoulder, my left shoulder. I've been hit,' he said.

I dropped my seat back and climbed into the back. His left shoulder was on the other side to me and I couldn't lean in front while driving like this. By now we were almost out of range, but I could still hear the rear gunner firing short bursts. However, there were fewer and fewer of them, which indicated to me that we were out of range, and if a belt-fed support weapon couldn't hit the enemy, a gang of Hajjis with AK-47s definitely wouldn't be able to hit us.

'Okay, slow down a bit and stop at the next base. I'll have a look at your shoulder,' I said, trying to keep him busy.

The left shoulder of his body armour had taken a round, our armour not having any protection at the shoulders. I used my knife to cut away the shirt underneath and had a look. He'd been lucky. By the time the round had travelled 200 metres, penetrated the steel of the vehicle and hit the body armour it had slowed down considerably, and any energy it had left had been just enough to break the skin and little else. I could see the base of the round below the skin but wasn't going to go all John Wayne and start digging it out. For all I knew, removing it might make things worse.

'George, it's okay. Just a flesh wound. Do you have any numbness in your arm? Anything feel strange?' I asked, trying to see if there might be any nerve damage or whether it was worse than it looked.

'No. Feel good. Just hurts,' he replied.

'I'll patch it up,' I said, removing a field dressing from my med pack, unwrapping it and stuffing it under the shoulder strap of the armour. I then climbed back in the front and started to earn my pay.

'Vehicle Two, send sitrep over,' I said. (Sitrep is short for 'situation report'.)

'Vehicle Two all okay. A few hits on the vehicle but nothing serious,' came the reply.

'Roger; out to you. Vehicle Three, sitrep, over,' I continued.

'No casualties. The vehicle's taken a lot of incoming but seems okay.'

'Rear Gunner?' I continued.

'All okay. Think I got a few,' Patrick replied.

'Roger that. George has stopped a round in the shoulder but is okay. We'll stop at the next location and reorg there,' I added. This was followed by several clicks signalling an affirmative from the team.

I couldn't help feel how lucky we'd been. My vehicle was like Swiss cheese, and I could only imagine what the rear vehicle was like. George would be fine— it was just a scratch and he would have a nice scar to show off.

By now we had an armoured Ford Excursion as our second vehicle, which was our client vehicle. As it was fully armoured, it was the safest place to be in a small arms contact, and unless on top of an IED, the crew had a good chance of survival. The downside was that it weighed about six tons and wasn't the most agile thing in the world. I put Paul and Karl in there because Karl was an excellent driver and had been flown to the US by the company to complete an armoured vehicle driving course, and Paul was really good with the clients— a born diplomat, I always said. If we had clients, it was the client vehicle's job to get away and our job to make sure they did. We were expendable, and that day we were empty and on an admin run.

George began to slow down as we approached the next US base. I informed the rest of the call sign and we pulled in and drove straight to the medical centre.

'George, stay there for a minute,' I said as I got out of the vehicle. Although George was injured, it wasn't life-threatening and I wanted a quick look at the rest of the team before we got him out of his seat. The whole team gathered around George's open door and asked him the usual round of questions. I quickly looked over the vehicles— the client one looked unmarked but the rear truck was full of holes and the rear deck where the rear gunner sat was full of empty cases from his returning fire.

'Okay, Geoff, can you go inside and warn them that we have a wounded man? I'm sure that George is capable of walking but let's play it by the book, just in case, but make sure they know it's not an arterial bleed or a head wound,' I said.

Geoff nodded and went inside. We then moved the driver's seat back and using the quick-release toggle removed his body armour easily. Some sets of armour have a quick-release mechanism that allows the armour to come apart in two pieces, front and back. It's designed for medics to get access to a casualty quickly and means you don't have to lift the armour over your head as you'd normally do. While we were doing this, Travis kept pressure on the dressing that covered the wound and, once we were clear, manually examined him as much as he could for further injuries.

'George, I think you're one lucky bastard! I can't see anything else wrong with you. Any pain elsewhere?' he asked.

'No, I feel okay. I need to stand up,' and not waiting for an answer, he swung his legs out and stood up.

'See, no problem,' he said, taking over from Travis and keeping the pressure on himself.

Two medics came out of the medical centre, thankfully calmly. I'd had visions of a full-on medical team, which is why I'd told Geoff to say that it wasn't life or death. They took charge and walked George in.

'Geoff, square away the vehicles and get some coffee. I'll stay with George and let Ops know what's happened.'

We all felt he was okay, and had we been unable to get to a medical facility would have probably treated him ourselves, but as they were there we might as well have used them. After all, I might be a good combat medic but for all I know there was nerve damage or anything that further examination might detect. Geoff then took the guys away after they'd said goodbye to George.

'I'll be in shortly. Better let our bosses know we've banged up an operator and a few vehicles,' I told George, before getting my sat phone out of my side pouch to call the Ops room. However, I noticed straight away that something was wrong. The faceplate of the phone fell off as soon as it was out of the pouch. A round had gone straight through it, and the only thing holding it together had been the pouch. At the time it didn't register; I shrugged it off and went inside to use a military phone. I had to follow our protocols and, like many professionals, was on autopilot until I'd completed my duties. I made the call and then went to find George.

'How's it going?' I asked. I'd been directed to a cubicle where a doctor was probing and examining the hole in his shoulder.

'It'll be a lot better when they stop poking me,' he replied, giving the doctor an evil look.

'Don't be a baby. A big boy like you should be able to put up with a bit of discomfort,' the doctor replied. George glared back at him, but said nothing.

'How does it look?' I asked.

'Should be fine. I think the vehicle stopped most of the energy. We'll give him a local and remove the round, then a few stitches and that's that. All in all, very lucky,' the doctor said without looking up from his examination.

'George, do you need me to stick around?' I asked.

'No, I'll be fine. You'd better catch up with the others and make sure they're okay. Oh, and bring me back something to eat.'

'Will do. I'll be back soon,' I replied as I began walking to the PX, where I knew the rest of the team would be. Coffee and food were always a first priority with us. I found them sitting on a picnic bench outside the Green Bean café, trying to look cool and already impressing the soldiers, especially the female ones, with stories of our recent encounter with Hajji. I stood by the table and dropped my sat phone on the table.

'Can I borrow your phone, Geoff? Mine seems to have stopped a round.'

Everyone looked in disbelief, even the soldiers sitting at the table. This just added to whatever stories the guys had been telling the women. Geoff pulled his phone out and handed it to me. Luckily, in our team both the TL and the 2ic carried satellite phones. I made another call to update Ops and told the team what was happening with George. We finished our coffees and went back to the med centre. Having now been stitched up, George was holding the bent and damaged round in his hand. We all liked mementos like that, and I have a few similar ones myself.

'The doc says I can go. Just gotta take it easy and get the stitches out in a week.'

'Great, Travis can remove them if you want. Okay, George, we'd better go. You go in the middle vehicle and Paul can take your place in the front one. All good?' I asked, and everyone nodded. I thanked the doctor and we went outside. I quickly told Ops what we were going to do and we got ready to hit the road again. We were heading straight back to our base, and I was going to make sure that George had some time off. I knew he wouldn't take the opportunity to go home— he wasn't like that.

We turned out of the camp and headed south, back the way we'd come, and back to our base location in the Green Zone. Several hours had passed and I'd given the exact grid of the contact to our Ops who would have told the military, so going back that way was probably safer now than at any other time. As we approached Baghdad there were several US Army Humvees parked up and soldiers on the ground. I waved as we passed and headed into the heavy traffic. I felt fine and, because we'd been in a contact earlier, felt like we'd filled our quota for mayhem for one day and wouldn't have any more problems. Fighting our way through the traffic, we were on the wrong side of the river and needed to cross to get to the Green Zone. As we approached, the traffic became heavier and I began to suspect that something had happened, so looked at my map and decided on a more indirect route to take us in. Usually we didn't stop, forcing our way through the traffic, even if meant pushing cars out of the way, but the amount of traffic made that impossible and if we wanted to keep our wheels rolling I needed to get creative. We managed to cross the river but were now skirting around the Green Zone looking for a way in. Eventually we managed to get close to Route Irish, the airport road, and came in from that direction. This had meant cutting down some narrow side turnings, but I knew where we were and that we'd come out right next to the checkpoint.

Communications in those days was very poor and you never knew what had happened until after you got in. This was often done on purpose. We had an intelligence officer who was convinced that telling us before a mission what was waiting for us would have a negative effect on our performance, and this was not uncommon across the board. Even though most companies had some sort of intelligence apparatus, it was always at the end of the day, when you'd completed your mission, that you were told what had happened. I was never told, for instance, 'Watch that route, there was a massive IED two hours ago.' It was more likely to be, 'Wow, you were lucky. That route you took had a massive IED on it this morning,' i.e. twelve hours ago, after you'd probably driven past the smoking remains of someone less fortunate than yourself.

I could see the main road ahead crossing in front of us, forming a T-junction. After 200 metres and a left turn we would be on top of the gate. We had one more small intersection and then we would be at the main road. But I didn't know that just a few hours earlier a huge car bomb had been detonated at one of the other checkpoints and that several small arms attacks had taken place in a unusually co-ordinated attack on the Green Zone, and that we were driving into the tail-end of it. The street we were on was wide enough for two vehicles at a push. I didn't like being closed in, but we'd run out of options. Everything else was solid, so it was this or be a sitting duck on the main road. We crossed the small intersection, and looking left and right all I could see was the rear entrances of the houses.

'Crossroads clear,' I said into my radio.

I felt more than heard the whoosh of a rocket-propelled grenade (RPG) as it was fired from a rooftop behind me. It struck the roof of the armoured vehicle, which instantly caught fire. I knew that the crew didn't stand a chance, and also that the rear vehicle was behind the now burning vehicle that was blocking the road.

'Debus,' I ordered over the net.

Fighting from the vehicles was suicide, and I wasn't leaving the rear vehicle on its own. Jumping out and scanning for targets, I could see several heads popping up from a roof 50 metres away and promptly opened fire.

'Rooftops!' I shouted.

I saw that the middle vehicle was an inferno and instantly put it out of my mind. Moving back was my plan. We'd come that way, so knew it was safe, and we didn't know what was waiting ahead. I signalled to Paul that we were moving back to link up with Geoff and his crew.

'Geoff, we're moving back to you,' I said into the radio.

Paul laid down fire as I ran back past the burning Excursion, the smell and heat assaulting my senses. I stopped at the intersection that we'd crossed and saw two men running out of the rear entrance of one of the houses, carrying rifles. I got down on one knee and engaged them. The first one fired wildly and I put two rounds into him in the centre. He went down silently. The other one stopped, unsure whether to run or fight. I didn't give him a chance to decide, putting three rounds into him.

'Paul, move now,' I said into my radio.

Geoff appeared on the other side of the intersection and, seeing the bodies, looked at me.

'That house!' I shouted, pointing at the open back door where the ambushers had come from. Geoff stood up, took a grenade from one of his pouches, pulled the pin and threw it over the wall into the rear garden. I knew then that we'd fight through until they were all dead. Escape wasn't the plan; retribution was. Being that close to the checkpoint, I knew the Army would respond pretty quickly and that we probably had five to ten minutes to get our pound of flesh. Paul came up behind me, and on the other corner was Geoff with Travis and Patrick behind him.

'Travis, point of fire, there!' I shouted.

I wanted him to stay at the intersection and be our fire support. He had a 360-degree view, and if the Army reacted more quickly than I thought, then at least he could stop them taking us out along with the bad guys. And if anybody came out of the back door other than us, they'd get a warm welcome from his belt-fed squad assault weapon (SAW). We were about to go way beyond our brief as security contractors, but I wanted these bastards dead, and dead today meant that they wouldn't be ambushing anyone tomorrow.

Geoff, Patrick and myself ran across the gap and framed the open doorway. I was closest, and I pulled out a grenade. Everyone nodded that they were ready as I pulled the pin and threw it through the open door. I heard footsteps running away as the grenade exploded, followed by a scream. Obviously they were coming out of the back door as we were going in. Hearing Patrick open up from the road, I went through the door into the back yard. It was small and full of rubbish and the grenade had made a mess of it. In front of me was a staircase leading to the roof, and halfway up a heavily bleeding Hajji was sprawled out, his weapon at the bottom of the stairs.

'The roof,' Geoff said, pointing upwards. I'd also assumed that they'd retreated to the roof. The usual thing for a PSD team to do would be to drive out of the contact, leaving Hajji feeling all victorious, and the last thing they expected was for us to stop and fight. They probably weren't prepared for that, and a secondary escape route wasn't part of the plan.

'I just saw three head up onto the roof. I think I clipped one,' Travis said into the radio.

'Roger that. He's down on the stairs. We're going up to the roof,' I said into my radio, not wanting Travis to engage us by mistake. I got two clicks in reply.

Patrick removed the magazine from the AK-47 on the floor and as we went past the insurgent I kneeled on him to see if there was any reaction. He didn't move and I was satisfied that he was dead. The staircase was narrow, and I signalled for Patrick to go round the side of the house. He nodded and ran towards the corner of the building. With one grenade left, I pulled the pin and lobbed it onto the roof. I heard more movement and then the explosion from the grenade before Geoff and I charged onto the roof. Through the smoke and dust I saw shapes and engaged them, firing short bursts on automatic, but it wasn't me that got them. The two survivors tried to get off the roof and ran straight into Patrick, who was waiting below. They didn't stand a chance.

'The Army's here,' Travis said into the radio.

'Roger. We're coming out. Make sure they don't open up on us,' I replied, turning back down the stairs. Patrick was waiting at the bottom, looking pleased with himself. 'Coming out now,' I said.

Keeping my weapon low, I left the rear garden and ran back to the intersection. Travis was talking to a sergeant while two other soldiers were trying to extinguish the still burning Excursion. I hadn't even thought of George and Karl.

'There are three dead insurgents in there,' I told the sergeant. He quickly organised a small detachment and they disappeared into the house to see if we'd missed anyone. As there were no rules in those days, we could probably have gone house to house killing everyone and nothing would have been said as long as it looked right. It was okay and, to be fair, we were only protecting ourselves. We would do it again and again, and I would still do it today. If an enemy attacked us, they got what was coming to them— it was that simple. I took it very personally when people who I'd worked with were injured or killed, and right now I had two dead, and a few dead insurgents wasn't enough payback as far as I was concerned.

'We have two in there,' I said, pointing to the Excursion.

'We'll get them out and take them back in,' the sergeant replied.

More military units had turned up and began cordoning off the road. We were very close to the Green Zone, which made this unusual, as it was rare for an attack to take place so close.

'Geoff, can you phone Ops and tell them what's happened?' I asked, rapidly feeling myself running out of energy and losing the will to live.

He nodded and walked off to find a signal on his phone. The flames were out and I knew that a medical team would soon be removing the bodies. It was something I really didn't want to see. The only consolation was that the RPG round would have done its job and they'd have died instantly. However, it did occur to me that I hadn't seen an RPG as we cleared through, which meant that we could have been hit from another location and that the gun team we took out were supposed to follow up in the confusion. Whatever the case, it was irrelevant now. Patrick and Travis came over.

'You okay?' Patrick asked me. I nodded. There wasn't anything to say. Survivor guilt is a very real and powerful emotion that doesn't help. I was already trying to get my head round the fact that we'd been hit twice in one day. The truth is that some convoy teams were getting hit three or four times a day, but they were driving from one end of the country to the other, escorting slow-moving trucks, so you could understand that, but not that George had been hit and then killed.

'I just don't understand it,' Travis said, obviously reading my mind.

'What?' Geoff asked, walking back over.

'George, clipped this morning and then killed later. How does that work?' Travis added.

'He should have died this morning. It was his time, but death missed him, so it's taken him now,' Geoff added.

We knew he was serious. Geoff was a mountain boy from wherever mountain boys come from in the US. A real believer. He often said that when your number was up, that was it, and in his mind, George was on borrowed time after the first contact.

'And Karl?' Patrick said.

Geoff shrugged. None of us had any answers.

'I've told Ops. I said we'd see them when we finished up here,' Geoff added.

'Thanks. Okay, we'll wait for the Army and head back in with them. They'll be taking George and Karl with them. The vehicle will stay here, but we'll have to go through it for anything that could help Hajji, and the weapons, even if they've melted. Understood?' They all nodded, and I walked back over to the Humvees.

'Well, we went through the house. It's been empty for a while. It's been a busy day round here,' the sergeant told me.

'Yes, I can see that. We got hit this morning. One of the guys in there was wounded in a small arms attack near Taji.'

'Shit! Busy day. We're going to take your guys out now. They'll be at the hospital in the Green Zone,' he said, meaning the morgue in the hospital.

'Thanks. We'll follow you guys in, but we have to get inside the vehicle and recover any sensitive items,' I added.

I could hear the doors of the Excursion being forced open. I didn't want to watch, but it was my duty. I walked over as the driver's door opened and smoke billowed out. The rest of the team came over— I was sure that they didn't want to look either, but they weren't going to let me do it alone. Karl was still in the driver's seat, almost unrecognisable as a human being, as was George. The medics quickly removed them from the vehicle and placed them in body bags before putting them inside one of their vehicles. I looked inside our burnt-out vehicle. It was totally destroyed, everything had melted, but we managed to recover the two M4 rifles, or what was left of them, and that was all we could do. The Army finished up and we slotted into their call sign for the return to the Green Zone in our remaining two vehicles that were still shot up from the earlier contact. We went straight to Ops and did the necessary reporting, and I then stood the team down and began writing the reports that would be sent back to the US for our own internal accountability and insurance purposes. I left out the fact that we'd followed through and attacked the enemy, just in case. The bodies would be returned to the relevant countries and the families would get a couple of hundred thousand dollars from the insurance. All companies had some kind of package for loss of limbs or death.

Exhausted, I walked back to my room. The team were outside the accommodation, talking about the day. A crate of beer had already appeared and we spent the rest of the evening getting drunk and toasting the memories of our fallen comrades. Word had got around, and nobody tried to stop us drinking. The people sharing our living area all understood— many of them did the same job as us. Some came over and joined us for a drink, but by midnight it was just the four of us.

We were stood down now, missing a vehicle and two team members, and another team would be brought in to cover for us. We had only a week to go until our next leave, and it was unlikely that we would get any missions before then. I was also wondering if everyone would come back off leave. My team was solid, but events like this often shook the toughest operator. Someone had to go to the morgue the next day and identify the bodies, but I had no intention of letting anyone from my team do it. The project manager could go. He was a decent guy, but he knew George as well as we did, and it was good for management to see the risk up close from time to time. The next time a stupid mission came in, they might think twice, although compared to my last company things were very sensible and I was yet to feel like an idiot just for doing my job. I had checked with the Army. They hadn't recovered any RPGs at the scene, which meant that whoever had fired the round that killed George and Karl was still out there. We'd never know for sure, but at least we had evened the score, which helped a bit.

I spent the next week rewriting my statements for various agencies. It seemed that we had to tell a different story to each one to make sure that the paperwork was done correctly, and then we had to produce evidence that the dead crew had been wearing their body armour, which meant dumpster diving at the medical centre to try and retrieve the burnt and blood-covered body armour that had been on the crew. This we managed, but once this was done the insurance company wanted to see the helmets. If they could prove they weren't wearing body armour and helmets, they could avoid paying out. Fortunately for us, we always did wear our protective equipment, but the helmets had melted inside the truck, so we got two new ones and dragged them behind one of our vehicles for a couple of miles until they looked like they'd been in a massive contact, which kept them happy.

Shortly after this, we were asked to go on a mission to recover the vehicle so that a forensic team could ascertain what kind of weapon had been used. Our testimony of an RPG wasn't good enough. I went along with another team to recover the vehicle, which was then pulled apart by a State Department forensics team that was in the Green Zone already looking for mass graves somewhere in northern Iraq. The one thing they did find was that the armour in the roof of the vehicles was substandard, which opened up a massive can of worms. The vehicles had been supplied by the Department of Defense, which had paid a ton of money from a company in Dubai for them. All our armoured vehicles were therefore pulled off the road while they were examined by an expert flown in from Texas, who decided that they were all weak on the roof and floor pan area and recommended that we buy new ones, from his company obviously. Because it was a government contract, corners weren't going to be cut, so we sold all the rubbish armoured vehicles to another company, which got them for a good price and didn't ask any questions. I know this because we would later see them out on the roads. However, I'm pretty certain that the armour in the roof would have made no difference, as a direct hit from an RPG will go through any civilian armoured vehicle. So unless we're talking main battle tanks, the outcome would have been the same, but rules are rules.

I thought we were coming to the end of the whole aftermath, but then the bodies went missing and it took over a week to get them back. They'd got mixed up with a shipment of soldiers' remains and had ended up in Germany, and by the time the mistake had been realised and rectified, a week had gone by. I didn't know the families, and didn't want to; it was something that the company had to sort out. One of the guys went to Karl's funeral, but I couldn't face it. What would the family think, looking at me alive and well and their loved one dead? They might not say it, but they'd be thinking, 'Why him and not you?' And then there were all the questions. People were always looking for more than the truth. A friend of mine was killed in a straight-out road accident in Iraq but his family couldn't accept it. The body was severely damaged, as it was a bad accident and the vehicle had rolled several times. The father, who was ex-military himself, was convinced that his son had been killed in some kind of shady paramilitary operation that had gone wrong. I saw him once on leave, and told him the story, but he point-blank called me a liar and said that it couldn't be true. To this day, he probably thinks there was more to it than he was told. Maybe it's hard to accept that in places like

Iraq or Afghanistan people do have accidents and die boring deaths, but in the early days of Iraq as many people were being killed by driving too fast in six-ton armoured vehicles as were being shot.

Eventually all the admin was done, and by the time my leave came round I was ready for it. Geoff had told me that he was coming back, but Paul said that his wife was putting pressure on him to stay at home. However, he wasn't sure that he could live without the money, but I tried to help, saying that it wasn't important enough to die over. I also think what had happened with George, that it could have been any of us that had swapped places was messing with his mind. It would have probably done the same to me. Travis said he would be back, because he intended to kill as many Hajjis as he could to make up for it. This worried me only because I knew that he meant it. I didn't care about how many we killed, as long as we killed the right ones.

As for me, I intended to come back, but the thing I couldn't get my head around, and still haven't to this day, was George being wounded in the morning and killed in the afternoon. Was Geoff right? Did death miss him and catch up with him later, or was it just bad luck or coincidence? I'm still not sure. I'm not a massive believer in coincidence, and I've seen some pretty weird events. Anyone who's seen enough combat becomes superstitious and can easily start to believe in strange things, but I find it easier to accept that George's time was up, and that was it. He was going to die that day, regardless. As for Karl, I'd like to think it was his time as well, and at least they made their last journey together. As the Vikings say:

Lo, there do I see my father.
Lo, there do I see my mother,
And my sisters, and my brothers.
Lo, there do I see the line of my people,
Back to the beginning!

Lo, they do call to me.
They bid me take my place among them,
In the halls of Valhalla!
Where the brave may live forever!

A friend of mine is Danish Special Forces, and his team say that prayer before every mission. I know many others that do. I'm of Norwegian descent and have done so for many years also— just another example of the superstitions of the fighting man.

7

Light Relief

I held it together until my leave, and then went home and tried to forget all about it. I'm good at that, and really didn't give it a second thought until it came time to return, but I'd felt very alienated on leave. There aren't many people you can talk to about this type of job, and in those days the whole Iraq and Afghan thing was still new. We hadn't created scores of twenty-something Afghan veterans like today, our own Vietnam generation, kids with more than one kill to their name. I used to avoid conversations about my job, as most people didn't understand or couldn't fathom why a sane person would put themselves in such danger for money. However, looking back, I don't think it was the money by that stage. It had been the reason early on, but as time went on it became a war of attrition as to who could outlast who. I wouldn't let Hajji wear me down, even though I was missing the point. 'Hajji' was a collective term— there were thousands of them, none of whom knew me or even cared. I was taking it too personally, like it was a war declared on me alone, and as time wore on I became a bit more sensible about it. But it took a couple of years. Initially I wanted to kill the entire country— no, the entire region— I hated them all that much. I would walk past Arabs on the street in London and hate them, even though they had nothing to do with it. I once started a fight with a Pakistani at Baltimore Airport because he was standing too close to me in the queue for passport control. That was my excuse, anyway. Truth was, I didn't like his face. I'd like to think that I've now become a bit more mature and tolerant. And don't confuse this with racism, even though it sounds like it. Like I said, I was letting the war get to me and cloud my judgement.

I emailed the others to see if they were coming back, and by the time I had to go back they'd all confirmed that they would be returning. I had considered quitting and had said to myself that if the others did so, I would also, but I knew deep down that they wouldn't. For whatever reason, they, like me, were locked into this struggle. I was the master of my fate and I controlled my fear, and this battle would continue until I was ready to leave for my own reasons. Anything else would have been cowardice as far as I was concerned.

Two days before my return flight I received a phone call from our Washington office informing me that an appointment had been made for me to see a psychiatrist in London before I flew out. This was quickly followed up with, 'Don't worry; it's our new policy for anyone who's involved in a work-related death. Everyone will have to; it's our duty of care.' I found this acceptable and looked forward to it. The appointment was for the following afternoon, so I headed over to Harley Street, which for those of you who don't know is famous for its massively expensive private doctors and hospitals, and is located in a very select part of London. Having grown up in London, I was familiar with its reputation. I arrived at a very grand Georgian terraced house that had obviously started life as a private residence but was now a doctor's office, and once inside was soon being ushered into a room not dissimilar to a large and luxurious living room— open plan, no desks or any furniture that would indicate a medical facility; just sofas, a big fireplace, some small tables, a selection of armchairs, and no couch. A very average-looking man in his mid-forties sat in one of the chairs.

'Please take a seat,' he said, half standing.

I looked around, and since I had quite a choice, sat closest to him. I didn't want to shout. I was also vaguely aware of the pressure a lesser person might feel to make the right choice. 'Am I being analysed right now? Will my choice of chair say that I am a closet cross-dresser with shoplifting tendencies?' That kind of thing. Considering myself mentally robust and recognising the need for mental health professionals— although not for me— I stayed relaxed and sat where it seemed most practical.

'Hi, my name's Mark. How are you?' he said in a relaxed and very neutral way. No mention of being a doctor or using his title, and he seemed relatively young. I'd always imagined highly strung Freud types self-medicating on morphine when I'd thought of headshrinkers. I nodded and waited for him to begin, which was the start of an uncomfortable silence, as he was obviously expecting me to gush forth about how hard my job was etc. But I waited. I wasn't being difficult, but I did find the situation a bit comical.

'So you work in Iraq? That must be interesting,' he said.

'Yes, it has its moments,' I replied.

Another silence followed. I really didn't have anything to say. I felt fine; well, as much as anyone can do when he risks his life every day.

'Do you want me to make this easy for you?' I asked.

'Yes, please do.'

'Okay, would it help if I told you why I think I'm here, and you can tell me what you think?' I offered.

'I think that's a good place to begin,' he said, obviously relieved.

I gave him the highlights of my career in private security in Iraq thus far, and to me it all sounded quite normal, but the look on his face spoke volumes about my new career choice as a sane and sensible direction.

'Well, that's not your average day at the office,' he said, seemingly unsure what to do next.

'I may have missed a few things, but it's hard to keep track sometimes,' I added.

'Missed a few things?' he said, looking even more surprised. I nodded. 'I'll be honest; the most traumatic event I usually have to deal with is a firefighter or police officer who suffers a rare event that upsets them. But this is a constant stream of chaos and mayhem,' he said.

'Isn't that what everybody does for a living?' I said, trying to be funny.

'Really?'

'Sorry, just joking,' I added.

'In simple terms, we as humans aren't designed to travel at a hundred miles an hour; that's why we have car accidents. And we're not designed to be bombarded by constant stimuli in the form of fire fights and car bombs,' he said.

'True, but what if you are?'

'Well, if you must, then there really isn't anything I can suggest. How do you feel about it? Sorry to lecture you, but I've never heard of such a thing,' he added, obviously concerned that there were people out there earning a living this way, or perhaps because he was in close proximity to one of them, who the following day would be back in the thick of it and didn't seem at all concerned about the prospect.

'I feel fine. I know it's not normal to do what I do, but I honestly can't see me doing anything else,' I replied.

'Ah, but do you enjoy it,' he said.

This was something that I hadn't really thought about. Yes, I enjoyed the money, although regardless of what the press might say, it wasn't millions. I was then earning $130,000 a year, when it was roughly two dollars to the pound, before tax, which unless you lived in a hollowed-out volcano in the South Seas you were going to have to pay. I'm sure there are loads of suits earning a lot more than I was, and don't even get me started about bankers. I've got friends who are still working in Iraq today, and the wages now are about £50,000 a year, again before tax. They are only paid when working, so if the rotation is eight weeks on and four weeks off, effectively they're paid for only eight months of the year. I knew of only one company that paid its men on salary, and they adjusted the wages so that on a monthly basis they paid less in order to even it out. Ultimately everybody was paid a daily rate, and that's how it still is today, so looking back on it, the money was pretty shit really. The smart people moved to places where they could avoid tax, but I wasn't one of the smart ones, I'm afraid.

'Yes, I do,' I said. (When you consider all of the above, I must have liked it.) 'But not in a despotic way,' I added quickly.

I didn't want to come across as some nut job who just wanted to get as much trigger time as possible and spend all his spare time brassing up the locals. There were plenty of those, and they, to be fair, would have probably avoided a psychiatrist at all costs in case they were rumbled and sacked.

'Well, just because it's not my first choice as a normal profession doesn't make it wrong. What I have to decide is whether doing this will affect you in the long term or if you're suffering already from any number of conditions that will harm you or others,' he said, getting back on track and remembering why I was there.

'Makes sense, but I did spend twenty years in the Army before doing this job, so it isn't much different from what I've been doing my whole adult life,' I added.

'I'm sure that helps. Put it this way; I wouldn't recommend it as a career choice for a school-leaver,' he added.

'Look, I feel the same now as I did in my twenties. I don't have panic attacks and I don't have sleepless, sweaty nights full of nightmares and similar. When I'm on leave, I function normally and don't have any problems. I have little respect for civilians and office workers, but I think, considering my career, that that's normal,' I said, in an effort to clear my name and speak up for myself and those like me.

'You don't like office workers?'

'Nope, never have, even as a child. I feel that unless you're willing to risk your life for others, you aren't a man. While I accept that not everyone can join the military, I don't see that as an excuse to be a limp-wristed office ponce whose greatest fear is a paper cut.'

'Generalising a bit there, don't you think?' he replied.

'Yes, but I'm very good at the job,' I said.

'So you don't feel as though you have any ill effects from your decades of exposure to risk and, dare I say it, unpleasantness?'

'Honestly, no I don't. I think that some people are naturally more mentally robust than others, and if you are, it's your duty to take on these sorts of employment. I don't like it in the way I'd love being an astronaut or king of the world, but I'm good at it and I get a lot of satisfaction from doing my job and getting everyone home. I know it's not possible to keep everyone safe, but I try,' I replied.

'So do you think you'll be okay? You're going back tomorrow, I understand,' he said, having a quick look at his notes.

'Yes, that's right. I'm sure I'll be fine. I do it because I can, and I'm responsible for a team of men. If I wasn't up to it, I'd say so. I wouldn't just be risking my life, and I'm man enough to admit if I've had enough. I don't intend to do this forever.'

'You seem fine to me, but keep an eye on yourself. I can't make a judgement based on the little I know about it and can only make a recommendation to your company, who asked me about this only a few days ago. Most of my patients I see regularly and have problems that I know about. Combat stress and post-traumatic stress disorder aren't my area, and the sort of environment you work in is very different to what I'm used to dealing with. The best person to judge is you.'

'Well, that makes sense to me,' I replied. There wasn't much else I could add, and I was grateful that he was sensible enough to recognise that.

'I suspect that one day you'll be about to get on the plane and you will just say no and not get on,' he added.

I nodded. It never happened to me that way, but I did once see someone suddenly freeze as we boarded the plane, just saying that he couldn't do it. I suggested that he took the flight— after all, his bags were now in the hold and it would look really strange, and selfishly I didn't want to be delayed— and that he should quit in Dubai. It made more sense, as he might change his mind, but he didn't and that's what happened. Luckily the company gave him an admin job in Dubai, but it was weird seeing him when transiting through, and we all avoided him, not because we felt he was a coward but it was as if what had affected him was catching and we would all go the same way. Again, it's that superstition that some social groups are more prone to than others. Either way, he felt it too and didn't feel comfortable, as he'd become what was essentially an office worker. It's not just me who hates them— most of us do— and he eventually resigned and went back to the UK to get a normal grown-up job that didn't involve being evaporated in a poorly armoured vehicle.

I thanked the doctor for his time and left. He seemed a decent enough sort and, true to his word, submitted a report that said I was stable and unlikely to spaz out anytime soon. I was informed several weeks later of the recommendation, but only after I'd pestered our HR department for a couple of weeks. I treated myself to a huge pub lunch and went home to finish packing.

The following day I was at Heathrow. I always seemed to get the same flight, a British Airways 777 that left at around ten in the evening and used to get into Kuwait at daybreak. I'd sit in the departure lounge and look at the other travellers, half of whom were Arabs going home after visiting the UK, but the others were me— men in their thirties or older, wearing North Face clothing and Oakley sunglasses and sporting expensive watches. I was no different in the expensive outdoor clothes department. We were all sitting there, with our own thoughts, preparing ourselves to go back, and occasionally I'd see someone I knew from the Army and we'd sit and chat. Then came the in-flight meal, probably a movie and the usual chaos at the other end, with loads of people holding cards for the new guys who didn't know where to go when they arrived in Kuwait. I'd be met by one of the admin staff and, depending on availability, would be taken straight to the US air base to get on a military flight to Baghdad or to the hotel to get a flight the next day. As contracts got bigger and manpower increased, the hotels were done away with because of cost, and the luxury of the hotel was replaced by rooms full of camp beds at the admin villa.

This time it was straight to Ali Al Salem, and by the end of the day I was in Baghdad again, suitably sweaty and tired after travelling for nearly twenty-four hours without a shower. I'd met up with the others at the air base in Kuwait and we'd flown in together, all looking like scarecrows and no doubt wondering what was going to happen next. We didn't mention the ambush and that's how it stayed. It was done and in the past. Now was not the time to dwell on such things, as we had a job to do, and we had all come back, which meant that we weren't ready to throw in the towel. I wasn't the quitting type and would keep going until the job didn't suit me any more. I could only guess the motivations of the others, although I thought it was part revenge and part payback. I could feel that, and was guilty of it too. Deep down, I wanted to kill as many of those bastards as possible. And they weren't all Iraqis, because a good many of the insurgents were from elsewhere. It was the scumbags who decided that they were going to take us on because some holy man in the mosque on a

Friday wound them up to do it, which is honestly how it works. You can't blame the religion, but you can blame the egomaniacs who preach their distorted version of Islam to the uneducated masses who believe what they're told. Ask any soldier about Man Love Thursday in Afghanistan. I don't have the time to explain it here, or the inclination to be accused of being racist, but ask a soldier or Google it.

Shortly after getting back we were told that we'd be going to Erbil in Kurdistan for one rotation. We had a few contracts there and we'd be looking after some Japanese oil types while they negotiated with the Kurds over oilfields. This meant moving from government to commercial parts of the company, which was the same but with fewer rules, if there could be such a thing. It also meant that because Erbil was considered safe, we could operate in two vehicles with four men, although I'm sure that the loss of two team members had a lot to do with our moving. Not for any negative reason, but the one big difference between US- and UK-based defence companies is the attitude towards their men. Blackwater might have been unhinged most of the time, but they looked after their manpower, whereas UK companies tended to prioritise the client first, followed by the bottom line, the vehicles and then the manpower. So I think we were sent to Erbil in order to give us a break and to help us get over it.

We left the following day, taking two new shiny armoured Land Cruisers that had just been delivered specifically for that contract. Vehicles differed, and in the end it was down to how much money the client was willing to spend. In the case of the Japanese, whatever it cost they would pay. Obviously the addition of armoured vehicles and a nine-week holiday in Kurdistan appealed to us greatly, and we left early in the morning for the long drive to the Kurdish capital. We arrived in the early evening after an uneventful drive and several fuel and food stops courtesy of the US Army. I don't know anyone who dislikes Kurdistan. As a place to work, it was a lot safer, and Erbil is a great city. Of course, it's not a modern metropolis on a par with London, but it's trying its best and has a lot of character. Most importantly, the Kurds didn't like Iraqis much and wouldn't stand for any shit from them. Considering what Saddam Hussein had done to them over the years, that was no surprise. Kurdistan has a lot of oil, and they knew it, but on the downside, although it didn't actually matter, we had to abide by the rules there, and that meant not shooting the police if they tried to stop us, and carrying weapons in public wasn't really tolerated. Even though some companies bent these rules, we'd been told to play the game, so we wore a pistol but kept it under our shirts, and if we wanted to carry something more substantial we kept it in a bag. We'd swapped our M4s for Heckler & Koch MP5s, very compact 9-mm machine pistols favoured by Special Forces around the world, and kept them in our man-bags when out and about. We were staying in a rather nice hotel— quite a new one that hadn't yet been overrun by westerners, although it wouldn't take long. The bar was very impressive and like a lot of new businesses in Erbil, they were thinking ahead. If you go there today, you'll be amazed at the levels of luxury, and I hope that in ten years' time it will rival Dubai. I preferred it to Dubai even then, but that's just me. A good friend of mine currently works at a hotel there, which is better than anything you'll find in London and costs about $500 a night for a basic room but can go up to thousands for the presidential suite. It has its own fleet of 7-series BMWs to take people to the airport, and millionaire playboy types stay there when they want to drop off the radar. Well, that's my pitch for the Kurdistan Tourist Board.

The job itself was very easy. We had two clients staying in the same hotel and we worked four days a week, and even then only for a few hours a day. Our clients would all fly out at least once every ten days for a long weekend, and we could please ourselves when they were away. We ate out most nights, and on one occasion found ourselves in a smallish hotel which was more of a restaurant with a few rooms above it. We knew the area, and I felt it was safe enough, as we all had pistols with us as well as our man-bags. Shortly after eating our evening meal I received a call from Talan, our local fixer. His entire family had been wiped out by the former Iraqi regime at the end of the war between Iran and Iraq when the town of Halabja was bombed by Iraqi forces using chemical weapons. Up to 5,000 people were killed and many more thousands were injured, and the remaining members of Talan's family died later through complications. Needless to say, he didn't like the Iraqis, and it was on this basis that we trusted him, and also the fact that he'd worked for us for three years and was very loyal.

'It's me, Talan,' he said as I answered my phone. The rest of the guys looked worried, mainly because they didn't want a fast ball mission ruining our time off and hoped it wasn't the office telling us to get to the airport and pick some VIP up. I shook my head to let them know that we were okay and they went back to enjoying themselves.

'Hi, Talan, how's it going?' Our clients were away, so there wasn't anything work-related to discuss.

'We have big party. My cousin is in town and you must come,' he said excitedly.

'Talan's having a party. Are we going?' I asked everyone. They all nodded. The thought of a Kurdish party was an interesting concept.

'Okay, we'll be there. Where is it?'

He gave me the location, which was another hotel close by, and we said we were on our way. We climbed into our cars and set off. When we arrived, from the outside all looked normal enough, but once inside, things changed dramatically. The place seemed pretty low rent, but we followed the noise to the bar and stepped into what can only be described as a Wild West bar, looking like something out of a spaghetti western— the only thing missing were spittoons. The place was packed with uniformed Kurds all drinking ferociously and generally behaving as drunken uniformed people do, but with slightly less nakedness than we would have done it.

'My brothers!' a drunk and unstable-looking Talan screamed as he lurched towards us, all red in the face and bleary eyed. He hugged us all, as though we were long-lost family, and began shouting to his friends and family in Kurdish. They all came over, and pretty soon we were surrounded by a dozen or so of his nearest and dearest, all trying to hug and kiss us in what can only be described as a huge, sweaty man-crush kind of way.

'Fuck, these guys are wasted,' Geoff muttered to me, while trying to maintain a smile.

'I know, but just go with it,' I replied, not wanting to offend anyone.

'It's only the first inch that hurts, anyway,' Patrick said.

'Helps if you relax,' Travis added.

'I'm not that bothered about offending anyone, if it comes down to it,' I said.

'It's not Thursday, is it?' Geoff asked, referring to Man Love Thursday. I shook my head. I didn't think it was something practised in Iraq as much; it seemed more of a Pashtun thing, or a Saudi thing or a Kuwaiti thing or even an Iranian thing. See a pattern here? We've all seen the video clip of an Iraqi having sex with a donkey, and I still laugh every time I watch it, but it's funny mainly because you could say 'Poor donkey' but the donkey looks supremely bored and doesn't seem bothered in the slightest.

'This is my cousin, Babik,' he continued.

Babik looked like he'd been drinking all day and stood there swaying with the smile of a very drunk man. We all smiled and waved, he tried to wave back, and then inexplicably started to dance, much to the pleasure of everyone else who immediately began to clap and cheer. Remember, we were still sober, so unless you've been the only sober man in a room full of drunk people, it's hard to understand the feeling.

'I'm going to get some drinks,' Travis shouted above the clapping.

We all followed him to the bar, where the barman was wearing a tuxedo with a sparkly bow tie and a seventies-style porn moustache. He smiled and asked us what we wanted.

'Could this night get any stranger?' Patrick said.

'You've said it now,' Travis answered.

Behind the bar were pigeon holes like in an old-fashioned mail room, but in each space was a pistol with a tag.

'You have weapons?' the barman asked, and we all shook our heads. We found out later that you handed your pistol in at the bar and were given a ticket, and when you left you collected your weapon on the way out. A sensible idea, but I wasn't comfortable about handing my weapon over for any number of reasons, including being too drunk to remember and waking up the next day on the other side of town minus one pistol— not something that I'd want to have to explain to my boss.

We sat at the bar and got slightly drunk, watching the floorshow of pissed-up Kurds wrestling, getting naked and pretty much doing the things that we did in the military when drinking too much.

'What do you think? Have a few more, then bale?' Geoff said.

We all nodded. It was a good atmosphere, but it was all a bit odd and not really my thing. Talan staggered over and, using me for support, whispered, 'We have prostitutes; they're on their way,' and then promptly crumpled to the ground.

'What did he say?' Geoff asked.

'Prostitutes, I think,' I replied.

'We have to stay for that,' Geoff added.

'Fuck that; I'm not touching anything out here,' Patrick said.

'I'm sure that none of us are, but I have to know what a Kurdish prostitute looks like. It's the fourth rule of soldiering, I think,' I said, trying to remember the order they went in.

The rules of soldiering are a constantly evolving list of things that all soldiers, regardless of nationality, should adhere to. Invented by me in Afghanistan a few years before, and constantly amended, it is also non-copyright so anyone can add to it. For instance, the first rule of soldiering is, always carry a camera. I must point out that this is done not so much in order of importance but rather circumstances, that after seeing someone nearly blow himself up with a hand grenade led me to say, 'Fuck me, the things you see when you don't have a camera on you!' and prostitutes by nationality was rule number four, probably.

'Very true,' Geoff said.

So we hung around, picked up our fixer, stuck him in a chair and made sure that he didn't choke on his own vomit. I was looking at my watch, thinking that it was getting very late and how sure was I that rule number four was worth the wait, when one of the Kurds who'd been outside ran in screaming.

'They are here,' Babik said, translating for us and trying to wake up his cousin.

'Well, this should be interesting,' Patrick said, looking mildly curious.

The whole room fell silent, but the noise of several people outside the bar could be heard. The feeling of expectation inside the bar was overwhelming as the prostitutes entered, a procession of half a dozen young men, all holding a rose, dressed in very tight shirts and trousers, fluttering their eyelashes. The Kurds all started whooping with delight and shouting and screaming.

'What the fuck!' was all I could say.

'Gentlemen, we're leaving,' Geoff said.

I pointed at my watch and waved at Babik. He came over.

'My friends, you must stay. There are more on the way,' he said.

'We'd love to stay, but we've got to work. I'm sure you can manage,' I replied, noticing that my team were already out the door and probably running for the vehicles. 'Maybe next time,' I added.

'Okay, but you must come again next time we have more people. Real party, okay?' he said, hugging me as I wriggled free and headed for the door without looking back.

I got outside where Travis and Patrick were having a cigarette and looking like they were going into shock.

'What was all that about?' Geoff asked.

'I think we've just found out what a prostitute in Kurdistan looks like,' I answered.

'Does anybody else feel real dirty?' Patrick asked. Most of us nodded, and we headed back to our accommodation.

As much as it had been very strange it had also been very funny, and slowly we were starting to get back into it again. I stayed in Erbil for a few more weeks but never saw anything remotely like that again, and have since put it down to being just one of those things. I couldn't say for sure that male prostitution was a particularly Kurdish thing, and have seen more of that kind of thing in Saudi and other so-called pillars of the Arab world, and it's for that reason that I don't work on the circuit.

The circuit, as it's referred to, is the world that you would imagine a regular bodyguard inhabits. Before the Hajji wars, bodyguards operated in a world that was almost impossible to break into. The only way you were going to get a job looking after a billionaire Arab was if you were ex-Special Forces and knew someone who was already on the circuit who could vouch for you. But the whole PSD phenomenon changed this. Suddenly thousands of men with solid infantry skills were needed to operate along the same lines that they'd been taught in the army. Gifted Special Forces operators weren't needed, and this meant that these PSD operators soon had a lot more experience of operating at the highest levels of protective services. Although not as safe as protecting some millionaire while he went to a casino or a party in London or Paris, PSD was and still is the tip of the spear when it comes to security. Many of the circuit guys ended up working in PSD, and many PSD guys ended up on the circuit.

The way it works now, especially with the advent of licensing so that the traditional bodyguard doesn't really exist anymore, the circuit is made up of the same companies that supply PSD operators to hostile environments, and also a few individuals or groups of men who work for themselves. The clients are mostly Arabs with oil money, and the job is mainly babysitting. There are several thousand Saudis who are considered royalty and a lot of them leave home in June to start their summer tour, which ends as late as October, depending on the start of Ramadan, which often dictates the start or end of the summer season as the date changes every year. The pay is similar, but basically, in London at least, you spend a couple of months in a suit going shopping and then going out to nightclubs and restaurants watching people getting drunk and acting stupidly. If you're a female bodyguard, you'll look after the women and the young children, so that means lots of shopping and visits to theme parks and cinemas. This is mostly because they are Muslims and, as such, the women stick with the women and the men stick with the men. It's not the doing of the operators; it's the clients' wishes. The days are long, as these clients party all night and sleep nearly all day, getting up in the afternoon but expecting the team to be ready at all times. You're treated like a dog, and basically it's shit. I don't work on the circuit, even though every year people ask me if I'm available. For me, my job is a serious business and I like to think that I'm protecting people because they genuinely need protecting not because some turd with more money than sense wants to show off. A lot of guys do it, and for some a good summer can carry them for the rest of the year. So it's horses for courses. PSD in hostile environments isn't for everyone. Some people do their time and get out alive; for them, that's fine. It's no more than the bullshit an average infantry soldier would have to put up with in the Army, and at least you get home most days and are very unlikely to get killed.

And then there's the celebrity circuit, which, to be honest, occasionally crosses over. I know people who do a bit of both, but it's not something that I'd ever consider either, because you can't do your job properly. Some 20-year-old trailer-trash singer isn't going to listen to you when you tell him to stop what he's doing. You'll be expected to let him do whatever he wants but at the same time keep him safe— something that's very hard to do. I know of plenty of people who have lasted only a day on a job like that because they've tried to be professional, only to be replaced because the client doesn't want to be told what to do. Just look at so-called celebrities like Justin Bieber; I can only imagine the crap that his team have to put up with. So for that reason I won't work on the circuit. I'm just not built for it, and even if I could earn more doing it, I'd decline because I couldn't square it with myself to protect people who I'd normally be aiming a rifle at. I could fill several books with anecdotal stories from friends, all about drugs, under-age male prostitutes, hundred thousand dollar bar bills and similar, but to me that isn't the way for an honourable man to earn a living, protecting oxygen thieves like that.

8

Stay Frosty

I was summoned to the country manager's office on our return from Kurdistan. I'd started to get a bit bored by the whole taxi service thing in Erbil and was hoping that he had something new and challenging for us. Unfortunately 'challenging' in Iraq usually translated as 'suicidal'. We'd moved to Anaconda, the US camp near Balad, which was close to Samarra in what I liked to call Bandit Country. The base was huge, with a cinema and all sorts of distractions to make life easier, and I was about to find out that we'd picked up a new contract that would feel very much like being in the Infantry again.

Our country manager was an ex-US Army colonel, not your usual Navy Seal or Special Forces type but Regular Army, which was unusual for a place that seemed top heavy in the secret squirrel, highly trained, one-man army sort of thing. I liked him. He wasn't pretending to be a super-soldier, just a regular guy with a lot of relevant experience, which was all we needed. He wasn't exciting but he knew what he was talking about and had the logistics sorted. A lot of companies would promise anything to get a contract and worry about the reality of delivering later, but we were lucky that we didn't have that kind of management. I'd already seen at first hand the fallout from that kind of bad practice.

'Take a seat,' he said as I walked into his office. I'd only met him a couple of times, and country managers didn't usually get involved with the servants unless something was really wrong.

'I see you've had a busy time of it lately,' he continued, looking through some paperwork on his desk.

'Yes, we have. But this isn't Disneyland is it? I answered.

'No, it's far from Kansas. We have a new contract; it's still Department of Defense, but more reconnaissance than PSD. Sound interesting to you?' he asked. I nodded. 'Great. You'll be getting an extra man and some new vehicles and equipment, but Ops will take care of that. But the short story is that between here and Mosul there are several ammunition sites that need clearing up, and before contractors can make these sites safe we need to send teams out to confirm that the sites exist, and if it's feasible to do anything with them. You go, you look, and you write a report. That's it,' he said.

'Sounds good, but you know as well as I that if there are any sites like that, they'll have been raped by the locals for any ordnance that can be turned into an IED,' I replied.

'Very true, and we have some reports of people moving into these sites and using the old bunkers as homes. I doubt it'll be anywhere near as straightforward as the Corps of Engineers think it will, but that's the mission.'

'Alright, I'll take it,' I said, as though I was buying a used car.

'Great. I'll make sure Ops give you as much help as we can.'

And that was that. He went back to his paperwork and I thanked him and left, not totally sure if I'd made a good deal. It certainly sounded different and interesting, and I liked the fact that we wouldn't have clients. All I had to do now was sell it to the kids. I had a quick chat with our Ops manager, who informed me that a new guy was coming in the next day and that two brand new semi-armoured Ford F350 Pickups would be turning up within the next week, and in the meantime he recommended massages and ice cream, which is always a good use of any man's time, I think.

When I told the team they took it well and seemed a little bit excited. The majority of the work in Iraq was the usual boring shit of collecting clients and taking them somewhere and bringing them back, running the gauntlet of God knows what along the way. This at least allowed us a lot more freedom and the chance to get out there and operate as we wanted, and to me and the others, that felt more like offensive operations rather than defensive. The enemy always had the advantage of knowing we had clients, so we'd run from a fight most of the time. But now we could take the fight to them, which I knew from experience was something they really didn't like, mostly because they were cowardly shitbags who couldn't fight. They lacked the Afghans' will and experience when it came to a real insurgency.

We took Ops' advice and went with massages and ice cream. The next day I got the call to pick up our new kit that was waiting for us at a little compound we had at the back of the base. We drove up in our existing vehicles and began the lengthy process of handing our old stuff back and signing out the new kit. Each man now had a new M4 rifle and one belt-fed SAW per vehicle. Any other stuff that might be illegal we'd pick up later. All the US bases had contraband boxes, of various colours and sizes, dotted around the camps, where US military personnel could dump contraband items with no questions asked. They weren't manned and were easy to break into to, and I'd made some very interesting finds— mostly grenades and ammo, and occasionally alcohol— but most items were of the 'bangs and bullets' variety, including on one occasion a fully functioning RPG and rockets for it. Obviously a soldier who'd lifted one during a search, or taken it off a dead insurgent thinking it would be a cool thing to have, later realised how fucked he'd be if it was found in his kit, so dumped it at an amnesty box. For us, these boxes were a constant supply of extra equipment, and if we needed something specific we had friends in low places who could get us things. Not military personnel but quartermasters from other companies, who were always dealing weaponry and ammo for a price or a favour. It wasn't some highly financed weapon-smuggling ring but mostly opportunistic people helping each other out. I don't think anyone was getting rich from it. So far it was Christmas, with new weapons, unlimited ammo, a choice of optic sights and weapon lights, and some other Gucci items. The SAWs were the airborne variety, folding stocks and short barrels, the same firepower but shorter and lighter— perfect for vehicle operations.

The F350 Pickup trucks were white unfortunately, but most vehicles were. There was a rumour that companies bought white vehicles in case the United Nations ever showed their faces. Then we could sell our old crap to them. I could believe it, and having worked all around the world, often in places where the UN were deployed, it's my considered opinion that they're a joke. The bad guys laugh at them, as they have no real power to make a difference. It's just a load of bureaucrats who couldn't make it in the commercial world and people lining their own pockets at the grass-roots level. Put it this way, when I was in Gaza, if you wanted a prostitute or a bottle of whiskey it was a European UN representative that you spoke to.

The pickups were semi-armoured, or up-armoured as we called them, and ours had armoured front and rear screens and Kevlar panelling on the roof and floor pan. The side windows were normal glass, and instead of armoured doors we had lightweight armour panels bolted to the inside of the doors which came up to shoulder height but at an angle, so you could hide behind but still look round to return fire. For us, this was perfect. It offered decent protection but didn't add a shitload of weight so, we could still move fast and go off-road if we needed to, and it was looking like we'd be doing a lot of off-roading just trying to find some of these locations. B6 armoured vehicles are nice and offer full protection from bullets and smallish IEDs, but they weigh a lot and can't go off-road or drive defensively. Some of them can weigh up to six tons and roll far too easily, so we were happy with the up-armoured F350s. Each one also had a homemade steel bucket in the back with an old car seat bolted inside it for a rear gunner, and also massive bull bars, ideal for shunting other cars out of the way and doubling as protection for the engine from rounds coming in from the front.

Our replacement was waiting for us when we went back to our accommodation. I said hello quickly but I had to go and see the project manager, so left him with the rest of the team, and by the time I returned, everything was fixed and the new guy had settled in. His name was Ivan and— no, I'm not joking— he was ex-Foreign Legion. Originally from Estonia, he now had a French passport. (If you serve your time in the Legion you're eligible for French citizenship.) He was, I'm afraid, stereotypical of what you'd consider to be a paratrooper from the days of the Russian occupation of Afghanistan— huge, square and very unfunny. I was hoping that it was because he didn't know us. The new order of march was going to be Geoff commanding the rear vehicle, with Travis and Patrick taking turns in the bucket, and Paul and Ivan with me in the front. Ivan would be in the back watching my flanks, although I'd already decided that, depending on the mission, we could move around to suit the requirements. I'd already been given our first mission and had prepared the tasking sheet, which I'd emailed to our Ops manager outlining how I intended to complete the mission. It also contained the ORBAT of the team— blood groups, which vehicle they would be in, and all contact info for the team. Should we encounter a problem, that sheet would be used as a quick reference for where we should be, how we intended to complete the mission, and how to get in touch with us. Ultimately that info could be passed to the military, who didn't know us, but all the information they would need to mount a search or rescue would be contained therein. I got the team together for my briefing, or 'prayers' as we referred to it.

'Okay everyone, our first mission,' I said. They all sat there with their notebooks out. When the briefing started, all joking finished. I kept it short and sharp for simplicity. 'Tomorrow start at zero seven hundred, travel from here to Baiji, then west into the desert. We have the grids; they're on the orders sheet which I'll give to you after. Between here and Baiji, usual roads. We're leaving early, so we may well be clearing that route ourselves. Normally we'd go later, but we're meeting up with a US Army call sign at

Baiji so have to RV on their schedule. Once we link up with them we'll head to the location, which was an ammo site containing ground-to-air rockets, so expect a large compound with hard cover or some kind of bunker system for the ordnance. If it's intact, the military will take charge and occupy the area; if not, we'll find out tomorrow as they haven't yet decided what they're going to do. We'll operate to our usual rules of engagement. If attacked, we fight. However, once with the military, we'll have to adhere to their rules of engagement and speed limits.'

There was an audible groan. The US military always drove at 55 mph, which we all felt was ridiculous. However, I bet they had fewer road accidents than we did, but probably lost more to IEDs due to making a slower, easier target, so maybe it evened out in the end.

'Once at the location our job is to take photographs, take measurements of the perimeter and make a detailed map, collect grids and anything else that might be useful to a follow-up operation, and that's it. Friendly forces— US Army, Coalition military and other PSD teams; enemy forces— most of the population. Comms— hand-held radios between us, Codan and sat phones. Back to base and safe locations— US Army camps. If we get into trouble on the way, we have to call in medevac and will rely on Army choppers to come and get us. This is a DOD contract for the US Army, and they have all our routes and rough timings, so we can expect QRF (Quick Reaction Force) from the Yanks if needed. Order of march will be myself, Ivan and Paul in the lead vehicle, the rest of you in the gun ship. Any questions?'

Every team leader gave a similar brief. Some stuck rigidly to the military system, but this meant that prayers could go on for hours while someone described in detail the ground enemy positions and likely numbers— every conceivable option and scenario. I liked to keep it simple, otherwise people fell asleep and forgot the important things because they were focusing on the unimportant shit. A good team needed less information. Sometimes on a fast ball mission the orders were as simple as 'We're leaving in five minutes and this is where we're going.'

'That's close to the Syrian border,' Geoff said.

'Yeah, about a hundred clicks from it. Shouldn't have any impact on us. Maybe that's why the Army are coming along, I don't know, but at the moment there aren't any problems between us and the Syrians,' I added.

'Are we overnighting?' Travis asked.

'No, as soon as our mission is complete we come back. The report has to be sent back asap. Fortunately for you lot, that's my job so I'll be spending my evening writing reports. We'll be putting sleeping bags and ration packs in the vehicles though, as from what I can gather, it could end up being a bit like an expedition later on, and some sites we may have to hold until reinforcements arrive. It's all new, so we've got to be flexible but mostly prepared for anything,' I answered.

There were no other questions and everyone seemed happy.

'Alright, now that's done I'd like to welcome Ivan to the team, and if there isn't anything else let's get the vehicles sorted and get ready for tomorrow.' I let the guys get on and pulled Ivan over to have a quick chat. 'How are you finding it so far?' I asked.

'Is okay, but you do not use Kalashnikov,' he replied with a very thick Russian-sounding accent.

'No, this is a US Army contract. We have to use the weapons that are supplied. In your case, as my side gunner, a SAW should be big enough for you.'

'But is only 5.56; PKM much better,' he said.

Now there's a common argument about calibre. NATO weapons mostly fire 5.56, which is smaller than the Eastern Bloc 7.62 but has a higher velocity and is more accurate. People have been arguing over this for a long time. My personal view is that any bullet will kill you if fired by a professional, but Ivan was obviously a fan of the Kalashnikov family of weapons, which are reliable but have no finesse. They are agricultural in design and build quality, and people say you can bury an AK-47 for a year and dig it up and it will still fire. That's all well and good, but what idiot's going to do that? Even the most highly strung weapon will work if you look after it— that's my belief, anyway— but most important to me was accuracy. Unlike the enemy, we fired aimed shots, not blindly unloading the weapon on automatic. Not only did you run out of bullets quickly, you missed most of the time.

'Maybe, but it weighs twice as much, and so does the ammo,' I replied. I was getting a bit pissed off with all the legionnaires I came across who thought they were the only people on the planet with combat experience. If I wanted lessons in fighting futile battles to the last man, I would bow to their greater knowledge.

'Ivan, it is what it is, okay?'

'Yeah, but I was just saying, Kalashnikov is better,' he added, trying to get the last word in.

'Go and see if Geoff has anything for you to do,' I said, determined to have the last word, and walked off, cursing my luck. However, Ivan would turn out to be an exceptional operator, massively not right in the head but hard-working and fearless, but until his dying day he'd be a devoted fan of the Kalashnikov and nothing would change his mind.

I spent the rest of the night checking my kit and marking my maps with all the necessary locations, RV points and safe havens should things go wrong, and the last thing I did was check over the vehicles. I knew they'd be ready, but there was no harm in double-checking. Water, rations, breakdown kit— all had to be there. We would be operating as a totally self-contained unit from now on. Admittedly we could scrounge anything from the military if we had to along the way. That was one of the many uses of the military locations on our routes— they were like service stations for us. We used them for food, shelter and admin, ammo, fuel, medical. Anything we needed we could find, but Murphy's Law says that you'll need something when you go off the beaten track and are in the middle of the desert without support, so for this reason we couldn't leave anything to chance.

We were lucky. Shortly after I'd got into bed it started raining, and it rained all night. Although this would mean our progress would be slower, it also meant that it was unlikely that we'd have anything waiting for us. Hajjis didn't like getting wet or cold, and I doubted that any of them would drag themselves away from a warm donkey to dig a hole next to the road. The rain stopped about thirty minutes before we left, when we were all having a massive breakfast (in my case because I didn't know when I'd be eating again). When you're on a new rotation or mission you have to play it by ear. We had to make it to our RV point on time, and you never knew what was going to slow you down. However, we did have the US Army ration packs (MREs—Meal Ready to Eat), which contained enough calories to keep you going. They were the work of the devil but they did their job, and the variety of menus was pretty decent compared to the British Army equivalents. The best ration packs I've ever eaten are the French and the Italian ones, and were the difference between a Ferrari and a Ford in quality compared to the US and British ones. We were all finished, but Ivan had other ideas, and after his third helping of everything finally admitted that he'd eaten enough, before proceeding to rape the dining facility of anything that he could eat later. By the time he'd finished, his man-bag was full of energy bars, cans of Red Bull, chocolate bars, potato crisps and many of the delights that were there for us to eat in moderation. But, like I said, he was a big lad, and a bigger engine needs more fuel, as they say. More importantly, I now knew who to see if I got peckish on the trip, plus he was in my vehicle.

'All call signs, radio check, over,' I said into my radio microphone. The people in my vehicle gave me two clicks, and as they were right next to me, those in the second vehicle answered with an affirmative.

'Roger that; moving now,' I replied, nodding at Paul and pointing towards the front gate.

He eased the vehicle out and pretty soon we were heading out onto the road that led to Tampa north. The road was wet and covered in mud, and I was concerned that the road conditions would slow us down or even make things more dangerous than they needed to be. The vehicles weren't weighed down with tons of armour but they weren't lightweights either, and once they started to slide there wasn't much even the most skilled driver could do about it.

'It's a bit slippy,' Paul said.

'We're going to have to keep the speed down until the road surface improves. Keep your eyes open and call out anything that doesn't look right,' I said into my radio. The last thing I wanted was an accident, but I also didn't want to get taken out by some opportunist insurgent because we were going too slowly. It was still early and there hadn't been much traffic. The roads leading to Tampa were quite small, mostly single carriageway, and it would be shit until we reached the main road. We just had to stay frosty until then.

'Parallel left, two hundred, Bongo truck,' Ivan said over the net.

I looked left and approximately 200 metres to our left, on a parallel track, a small truck was trundling along. Ivan had the SAW resting on the open window ledge of the rear left door and was aiming at the truck. We always made ready before leaving, making sure there was a round in the chamber. All you had to do was flick the safety off and pull the trigger. Most belt-fed machine guns operated differently: you pulled the working parts to the rear and they sat there until you squeezed the trigger, sending the working parts forward, feeding a round into the chamber and unleashing a lot of unpleasantness for the other end. I looked through my binoculars, and the driver didn't look like a farmer. In this area that was the common Bongo driver.

'If he makes a phone call, give him a warning burst,' I said to Ivan. 'If he makes a call, we'll give him a warning,' I said into the radio.

We were far enough away from the base that they wouldn't hear, and it was early, so who would he be calling at this time of the morning? Probably a friend in the village up the road to let them know we were coming. If I was wrong, he just got a fright; if I was right, he knew we were on to him.

'Firing!' Ivan said loudly enough for me to hear, followed by a short burst in front of the vehicle, which came to a sudden halt.

'Rear Gunner, watch him. Drivers, increase speed,' I said into the radio.

We'd have to chance it; there was no alternative route and we were close to the main road. Paul put his foot down and I could feel the vehicle sliding as the engine tried to put the power through the wheels, but he kept it relatively straight and we were quickly approaching the junction onto Tampa. It was clear left and right, so we stayed in our formation as we turned right onto the main road. The rear of our pickup tried to overtake us, but Paul countered the skid and we were soon powering along Tampa's much better road surface.

'Two clear,' Geoff said over the net, letting me know that his vehicle was now behind us and that he'd made the turn without incident.

'Good shooting,' I said over my shoulder to Ivan. He nodded and clicked his safety back on. 'Anyone sees that vehicle again today, we'll consider it hostile,' I said over the net.

I couldn't have said with 100 per cent certainty that the vehicle had been a threat, but I hadn't been willing to take a chance. My gut told me that it was, so I'd be keeping an eye out for it. Not that easy, considering the amount of similar vehicles on the road, but I'd do what I could. If the traffic wasn't against us we could be at out RV point on time. Baiji was only a couple of hours north, and the fun would begin after we linked up with the military.

The rest of the drive was uneventful. I was tempted to stop for a break near Speicher, but by the time we got in we'd only have five minutes before we'd have to turn around and come out. I made a mental promise to stop there soon (they did the best frappuccino), and we arrived at the RV point with twenty minutes to spare. The Army was already there but, to be fair to us, it was a semi-permanent checkpoint that they'd been manning for a few days. We parked next to the Humvees and got out, glad to stretch our legs. While the drivers checked over the vehicles, Geoff and I went to find the man in charge, a Corps of Engineers officer called Rodriguez. We introduced ourselfs and asked what the score was with the military. He told us that with the continued search for weapons of mass destruction, the people in charge thought that there was a good chance that this ammo site could house such weapons or had done in the past, but definitely had advanced missiles of some description.

However, it became apparent as time went on that the WMDs that we were so sure had been all over Iraq had never really existed. During my time there, I saw many ammo supply points that contained missiles and even weapons going back to the Second World War, many from the UK and France. I have pictures of missiles in their containers with Aérospatiale stickers all over them, and I've seen many types of weapon sold by all manner of countries, but these countries, although happy to sell these weapons, rarely sold the delivery systems to go with them, so we commonly found piles of missiles but no launchers. But now, with hindsight, does anyone actually believe that there ever existed such a threat to us in the West from chemical weapons? It's true that the Kurds were gassed in the north, but no advanced weapons programme ever materialised. Still, when have we ever allowed the truth to get in the way of a good invasion? The Army would occupy the site if it was deemed necessary, and were relying on us to find it as they didn't know where it was. Their intention was to follow us, let us do our survey with Captain Rodriguez, the main force would supply security, and we would leave when we'd finished. I had a quick chat with the staff sergeant in charge of the platoon we'd be travelling with, just to go over details such as actions on enemy activity, a brief heads-up on tactics and what we would do, and made sure that they tried not to brass us up by mistake. That was always a massive concern of mine. I don't mind being shot at, but I'd feel really stupid getting taken out by my own side, so I wanted to make sure that everyone in the platoon knew we were there and that we were on the same side. I'm not putting the US Army down, but even retards make it into the military, and that's all countries— even mine. There isn't an army on this planet that doesn't have its fair share of idiots.

We didn't have comms with the Army unfortunately, as our radios were on different frequencies. However, I took my driver's radio, as he was sitting next to me so could live without it, and gave it to the platoon commander, not to Rodriguez. If it all went loud between Baiji and the ammo site, a Corps of Engineers officer wasn't going to be any use to me. When they were ready, we set off in the lead, remembering to keep the speed down, which none of us liked, but after we turned off the main road the going was slowed down by the terrain anyway, so it didn't really matter. The map told me everything that I needed to know, and I was confident that I knew where we were going. Iraq is pretty featureless and flat in the boonies; it only starts to get a bit more interesting when you go north towards Mosul, and after an hour of cross-country and small tracks I'd calculated that we were about 5 kilometres from the location. As we got closer I could make out what looked like a perimeter of earth that had been pushed up to form a berm. I got on the radio to tell everyone and we pushed on. I had the window open, and when we were roughly 600 metres away I heard the unmistakable sound of rounds passing by. I was too far away to hear the weapon, but at that range I wasn't concerned.

'Contact, front,' I said into the radio.

Give the Americans their due; the .50s on the Humvees opened up immediately, suppressing the enemy. We reversed, getting behind them, as one of the most dangerous places to be is between the two, and our weapons would have been ineffective at that range. I was also satisfied that the location to our front now engaging us was the site we were looking for. With the Humvees between us and the enemy, I was happy.

'We're staying firm here, until I know what the plan is,' I said into my radio, before getting out of the vehicle and going to find the platoon commander.

'Looks hostile!' he shouted above the noise of the .50 as I approached.

'Yes, I don't think they want to leave!' I said, the noise increasing with the sound of the Mk 19, a very common weapon mounted on vehicles. The Mk 19 is effectively a belt-fed grenade launcher that can lob a grenade over 2,000 metres. Personally, watching them destroy something gives me a bit of a hard-on, and the one behind me was making short work of the berm where the fire was coming from, but we were still receiving incoming rounds, although not accurate and becoming more sporadic. It could still ruin your day if you got hit, even at this range.

'What's the plan?' I asked, knowing that the Army was about to have its hand forced by the enemy's determination. Obviously the location was of a strategic value to the enemy, so we all knew that the Army would probably be expected to take and hold the site, at least until somebody decided on a more permanent solution. The other issue was that while we were waiting, the enemy were probably bugging out, taking as much as they could carry towards Syria.

'Speicher isn't far,' I added.

'Good idea,' he replied, getting on his radio to request air support. Apaches from Speicher could be with us in minutes and could secure the area better than we could. More importantly, they could chase any bad guys and catch them out in the open. I quickly ran back to my vehicles and told the team. Ivan looked very excited, but we all were. There isn't much in life more impressive than a ringside seat to some airborne mayhem unleashed from an Apache. It's enough to give any man goose bumps, and if it doesn't you need to hand your man card in at the door and get out. I also reminded everyone to stay tight with the Humvees, as I didn't want to get taken out by mistake. I'd seen A-10s take out a friendly call sign in the first Gulf War. It happens more often than anyone would care to admit.

I went back to the lead Humvee, and judging by the smile on the platoon commander's face, we were getting air support.

'Five minutes or the next one's free,' he said.

I gave him a thumbs-up and we continued suppressing until we could see the Apaches approaching from our six o'clock. We stopped firing as they flew in, but we could feel the rounds in the air. The Apache has a 30-mm chain gun that has an effective range of 1,500 metres. Its rate of fire is about 600 rounds per minute and it can literally send a wall of lead towards the enemy. It can also fire a mixture of explosive and incendiary ammunition. I didn't know what these were loaded with, but the remains of the berm disappeared in a cloud of dust before they boxed round us and carried on beyond the compound. I was hoping that they were on the hunt for any runners, but suddenly it went quiet.

'I think I've just come in my pants,' Geoff said behind me. I turned around and my whole team were standing there with binoculars and scopes, apart from Ivan, who had a video camera and a strange look of ecstasy on his face.

'Did you get all that?' Travis asked him.

He just nodded his head, still smiling. I knew we wouldn't be moving on just yet, so told everyone to have lunch while we waited for the all-clear to move forward from the helicopters. I wasn't going to move forward with those things looking for targets, and we were now very much under military jurisdiction. Back in those days nobody cared if we were involved in offensive operations, but in present-day Iraq you'd get arrested in five minutes for doing such a thing. However, at that time we did what we wanted. I sat back in my truck and began to rummage through the MRE. I started with the pound cake, which is quite tasty, and I still had my thermos of coffee. Some people have a cigarette after sex, but I prefer coffee and cake after all enemy contacts. I could hear some explosions in the distance, and pretty soon there was smoke on the horizon, although it was too far for us to see anything. The platoon commander came over a few minutes later.

'Well, the Apaches are heading back to resupply. They got several vehicles heading away from the site,' he told me as I handed him my flask.

I couldn't tell you what the rules of engagement were for the Apaches, but it was pretty black and white; anything out there would have been a legitimate target. There was nothing as far as the eye could see, but we found out later that some vehicles had stupidly tried to engage the helicopters and had been brassed up. That was a sure-fire way to get yourself killed.

'So what's the plan?' I asked him.

'We have to wait for clearance to move forward from our Ops room; then we can carry on.'

'Okay, let me know when you're ready to move on,' I said.

As he walked off, I told the rest of my team and we settled in for a long wait. There was a lot more helicopter activity, and I'm guessing that someone further up the food chain had decided that we might have stumbled on those pesky WMDs. I have to admit that it was very unusual to meet that sort of resistance, as the enemy knew we had air cover at our disposal, and they could have run before we got there and still got away with a lot of stuff. But, as we were to find out later, we'd stumbled across a training camp. Its proximity to the Syrian border made it ideal, and all the ordnance that was already there had made the location perfect. Parts of Iraq had yet to be fully policed by Coalition forces, and there hadn't been a military presence in the area. The Army was stretched pretty thin up there, as places like Mosul and Fallujah were taking priority, so a small compound in the middle of nowhere was easily overlooked. We waited there all day until reinforcements eventually arrived and the Army pushed into the compound. We stayed in the rear and, when given the all-clear, were allowed in, and it was obvious that the enemy had turned it into a home from home. Their discipline had been good, though. From the air it would have looked like civilians were living there, as everything was under cover or inside the bunkers. Weapons and ammunition that hadn't been taken was still in boxes stacked up inside, and there was food, stores and communications equipment, but considering what was supposed to have been there, it was apparent that a lot was missing. No doubt missiles and ordnance had been recycled to make IEDs and other fun items designed to ruin our day. The Army engineers were checking everything for booby-traps, although I doubted that the enemy had had a chance to leave us any presents. There were also several dead bodies— not as many as I'd expected to see— but what there were didn't look like they'd be having open caskets. Those 30-mm rounds certainly did their job, as did the grenades from the Mk 19s.

I gave my GPS to Geoff, told him to mark the perimeter and he headed off. All he had to do was walk the perimeter with the GPS and the unit would mark the length and location of the perimeter walls. When we returned I could superimpose that onto a map using my computer, and this would form part of my report. I could then send it electronically or print off a map with all the relevant waypoints and locations. I do love technology— when it works.

As Ivan was a keen cameraman, I gave him the job of photographing everything. He was very happy to do it, and even now I imagine him inviting friends round to his bunker somewhere on the Russian Steppe, giving slide shows to his survivalist friends, containing hundreds of high-resolution pictures of dead bodies and destruction. Within two hours my mission was complete, so I went to find out what was going to happen next. I thought that I'd better have a chat with Rodriguez and luckily found him with the rest of the headquarters element that had now arrived, so all the grown-ups were in one place.

'Captain Rodriguez, we've done what we came for; what's the plan for you guys?' I asked.

'We're going to stay here, for now; at least for tonight. After that we aren't sure, but we may be blowing everything in place,' he said.

Blowing in place was something that had caused more problems than it solved. During the invasion, the pace was often so fast that the Army didn't have the resources to hold every ammo dump that they took, so many were destroyed using demolition charges or artillery. While some of the munitions were destroyed, some survived and were then dispersed over a wide area, still live and unsafe and also available for enterprising locals to use to make bombs. Those locals who weren't killed by the unstable munitions could then cart them off and use them for whatever they wanted.

Ultimately it wasn't my problem. I was there to survey the site and pass on my findings, and I wasn't going to get involved in the military's planning, good or bad. That was above my pay grade and wouldn't have made me popular. Sometimes you just have to know when to say okay, walk away and let someone else deal with the problem.

We had just enough daylight to get back to our base, and that was my intention. We'd completed the mission, even though the parameters had changed considerably, but we'd dealt with the changes and now there was nothing left but to go and make my report. I wasn't entirely sure how I was going to word it, but I'd speak with my boss and hopefully between us we'd be able to come up with a solution. I told the kids to get ready and got as many contact details from the military for any follow-up questions and so I could include them in the report, and in that way possibly avoid answering any stupid questions. The DOD could ask the Army directly what was going on with the site. After saying our goodbyes, and retrieving my flask, we left. We didn't have the time to mess around, so went back the way we'd come. As we hit the main road again I had a sneaking suspicion that we'd be back this way soon enough, but I didn't like the idea— that whole area felt very wrong. I suspected that the enemy there wasn't your usual Iraqi with nothing better to do; they seemed a bit more professional and a whole lot braver. We got back in just before dark after an uneventful journey and I told the team to get ready for whatever tomorrow had in store for us. I then spent an hour telling the project manager the story, and he suggested that I first write a short account of the events leading up to our entry to the location, and then the report and the contact details for the military. It seemed straightforward enough, and it didn't take me long to put it all together. We had nothing on for the next day, but I wanted it all finished while it was still fresh in my mind, and when I'd completed it I went to the dining facility. I'd only just sat down when I heard a voice that I recognised.

'Too good to sit with us Grunts?'

I turned around in my seat, and saw that it was John Forbes, my old 2ic from my first contract.

'My God, they let anybody in here these days,' I replied as he sat down opposite me.

'So what do you know?' I asked.

Even though we hadn't seen each other for a while, we just picked up where we'd left off. This is very much a military thing. I sometimes bump into people who I haven't seen in over ten years and we carry on as though we'd seen each other last week. It's something that civilians can never seem to get their heads around.

'Just coming back off leave. I got a ride on a Blackhawk going to Speicher, but it was detoured to here. I'll try and get further tomorrow,' he said. Anaconda was probably one of the better places to be stranded.

'Common problem; so who are you working for now?' I asked.

'Armor Group. We're at an ammo site near Tikrit.'

'Any good?' You were always looking for something better, so it paid to know what was available.

'Fucking suicide! Soft skin vehicles, daily runs to Baghdad, no way to vary your route, and a project manager who's trying to get everyone killed,' he almost spat.

'Nothing new, then,' I laughed, but unfortunately it wasn't funny. Armor Group had more than its fair share of casualties, a lot of it down to poor management and shit vehicles. It was the same with a lot of outfits, but Armor seemed unluckier than most.

'How long have you been with them?'

'Just after you left, I jumped. The money's good and you're paid on leave, but at the moment it's that or convoys. Not a lot of options.'

I told him about my contract and gave him the email address of HR and recommended that he gave them a call, but he didn't seem that keen after I'd told him what had happened earlier. Looking back on it now, it does sound a bit suicidal, but at the time things seemed to evolve and you didn't really notice the danger. Well, not until you bumped into someone doing something more sensible, and right after you told them what you were doing, they always seemed to get that look— a sort of cross between not believing you and 'Are you fucking serious?' John was starting to get that look as I casually spoke about sitting there on the start line with an Army call sign, getting ready to go into a terrorist training camp that had just been levelled by helicopters five minutes from the Syrian border. When you put it like that, it does sound a bit insane, but at the time none of us saw the problem. I guess that's how the First World War dragged on. People get used to anything, and before you know it, the most insane situation is daily life and feels normal; anything else feels alien. I felt that way for a long time after I eventually left Iraq. It took me ages to readjust to everyday life in a non-hostile environment.

'So what happens if you can't get a ride on a chopper? I asked.

'We're only an hour or so north of here. Worst case scenario, the PSD team comes to get me, but we've only got one and we had a guy stuck here for ten days last month,' he replied.

'Wow, that sucks. What a horrible way to spend ten days of your rotation, stuck in a safe location with good food and shopping, not to mention a cinema and women,' I added sarcastically.

'Yeah, we do a nine weeks in and three at home rotation, so he ended up doing less than eight, but not his fault, so didn't cost him any leave,' he said.

I spent an hour or so telling him about the casualties and all the gossip. His contract sounded a lot worse than mine, so I wasn't bothered. Like me, I don't think he realised how stupid his missions were, and his accommodation was shit, with only a small dining hall run by Indians and no facilities. So far I'd done some pretty stupid runs, but he won hands down when he told me how they once drove all the way to Baghdad from Tikrit, spent most of the day at the client's main office at the BIAP and then drove back, only to be sent back again that same afternoon to pick up an apparently vital CD that a client had forgotten. They drove all the way back to Baghdad, the trip being 100 miles each way, so in total 400 miles, to pick up a CD which turned out to be a driver disk that you get with a printer, which could have been downloaded. On the drive back they totalled one of their vehicles. By then it was dark, the headlights didn't work, and it hit a pothole at speed and took off, smashing the suspension. They had to destroy it because they had no way of recovering it. If they'd left it, by morning it would have gone missing, and all this because of a client's forgetfulness or stupidity, probably both. Not only the cost of a vehicle but, more importantly, risking twelve lives for a fucking CD that was available online. I thought I'd heard it all, but that really took the biscuit! And the worse part— where was the project manager? Why didn't he tell the client to wind his neck in? Sorry, I forgot that he's the one who wants to get everyone killed. You may think I'm being hard on the management, but really from our point of view that's exactly how it felt sometimes. Every time I complained about a mission being stupid or questioned why we were doing something that didn't make any sense, I was always told the same thing. 'If you don't like it, you can fuck off home.'

I realised how lucky I was with my new contract. Once we were out on the ground, we could do what we needed to do to survive. I was aware that reconnaissance of ammo sites that might end up being abandoned wasn't that important. I knew the realities and had already decided that if I was given a mission of such stupidity, I would drive to Speicher, park up and spend the day shopping, then go back and write a bogus report. I wasn't going to die for nothing. Unfortunately for me and my team, I'm not that way, so never felt that any of the missions required that level of skiving.

'Shit, John, that's fucking retarded. You've got me there. I thought the Thanksgiving Day mission was bullshit, but that wins hands down.'

'I know; it's really special,' was all he could say in reply.

'So what are you going to do? Stay on the contract or move on?' I asked.

'Nowhere else. Armor's a good company, the only other contracts are convoys, and I don't fancy spending my days escorting slow-moving trucks from one end of the country to the other.'

'Fuck, no. Those guys get hit several times a day. No amount of money is worth that,' I added.

I'd always said that I'd leave when my only option was convoys. It was the one thing I really didn't want to do. The whole thing sucked, in my opinion, but I do know some guys who really liked it. I guess you either love it or hate it, but I'm fairly sure that I wouldn't have enjoyed it. We ended up getting coffee and I took him over to our accommodation, showed him our set-up and then took him back to the transit accommodation. Before I dropped him off, I made him promise to send his CV into HR and at least have a go at moving. He said that he would and we said goodbye. I went back to my room and lay awake, unable to sleep.

Conversations like the one I'd just had always made my blood boil. The lives lost through stupidity. Even now, writing this, I'm getting angry, mainly because it's something that I've never been able to come to terms with. No amount of soul-searching has ever led me to a satisfactory answer as to why this sort of thing happened, or how some of these people were employed in the first place or kept their jobs when they were obviously not fit to clean toilets let alone manage a project and gamble with men's lives. There are a few project managers out there now who if I saw on the street I would do something stupid. I know that for a fact. I doubt that I'd be able to control myself, and I know that I'd probably end up in jail. But it would be okay; I could lived with that. As for John, he left Armor and went to work for another company. I subsequently heard, second hand from a mutual friend, that he was killed a year later by an IED near Taji. Apparently the IED was so large that they didn't find much, which on the upside means that it was probably quick, but that was the reality of working in places like Iraq. Most of us have lost our fair share of friends, and that will never change as long as men like me do this kind of work.

A week later we were back on the search for ammo sites. Having spent the last week answering questions and writing follow-up reports, I was starting to worry that my job was now going to be 90 per cent paperwork. I didn't mind, but it was hard being both a team leader and an administrator. I decided to give it a bit longer. Perhaps it was due to the whole thing being new and it would settle down, or had a lot to do with the resistance that we'd met earlier and the possibility of the military being directly involved. If our missions were going to turn into bug hunts then it made sense that the military took the lead. While nobody cared if we got involved in offensive operations, it wasn't our job. Once in a while was fine, but we couldn't be re-tasked as offensive without somebody noticing, and then we'd become mercenaries. We were already close to it, but we hadn't crossed that line, which harked back to the 1970s in Africa when gangs of European contract soldiers did the dirty work of governments, often with the British and US governments looking the other way because it suited them. However, that was unlikely to happen in Iraq, and we were dangerously close to that line. I decided that I'd see what happened over the next few weeks and would voice my concerns if I felt it necessary, and that I'd also speak to the team about it.

This mission meant going past Baiji and into the desert, but quite a distance from the Syrian border. I wasn't unduly worried— every mission has its own dangers and risks— but after our previous encounter I was concerned about the possibility of civilians being on these sites or booby-traps being left for us. If the site was deserted, that would be a combat indicator as far as I was concerned. The locals would have been warned and would then avoid the location, so either way the risk had just increased. I could see the site as we approached, but this one was a lot smaller, and smoke was coming from inside the compound, which to me meant people.

'Paul, drive us around the perimeter, but keep a good few hundred metres away from the berm,' I said.

Skirting around the site, we saw nothing unusual. The berm was intact, but there was a lot of rubbish in the trench that ran around the perimeter at the foot of the berm— mostly empty water bottles.

'Right, we're going in. Keep it tight; there's a good chance there are civvies in there,' I said over the net as Paul drove slowly into the compound.

The site itself was small but had several concrete bunkers that had been used to store artillery rounds. These were now a commodity, and the 155-mm shell was a favourite in the making of effective IEDs. It was small enough to carry, yet devastating, especially when several were daisy-chained together to form a larger IED, all detonating at the same time. The biggest I'd seen, probably made up of seven shells, fired a Humvee about 20 feet into the air, killing the crew. I could see straight away that people were living there. We quickly debussed and I decided that we could do our job but needed to be as quick as possible. I delegated all the tasks among the team and told the drivers to stay with the vehicles. Not keen to piss anyone off, I told everyone to keep it low key and friendly, as we might have to go back there or to other locations where the word had spread. If we got all hot and heavy, people would be itching to take us on, whereas if we acted decently that would also get around and we'd be less likely to get a hot reception at other locations.

There were quite a few kids and the usual camel-faced locals. Obviously the well-educated locals with money didn't live in old ammo bunkers and, as in any country, the poor and the stupid had to survive on their wits. Each of the bunkers had more than one family living inside, and it all looked pretty desperate. The kids were wandering about barefoot, covered in dirt, and there wasn't any power. This lot must have been poor if they couldn't afford a generator. Usually the first thing to appear was a satellite dish— it didn't matter how remote or poor people were, they always seemed to manage that. I'd seen houses with three walls and no roof that had a generator and a massive satellite dish, but this lot hadn't yet evolved to that level. I guessed that they were poor before we invaded, and that living in an ammo bunker was a step up the ladder compared to wherever they'd come from. They watched us with interest. The locals were usually inquisitive and always approached to see what you were up to. But this lot were different. I asked if anyone spoke English, but knew I was wasting my time. Within thirty minutes we were done and there wasn't any ammunition left. I'd taken a lot of pictures, including the inside of the bunkers, and assumed that the local villains and insurgents had raided the place early on, taking anything of use. I took a couple of boxes of MREs out of the back of my vehicle and dumped them on the ground, making the universal gesture of eating, to let them know that we hadn't just dumped a box of land-mines in front of their houses.

'Man, this is a shit way to live,' Travis said to me as I closed the tailgate of the truck.

'I know, poor bastards; it's always the poor that suffer,' I replied.

I'm no crusader. I come from a very comfortable middle-class background and never went without anything as a kid, but I've been a soldier all my life and the one universal truth I've discovered is that the poor and the weak always get the shit end of the stick. I've seen it all over the planet. And the one thing that did really piss me off was that the Ba'ath party members who'd got rich with Saddam Hussein had simply taken their uniforms off and were still getting rich by taking us for a ride and holding their hands out. Many were getting into politics or supplying services to us, and the Coalition was paying top dollar to these shitbags. Well, I guess that's capitalism at work. What was even more annoying was that a lot of them ended up as US citizens. With the US Government's expedited visa programme, any Iraqi who had worked for the Coalition could and still can apply for a visa and, within five years, citizenship. Now a lot of Iraqis worked in Security in the later days when Iraqi PSD teams members became the norm, and these guys risked their lives and died, but a lot of these former regime scumbags slipped through the net and are now rich businessmen in the US, laughing at our gullibility and stupidity. These are the things that anger me. These injustices are what make our democracy weak and easy to circumvent, and it's not just the US. The UK is arguably even worse— we let anyone in.

Geoff pulled a couple of cases of water out of his truck and dumped them on the ground.

'Well, that was strange,' I said as we all gathered round before leaving.

'I guess we can expect similar at other locations. After all, real estate is hard to find,' Travis added.

'Especially bomb-proof accommodation,' Geoff said, pointing at the bunkers.

'Anyone see any ordnance?' I asked.

They all shook their heads. I was satisfied that this place didn't have any ammo left and was hoping that the site would be ignored. I would put in my report that the families were living there, and knew that there was a good chance that nobody would be in a hurry to make a load of families homeless. At company level, people didn't really give a fuck about what happened to the locals, but the Coalition and Government do-gooders didn't want to seem to be victimising the population— if anything, quite the reverse. A lot of money and resources were wasted on projects that locals didn't even want or understand, just to make some bureaucrat feel good about himself. We mounted up and headed back.

'PSD call sign ahead,' I said over the net.

About 300 metres in front of us was a two-vehicle convoy. Paul flashed his lights and I waved as we drew closer, the rear gunner waving us forward. We were about 200 metres from the rear vehicle when it disappeared in a ball of flame and smoke.

'Contact, front. The PSD team in front's been hit,' I said over the net as I swivelled in my seat and began looking for targets. The team in front began shooting, but I still couldn't see anything on our flanks and I was concerned that we'd get drawn into the contact and end up taking fire from the team to our front. The rear gunner should have informed his team that we were behind them, but people do panic at times like this and often end up shooting in all directions. We cleared the smoke and I could see the rear vehicle slightly ahead burning by the side of the road, having obviously taken most of the blast. The lead vehicle had carried on going and was a good 300 metres further on. We were the closest.

'We're going to stop. Secure our rear,' I said over the net.

My rear vehicle stopped to provide security for us as we tried to help. Now technically we should have driven on, but who would? We were the closest to the burning vehicle and if anyone was left alive, we were their only hope, as the front vehicle would take several minutes to get back, assuming that it wasn't damaged or had any casualties. I was taking a chance, but these situations are those defining moments that you read about, when people spend the rest of their lives wondering why they hadn't helped and all that other self-doubt. The problem is, most normal people have these defining moments only once in a lifetime, if at all, but we had them on a weekly basis, so it was obvious to me what had to be done.

'Pull over next to the burning truck. And make sure their front vehicle can see us when they come back. I don't want them engaging us, thinking we're insurgents,' I said to Paul.

That was a real possibility. They drive back, all shaken up, and see people with guns trying to get into their rear vehicle. It's not a stretch to think of them engaging us, believing we're trying to finish the job. They had the same vehicles as us— diesel powered, so unlikely to explode. The cab had taken all the blast and it was this part of the vehicle that was on fire. The rear deck where the gunner sat was just fragged. The gunner was missing, and I immediately assumed that he'd been thrown out by the blast or by the vehicle swerving to the left.

'The gunner's missing. He might be in the grass,' I said into my radio.

Iraq is one of those places that when it's hot the land is brown scrub, but overnight it literally turns green when it rains. We'd had a couple of weeks of bad weather and the sides of the roads in many places had become overgrown with tall grass, easily tall enough for a man to hide in. We still hadn't received any incoming; whoever had detonated the IED had probably seen us at the last minute and was long gone. My team had evened the odds, and Hajji wasn't stupid. He didn't like a fight.

Ivan had got our fire extinguisher out of the back and was trying to beat back the flames. By now the front vehicle of the stricken team was pulling up, and the TL came running towards us. He looked fucked, especially when he saw that there was no chance anyone had survived in the cab. Their vehicles were soft skinned F350s with no factory armour, only what they'd improvised themselves. Having operated unarmoured vehicles myself, I knew that the chances of surviving a large and well-placed IED were virtually non-existent. I knew what he was feeling.

'Your gunner's missing— I think he might've been thrown clear. We'll carry on here. I have a truck behind us looking. Try and find him,' I said, more as an order.

I know what it's like. Even the best of us finds it hard to hold it together at times like that, and if someone gives you an order that makes sense, you'll follow it. It's easier than having to think for yourself, and he knew there was a chance that the gunner was alive, and that meant everything. The crew were dead for sure, so he was of more use looking for a survivor than crying over the dead. He nodded and ran back.

'Geoff, the TL's heading back to you. These guys are done,' I said over the net, so that Geoff could look out for him.

Luckily we carried full-size extinguishers, not the small ones you usually get in vehicles, and Ivan had managed to put the flames out. As there was no armour, the windows had shattered, or had been open. Either way, we could see through the smoke inside the cab that the right-hand side was peppered with shrapnel, so there was a good chance that that and the concussion from the IED had taken them out. Nobody wanted to burn to death trapped inside a metal box, and I hoped that these guys had gone out quickly. We could see two charred bodies in the front seats, the passenger still holding his rifle, his hands fused to the metal. That was one of those images that stay with you— even in death, still armed and ready.

'You okay?' I asked Paul, who was standing there with his mouth open.

He pulled himself together and nodded, turning his back on the carnage. 'Okay, I'm going back there. You hold the front. If you see anything, let me know,' I said, pointing to the rear where the search was still going on.

I ran towards my rear vehicle where Travis was standing in the bucket, using the roof of the vehicle as support. He had the bipod legs down on the SAW and was resting them on the roof covering our rear.

'Any survivors?' he asked.

I shook my head as I ran past. He had a good view from up there and had seen us trying to put the fire out. He knew what I meant. I ran over to where Geoff and the other TL were kneeling in the grass and saw the gunner lying unconscious. I could tell immediately that his left leg was broken due to its strange angle, but other than that saw no other injuries.

'He's alive!' the TL said to us.

'We need to get medevac in here, okay?' I said, pulling my satellite phone out of my vest. I got my GPS out for the exact grid and turned the phone on, but it took a few minutes to find a satellite signal, and I then left the TL to deal with his gunner. As long as he was occupied, he'd be okay.

'Front vehicle?' Geoff asked.

'Not a chance,' I said. 'Paul and Ivan are up front holding the ground there. We'll call in medevac and hopefully get some Army support. We'll have to play it by ear until then.'

'Roger that. Patrick's pushing the traffic over to the other carriageway so we don't have any vehicles getting too close. We're a sitting duck for a snap ambush,' Geoff said.

I could see Patrick a few metres behind us, waving the traffic off to the other carriageway. They were all crossing over into the oncoming traffic— better that than mixed in with us. The sat phone was ready, so I called the first of the many pre-programmed numbers I'd stored in its memory. When I eventually got through I gave our location and asked for QRF support from the nearest military call sign.

'Okay, all sorted. Medevac is on the way. How's he doing?' I asked the other TL.

'I don't know. Can't find any other injuries,' he replied. We carried on holding the ground.

'Choppers,' Travis said over the net.

I looked up and could see two Blackhawks getting closer. I popped a smoke grenade so the pilot could see us and also see the wind direction. There was enough room, and the first one came straight in while the second provided cover from the air. Two crewmen ran over to us and we gave them all the info we had. I pulled the second one over and told him about the bodies in the first truck, and he nodded and went back to help his colleague. After they'd put the two fatalities into body bags and loaded them, together with the casualty, they gave us their details, location and unit, and left. I could tell that the other TL wanted to go with the casualty, but he still had one vehicle and one member of his team to worry about. He could either slot in with us or wait for the Army ground unit. I hoped the latter. We managed to keep the other TL out of the picture while we bagged up the dead crew, but I don't know why I made such an effort. He was obviously a grown man and, like us, had seen his fair share. Maybe I just hoped that someone would do the same for me, or perhaps I was topping up my karma, but whatever the reason, it felt like the right thing to do. And it wasn't pleasant. Some of the body parts were missing and some of the vehicle interior had melted into the bodies. They were still hot, but we managed. The sensible thing would have been to wait for the ground units, but sensible wasn't around.

'Suspect vehicle,' I heard Travis say over the net.

'Where?' I asked.

'Two hundred metres at our six. Black BMW,' he replied.

Using the vehicle as cover, I looked through my binoculars. The traffic was building up at our rear, and a single car had pulled out and was parked broadside to us. Its side windows were slightly open but I couldn't see inside.

'Okay, keep an eye on it. If anything happens, let them have it,' I replied, feeling that some payback was due about now.

Even if they had nothing to do with the IED and were an opportunist crew, we'd be ready to give them the good news if they tried anything. The radio traffic had warned the rest of the team off, so everyone was ready.

'How are you coping?' I asked the other TL.

'Okay. Thanks for stopping. You could have carried on going; you were in the clear,' he said, shaking my hand. He was getting himself back in the game. I'm sure he would have functioned fine if we hadn't been there, but we had been, and he'd let us get on and help him.

'No worries,' was all I could say.

'I better go see if my driver's okay,' he said as he walked back to his vehicle. The driver had stayed in the vehicle the whole time— it was his job to do so— and many of us had a firm drill about the drivers being in control of the vehicles at all times, but I was surprised that he hadn't ventured out. But then again, who could blame him?

'Contact, rear,' I heard over the net.

A second later, the SAW and the rest of my team opened up at the rear, and I ran back to see the BMW being hit by several hundred armour-piercing rounds. It pulled forward as if trying to get away, but stopped within a couple of metres. Everybody emptied their magazines, and Travis finished a belt of two hundred. All massively excessive, but understandable, given the circumstances.

'What happened?' I asked Geoff, who was aiming over the bonnet of the truck.

'Fucking idiots! They obviously didn't realise we were all watching them. I had the binos out and saw a weapon, then a muzzle flash, and that was that. We let them have the good news,' he replied.

I tried not to laugh, mainly because I imagined what was going on in the car. They must have thought we were in disarray and that they'd get an easy kill, only to get the reaction that they did. I only hope they had a few seconds to realise how wrong they'd got it before they went straight to hell.

'Where the fuck is this ground unit?' I said.

'Ground unit approaching,' I heard Paul say over the net.

I raised my eyes. 'Typical!' I thought to myself, as I walked back to the front of the convoy. Four Humvees were coming from the opposite direction, and I made sure that I kept my weapon down as they approached. I told the platoon commander what had happened, and then took him over to the other TL. I also made sure he knew that we'd had nothing to do with it and were a different company, mainly because I didn't want to get caught up in any investigation but also because we needed to carry on and get back to our location. Informing him of our intention to move on soon, I said that he needed to let us know what the plan was going to be with the other team and their only remaining vehicle, and then told the rest of my team what the plan was. By now the Army was policing the traffic, and I got my team to reorg so that we were ready to go. Two of the Humvees went to investigate the BMW that we'd used for target practice, and when they returned they had several weapons and looked a bit green. Apparently the four bodies inside the car looked like they'd been hacked to pieces. Well, several hundred rounds will do that to you. I knew that I'd be writing another report, even if it was just to cover my arse, because we'd got tangled up with another team and had had a contact, even if it was one-sided, for us, anyway.

The platoon commander gave us the nod to go. They would take the other vehicle back with them, and the other company would have to arrange recovery. The burnt-out vehicle would have anything salvageable stripped out and the weapons would have to be recovered. I'd done enough, and knew that one of the rifles still had bits of the owner melted onto it, so I wasn't going to help that much. I gave the other TL my contact details and email address in case his company needed anything from us, saying that I'd write a report and if necessary send it to everyone who needed a copy. I was sure that the other PSD team would want one, as we all liked neat paperwork, especially when dead PSD operators were involved, and insurance companies were always looking for reasons not to pay out on life policies. I'd never known it to happen, but there was always a lot of report writing to satisfy the vampires.

We mounted up and headed back. I'd totally forgotten about the poor bastards living in the ammo bunkers, we'd been so wrapped up in the last few hours, and that's all it was— two hours tops, maybe less. All that activity and mayhem stuffed into about 100 minutes. No wonder people had sensory overload and mental problems. I'm sure that the average human wasn't designed for that level of activity. When I went to the office and told them what had happened, they weren't surprised that we'd helped out and, even though it wasn't our problem, I think our project manager would have been disappointed in us if we hadn't. He was old school, and we were grateful for it. We didn't need any politically correct boy scouts in a place like this. I wrote both reports, the survey and the contact, and emailed them in, and although we didn't usually drink, that night we all sat in my room and finished off a case of beer and a bottle of Wild Turkey whiskey that Geoff had been saving, having convinced him that saving things like that was stupid, because if he got greased tomorrow we'd all be drinking it and he would miss out. Logic like that you can't argue with.

'Well, Travis, good shooting today. There's four fewer shitbags to worry about,' I said, lifting my glass in salute, followed by everyone else.

'My pleasure,' he replied, looking satisfied with four kills.

'We did the right thing, didn't we?' Patrick asked.

'What, stopping?' I replied. He nodded. 'On paper we could have driven on, but we did the right thing,' I said.

'Johnny Cash,' Geoff said.

'What?' I replied, not then being familiar with the American singer.

' "Drive On",' he said, disappearing to get his Johnny Cash CDs.

'That was a goat fuck. Did you see the vehicle that got hit? And it gave them no protection at all,' Travis said, shaking his head.

'No, and I didn't enjoy peeling those guys out of the vehicle and shoving them in body bags.'

'Was not fair. Was at wrong end to engage BMW,' Ivan said, looking truly annoyed at being denied a kill, even a partial one.

Although most of us had fired at that range, I was sure that most of the damage had been due to the SAW, as the more stable weapon at the time. But 200 metres is nothing for a professional with a good weapon, so everyone could claim a partial kill apart from Ivan, Paul and myself, who didn't have the opportunity to fire.

Geoff came back in with his iPod and speaker dock and started playing 'Drive On'. I'm a Johnny Cash fan now, but back then I hadn't been exposed to his music, and it was only when I started working with Americans that I found myself adopting some of their culture. Johnny had a lot of interesting things to say, and 'Drive On', especially in those days, was relevant. Some of us saw a lot of shit that would have finished a weaker man, but we kept going. Even though we worked for a company and could have left at any time, we still felt a loyalty to the group that only a man bred in the military can understand. You can't expect a civvy to have the same level of loyalty to a regular job; you won't see a civvy risking life and limb to get a proposal finished or a presentation completed. It now seems stupid that for years I hated civvies for what I saw as cowardice, and felt that you weren't a man unless you'd risked death for something that you believed in. But I was wrong. People like me, and those with whom I worked, did what we did so that civvies didn't have to, but I knew that we'd always have that something that they never would— that knowledge of ourselves that only a man who's seen the tiger's smile knows about himself. I still believe that you can't know yourself until you've faced death, and that what you did next would tell you what you needed to know about yourself.

We spent the rest of the evening drinking and talking shit. Johnny Cash had a lot to say that night, and most of it made sense, but deep down we felt relief. Nobody said it, but we all thought it: if that team hadn't been there it would have been us, or if we'd left a minute earlier we could have been the lead team. Maybe karma exists, and leaving the water and rations at the ammo dump delayed us just enough. I like to think that act of kindness saved our arses that day. Our vehicles were only semi-armoured, and whatever hit that team was big— probably big enough to have killed the crew in one of our F350s just as easily. It's these little things that mess with your mind; they're the things that keep you awake at night, and when you go over these events there's no logic. But I think it's a bad idea to look for logic in such things, although it's human nature to try and make sense of the most random act, and it doesn't get any more random than driving around Iraq just waiting to get hit. After all, it's a numbers game. Even after all the alcohol, I lay awake that night when the team had left— to have their own sleepless nights, no doubt— but I did exactly that, tried to make sense of it all, to put it into perspective. But mostly I thanked my God for giving me the sense to drop those rations before we left.

9

Mass Hysteria

We continued with our mission to survey remote sites, and for the most part found them to have been raided of anything useful, and occupied by families. Those that weren't had been destroyed, probably by Coalition forces, and required some form of clean-up. This was tendered out to explosive ordnance disposal (EOD) companies specialising in this kind of operation. Generally, once a contract had been awarded to a company, they'd come in with their own security contractors, in some cases from our company, or whoever they employed, and a perimeter would be put in place. On the larger sites, some with a perimeter of 10 kilometres or more, the original walls were used, but the smaller ones required something being built, and in the early stages bulldozers were used to create earth berms, which was quick and easy. The one thing they all shared was a debris field of some description. Military units had blown the bunkers or ammo dumps using demolition charges, but all that this had done was spread a lot of dangerous ordnance over a wide area, and this had to be enclosed before the clean-up could take place. Once the site had been secured, watch towers and a front gate for access control built, accommodation and offices (always in the form of trailers) dropped off and all necessary life support was in place, the clean-up could begin. Some of these sites had quick turnarounds and stayed very mobile, while others operated for years and became collection points for all the old Iraqi stuff that had to be destroyed. These became almost permanent, employing locals for security and PSD teams for road moves and days out to local bases for the clients, who were mostly ex-military EOD guys from the US or various European countries. They'd spend the day on litter patrol for unexploded items before centralising them in huge piles and blowing them up properly.

I knew several PSD operators who lived and worked on these sites. The work was dangerous, largely due to the remote location and the fact that most of these EOD companies were based in Baghdad, which meant a lot of road moves between the sites and the bases. This often involved using the same routes and long drives over 100 miles, making the numbers game slip into the enemy's favour. One friend of mine, based near Tikrit, could guarantee that on at least five days out of seven he'd have to do the trip to Baghdad. They suffered outrageous casualty figures, even losing clients, but the work continued regardless. All the clients were ex-military, so were more willing to take the risk than the average client, which didn't help, and of course the management didn't mind playing with men's lives to get the job done. Saying no to the client risked making them look bad.

We'd recently surveyed a site that was still intact and very remote. The Army had moved in the same day and we'd relieved them quickly, and within a week we had a guard force of Gurkhas providing the physical security of the site and a PSD team there to watch over the EOD guys who were making everything safe. The location, in northern Iraq, was not a million miles from the Iranian border and people were therefore taking the operation very seriously. We had regular resupply from the Army, and the company were sparing no expense. They were thinking of the long game and could see the financial sense in starting their own EOD division. Armor Group had Mine Action, a very successful EOD section that we came across regularly, so it made sense, and to get the best contracts you needed to be better and cheaper than the competition, so a bit of investment went a long way. In addition, having your own company as the client was the ideal situation: when Mine Action won a contract, that guaranteed work for Armor Group, so was a very good idea.

Having been tasked to relieve the PSD team there for a couple of weeks, we again prepared for a camping trip. The location had trailers for living accommodation, a small control centre of three interlinked cabins, and a separate shower and mess hall. The military paid regular visits and sometimes overnighted in a spare cabin. One of the reasons they liked coming over was the food, as we had a kitchen and cooked for ourselves using locally sourced food (which mostly meant raiding KBR supplies whenever we got the chance), and also because we had sit-down toilets. The military were based in a former Iraqi Army barracks down the road, with hole-in-the-ground toilets that meant you had to squat. I've spent most of my adult life in the Middle East and have never got used to squatting over the shitter. I hated shitting in the field in the Army, and I hated squatting over a hole in the ground, but unfortunately it's a reality of the Middle East. In my opinion, asking a westerner to adapt to this is just one step too far. I've seen Iraqis standing on a normal toilet because to them a sit-down toilet is just as alien a concept as squatting is to us. If you ever find a toilet with a broken-off seat and footprints around the lip, the chances are that an Iraqi's been using it.

Getting to the location was an expedition in itself, and it didn't help that the weather was shit. Being that far north, we had snow and subzero temperatures. A phrase I commonly heard in northern Iraq was 'This is the worse weather we've had in over twenty years,' but this seems to have been the case in every year since I first deployed right up until today. We finally arrived late in the afternoon, and our vehicles were brown instead of white, as we'd got bogged in a couple of times and had spent a few hours pulling each other out of the shit with tow straps and brute force. But it was also one of the things that made the site a bit more secure; if we couldn't get to it easily in modern off-road vehicles, Hajji couldn't reach us either. You could get there on foot, but that would be a long trip, and if we had any mortar attacks we'd have choppers in the air looking for the culprits before anyone could get away. That was a big advantage of the remote site compared to operating in built-up areas, but there are pros and cons to everything and it all evened out in the end.

I went and found the team leader I was there to relieve. He and his team had been there for twelve weeks— and it looked like it. There was a massive stockpile of MREs, something I was also guilty of, as sometimes you couldn't be bothered to cook, and it was too easy to open an MRE and eat all the goodies. However, pretty soon you couldn't shit, because most military ration packs are designed to stop you from shitting. Obviously not stopping to take a dump made you more combat effective, but the downside was that you got bloated and felt horrible. I've never been able to explain this one. An MRE has a lot of calories and is designed to keep you going during combat, but when you're burning a lot of energy, after a few weeks of living on them you start to lose weight, and those guys looked really bad. Their clothes were hanging off them and they looked like ghosts. I knew Mike, the TL, quite well, and he looked like a different person. I was shocked and made a mental note to be disciplined enough to try and look after myself, and it should have been easier for me, as the intention was for us to be there for only two weeks. The medic was also going back, even though he was meant to stay on, but two nights ago he'd decided to self-medicate using the ketamine from one of the trauma packs and was now a dribbling wreck. Luckily for me, my team had two very good medics, so I decided to delegate them and gave them the med packs to sort out. I did the handover and we watched the old team drive out, none of them looking happy to be leaving and just looking physically and mentally drained. Their vehicles had already been at the front gate ready to leave when we'd arrived. As we stood outside waiting to see them off, Mike came over.

'That's us off, then. Watch yourself here,' he said mysteriously.

'I'll try. Anything you need to tell me?' I asked, just in case he'd forgotten something.

'No, but this place isn't right,' he said as he got into the lead vehicle and drove off.

'What do you make of that?' I asked Geoff, who'd come over to wave them off.

'Beats me. I've not seen anything like that since we invaded this place.'

'Same here. Alright, get the guys together and we'll have a briefing in ten minutes in the kitchen,' I said and went over to the accommodation to unload my kit.

The rooms were okay, nothing to get excited about, and the separate shower and toilets were a pain, as the last thing you wanted to do in the middle of the night was go outside in subzero temperatures for a piss. That was when empty water bottles came in useful— not the best thing to do when you're half asleep, but a necessary evil. The kitchen was a large trailer split in two. On one side you had bench seats and a coffee-making station; on the other was where you actually did the cooking, as well as a store for the food and a walk-in refrigerator. I made myself coffee and sat down with the rest of the guys.

'All settled in?' I asked.

They all nodded, and seemed happy as they knew they only had to put up with it for two weeks. They'd all seen the previous lot and weren't happy about the look of them, but we put it down to the long rotation they'd just done. They'd be on their way home by the next day, so would have a few weeks to get over it.

'Okay, here's the news. Firstly we've got no clients for at least a week. They're all in Dubai getting drunk. The bunkers are locked and alarmed— we monitor them from the control room. We've got four Gurkhas who do twelve on, twelve off and are responsible for the site security. Until the clients get back the front gate stays locked, as we aren't expecting any visitors and there's no local workforce turning up every day. Unfortunately one of us will have to stay up at night as duty bod. The Gurkhas are fine, but we've got to have an expat in control at all times, so all of us, including me, will do a night each. When you've been on nights you'll get the next day off. All with me so far?'

The kids all nodded. Even with the night-shift, we should be able to have an easy time of it.

Gurkhas were a common sight in Iraq then. They mostly come from the Gurkha regiments of the British Army and were all from Nepal, having originally been employed as mercenaries since the 1800s and are now part of the British Army. They're a tough and fearless bunch, and many ex-Army Gurkhas then filled positions as static guards with nearly all of the companies operating in Iraq as they were cheap and willing to work brutally long rotations. Most of them lived in remote regions of Nepal and the Himalayas, and some of them spent 90 per cent of their leave just getting home. I knew one who'd done six months in country and got four weeks off, and it took him more than ten days to get home. He lived in such a remote area that most of the journey had to be done on foot, and he managed to get only about five days at home before trekking all the way back. However, even though they were cheap compared to us, the money they did make allowed most of them to live like kings back in Nepal. They're a funny bunch. Fiercely loyal to the British, they like to drink, fight and gamble, and are famous for carrying the kukri, the heavy bladed, curved knife that they aren't supposed to unsheathe unless it draws blood. I've seen some cut their own thumbs rather than re-sheath it unbloodied. But as with all things, there are exceptions, and we sometimes came across Indian Army Gurkhas. In Nepal it's a massive honour to be accepted into the British Army. The selection process is tough, and many more than are needed turn up to join, but the ones who don't make it often end up joining the Indian Army and, although still Gurkhas, aren't anywhere near as disciplined or professional as the British Army variety. So not all Gurkhas are created equal. I remember my grandfather, who was a soldier during the First World War, telling me when I was a kid that they used to terrify the Germans. He and one of the Gurkha Rifles battalions were on the line with his cavalry unit, and kukri-wielding madmen would get in amongst terrified German soldiers during vicious close-quarter trench battles, taking heads as trophies. Apparently a kukri in the hands of a pro could take the head off a cow with one blow. It sounds incredible, but I've seen stranger things.

'During the day, we'll be on standby for whatever happens,' I continued. 'We've got to man the control room 24/7, so that'll be our base during the day. Also, we've got to make check calls every three hours. There's a satellite phone base station and also internet in there, and at night the night-shift guy will live in there. We're fairly close to the Iranian border, but not close enough to be accused of being in Iran. We know what those pricks are like for that shit. No fixed mealtimes— there's a lot of frozen food and stuff we've brought with us, so cook for yourselves or, if you want, we can all muck in and cook regular meals. I'll leave it up to you lot to decide. We're all grown men; I'm not going to tell you how and when to eat. We'll worry about the clients when they get back. We can expect visits from the Army, and they do overnight here also, but we won't get a warning— they'll just turn up. We should see them coming, as we do occupy the high ground and have a good field of fire. Keep your pistols on you at all times and your radio just in case we get overrun. Unlikely, but you never know. Keep rifles and armour in the accommodation for now. Any questions?' I said finally.

'Internet, you say?' Travis said.

Internet access was a big issue. Very few companies supplied internet to their guys. Only the offices had it, never the accommodation, and most of us had to go to the MWR, which meant queuing up to get on a military-supplied PC. It was like an internet café having a limited time to use it and speeds slower than dial-up. Smart phones and all the mobile stuff we take for granted these days wasn't on the market then, and mobile phones were just that— phones— so not many of us were lucky enough to get on the internet more than a few times a week.

'Yes, there's a wireless hub, and there's no password, so anyone can get on. The range is limited though, so you've got to be close.'

I knew that the control room would be the heart of the contract and that everyone would be in there, which was good because it meant that it would always be manned, and even at night the person on duty wouldn't be alone.

'Internet is for girls,' Ivan said, and I wasn't surprised. We all liked him a lot, because he was a solid operator, but his idea of porn was cleaning his weapons and talking to them. I once heard him tell his SAW that it shouldn't feel bad that it wasn't a PKM but should feel inferior about its small calibre.

'Does anyone know what was going on with the guys we relieved? They looked like they'd spent a year in the jungle or something,' Paul said.

'That I can't answer. I tried to talk to the TL but he seemed a bit distracted. I'll have a word with the Gurkhas later to see if they can shed any light on it,' I replied.

'Don't forget the message of doom. "This place isn't right," he said as he was leaving,' Geoff told the others.

I'd hoped that he wouldn't mention it. Soldiers are a superstitious bunch, don't forget.

'I'm sure they were just a bit stir-crazy,' I added.

'The weather's not looking so good. Any word on that?' Travis asked.

'No, we'll just carry on. Obviously when the clients get here things might change. You can't blow shit up if there's lightning or adverse weather. Also, before I forget— Travis and Patrick, you're the medics for this trip. The site medic has been sent back for self-medicating, so go to his old room and take charge of the medical equipment. I want you to go through it and then let me know what shape we're in. Also, as we aren't signing for anything, we can steal what we want and blame it on him. He's going to get fired anyway, so it won't make any difference as far as he's concerned. I doubt he'll care, anyway.' The medic had his own room, which doubled as a clinic, and should have been well stocked. 'If there's nothing else, get yourselves comfortable and let me know what you want to do about meals and admin. Anything for me, I'll be in the control room with Geoff going through the protocols in there,' I said finally.

We all dispersed: Travis and Patrick on the hunt for the medical packs; Geoff and myself to the control room to get to grips with that. There was a comprehensive set of standard operating procedures (SOPs) in the control room, but they looked far too thick to read. Like all SOPs, they were ignored until needed as a guide for anything the handover had missed. The camp had a very limited CCTV system as well as a computer screen with a graphic of the camp showing the perimeter and the bunkers. The bunkers and the perimeter showed green, but if breached would flash red and an alarm would sound. It was all very basic, but very unusual for Iraq. I hadn't come across any electronic security thus far, and obviously the company was going to use this as an example for any future bids for this kind of contract. We also had a Thuraya base station on the roof of the cabin— a satellite antenna that gave us satellite comms. The sound quality wasn't great, but we could make our check calls. We also had a desktop PC that we could use to send an email in case the sat comms were down. As we were calling another sat phone, the problem could just as easily have been at the other end, and even today sat phones are only slightly better than smoke signals. I made the call and sent an email confirming that we'd taken over the site and commenced our duties, and Geoff and I went through the procedures for the control room, familiarising ourselves with the system used to monitor the bunkers.

'Do you know what's in the bunkers?' Geoff asked.

'No idea, but I'm guessing it's more than pistol ammo with this level of security,' I replied.

It was very unusual to have a site sewn up as tight as this one was. I found out later that the existence of the site wasn't common knowledge, but whether that was because of the proximity of Iran or something illegal was going on there, I don't know.

'Okay, if that's it, I'm going to see what the guys are up to. I'd better make sure they aren't stealing everything that isn't bolted down,' Geoff said.

'Do me a favour. Send the head Gurkha in.'

Gurkhas have a very strict caste system, which relates to their position back home. Rank in the Army or there in Iraq wouldn't count. A guard commander working for us would only take his orders from a guard if that person was higher in the caste system, very similar to the system in India, so wherever you went, if you were working with Gurkhas, there'd always be a head man. A few minutes later there stood the Gurkha king as the guys named him later. His name was KK, pronounced 'kay kay'. Don't ask; they weren't his initials, but it was easier to pronounce than his real name.

'So what's the story here?' I said.

'You British Army?' he asked.

Gurkhas can be a bit sneaky, especially if they think they can get something out of it. Being English, I was in the minority, working for an American company.

'Yes, of course,' I replied.

This would make a difference, as it was something that he could be loyal to and also get his guys behind. He would also expect me to watch out for him and his boys, which of course I would. In his inscrutable mind it was now us against the Americans, if you know what I mean, but to be honest the Gurkhas did get shat on quite a bit, and were used almost like cheap labour. Being British Army meant that I had a soft spot for them and recognised their sacrifice for the Empire, and also meant that I treated them as equals, whereas in the American system they were classed as Third Country Nationals. It wasn't the Americans' fault. They weren't familiar with the history of it all, and having never fought with them, didn't see them in that same light us the Brits did. However, the Yanks who worked with us soon realised and treated them very well, but I dare say that if you dropped a Gurkha in the middle of any American city, most of the inhabitants wouldn't know what he was.

'Very good. What regiment?' he continued.

I told him, which was even better, because I'd been in the Light Division, which meant that we came from the same place. Our officers went to the Gurkha regiments, and we shared a common history, so KK was now a very happy man.

'Take a seat,' I said. I was very keen to find out what had turned a PSD team into such a state. He sat down and relaxed.

'You want tea?' he asked.

'Sure, why not?' I replied, and he winked at me and barked some orders in Nepalese into his radio.

'Big problems here,' he added, shaking his head and tutting like Yoda.

'Really? Why?' I enquired. He leaned forward and continued as though we were in a public place and he didn't want to be overheard.

'We got here twelve weeks ago. No trouble, very easy job. Clients are good. Then two weeks ago …'

He stopped in mid-sentence, the door opened and in came one of the other Gurkhas with a tray of tea. He put it on the desk, KK said something, and the other Gurkha looked at me and smiled very happily and then left, kind of bowing and smiling as he went.

'He also very happy you are one of us,' KK said, picking up his tea and savouring the aroma as though it was a fine wine. I recognised the smell myself and it took me back a few years. I picked up my cup and took a sip, and my expression said enough.

'Gunfire!' KK said happily.

Gunfire is a tea traditionally served to the enlisted men by the officers on Christmas Day. It's black tea laced with rum, and while it's quite a violent drink, it's a life-saver when the weather's cold like it was then.

'Very good.' I wasn't going to argue about the rules regarding drinking on duty. I'm sure he policed it well enough.

'We only have it once a day,' he quickly added. Obviously the Gurkha king had supernatural powers and, as if to make a point, he added, 'It will start soon.'

I was about to ask him what would start soon, when the alarms sounded and the security display lit up like a red Christmas tree, with all the bunkers showing as open. I ran outside, grabbing my rife that I still had with me, not having had a chance to secure it anywhere, and ran to the closest bunker. The Gurkhas on the front gate were static at their posts and the rest of the team came running outside to join me at the obviously secure bunker. The weather wasn't helping, as the wind was howling and we were at the onset of what felt like a blizzard, and I was struck by the whole horror-film vibe that was suddenly making itself felt.

'What is it?' Geoff shouted above the wind.

'I don't know. All the bunker alarms just went off. Everybody check the bunkers; we'll do the perimeter,' I shouted. They all dispersed, and I walked off with Geoff to check the perimeter. 'I'm not sure what's going on here,' I continued.

'Me either, but something's up. I don't spook easy but there's a very strange vibe here.'

I nodded. I hadn't wanted to seem irrational, so hadn't mentioned it. As we'd only just arrived, I hadn't yet had a chance to take stock, but there was a definite feeling or atmosphere. I remembered Trenchard Barracks at Celle in West Germany, which had been my first posting when I left the depot and joined my battalion. It had been an SS camp during the war and was right next door to Belsen concentration camp. That place had a horrible atmosphere, and lots of strange goings-on had been reported by members of my unit. This felt similar, but I shook the feeling off and continued checking the wire. As I expected, the site was secure, and we carried on in silence and came back round to the front gate, where the rest of the team were.

'Nothing?' Ivan said.

'All the bunkers are secure. Must be the weather,' Patrick said. I nodded and signalled for them to go inside the control room.

'Okay, I really don't know what the score is here. I was having a conversation with KK, the head Gurkha, but the alarms interrupted me. Carry on as usual, and as soon as I have something I'll let you all know,' I said.

'We want to eat at the same time, for dinner at least, so we'll split the cooking among ourselves,' Paul said.

'Sounds good. Everyone fall out and I'll catch up with you all at dinner.'

As they left, I stuck my head out of the door and called KK over. I sat down and waited for him.

'So what happened, and what's the problem here?' I said bluntly. He could see I wasn't fucking around. The look on my face and the tone of my voice said it all.

'It was the clients,' he said, looking nervous.

'Just tell me. I won't say I heard anything from you,' I pressed.

'I don't know English word. Better I show you.'

He stood up, went over to the corner of the room where the battery charger for the radio sat on a small table, and took all the equipment off the table. I got up and walked over. I hadn't noticed it before because of all the crap on the table.

'Geoff, can you come to my location?' I said into my hand-held radio that I was now carrying clipped to my belt.

'Roger; on my way,' he replied.

'Just wait a second,' I said to KK. Geoff was there within a minute.

'What's up? Holy fuck, you're shitting me!' he said as he saw what I was looking at.

There on the table somebody had written the alphabet in a circle, probably with a Sharpie marker, each letter being about 4 inches high. In the centre of the alphabet circle were the words 'Yes' and 'No' with a box drawn around each one, and the word 'Goodbye'. There were also the numbers one to ten.

'What you call this?' KK asked.

'It's a Ouija board,' Geoff answered.

'Ah, we call it spirit board,' he replied, shaking his head.

'And what's it doing here? Didn't the clients have enough work to keep them busy?' I said.

'Obviously not,' Geoff replied.

'What happened, KK?' I asked.

'Two weeks ago, one client, Dutchman, I think, did this. He was drunk, and he and three others stole table from here and went to their room,' he said.

'Didn't the team leader stop them?' I asked.

'Said they were playing cards,' KK replied. It made sense; obviously they weren't that drunk. 'It was later, after midnight, they came running out of room screaming like madmen. It took all of us to calm them down. After this, strange things happened. Alarms were just the beginning,' he continued.

'Stop being so mysterious. What else?' I snapped.

'Things went missing. Chairs in recreation room moved on their own,' he said finally.

'Really?' Geoff said, looking unconvinced.

I'm an open-minded sort of a person and like to think that we live in a wonderful world with almost limitless possibilities. I also like to think that I've not been restricted in my view on things by a Catholic upbringing that had double helpings of evil nuns and touchy-feely priests during my schooldays, but I'm also a realist, and none of this was making sense to me either.

'Right, KK. Thanks. I'll be on duty tonight if we have any problems,' I said.

He nodded and left. I quickly tried to make the check call but had no luck with the phone, so sent an email stating that the alarms had activated and the weather was messing up our comms. Obviously I didn't mention werewolves and vampires.

'So what do you want to do?' Geoff asked.

'Well, first we need to get some garlic and holy water and sharpen some stakes! What do you think? Nothing! They've obviously all been here too long, and the Gurkha king is trying to put the wind up us,' I answered.

'Shall we tell the team?'

'Yeah. If they hear it from the guards they might think there's more to it than there is. Tell them exactly what KK said, and please don't add any witches or goblins in an effort to be funny. This place is creepy enough, and we all have weapons. I don't want anyone shooting someone by mistake, thinking it's a ghost lurking in the shadows. Tell them not to mess around. That's how accidents happen,' I said seriously. A load of scared people with infantry weapons would be a recipe for disaster. 'Fucking Ouija board. As if we don't have enough problems out here, without people doing stupid things like that,' I added, truly dumbfounded at the stupidity of people.

'Listen, I'm not saying I believe in that kind of thing, but it's never a good idea to fuck with things you don't understand. I heard of a kid at my school ...' Geoff began, but I held up my hand to interrupt.

'Geoff, we've all heard about a kid at our school who jumped out of a window after using one, or your cousin's friend who fell under a bus. We've all got a story like that. It's an urban legend. But you're right. Don't mess with things you don't need to— that's how bad things happen. If you're a believer you'll bring it on yourself— unconsciously you'll cause something to happen— that I do believe,' I said, trying to nip this shit in the bud before a load of already superstitious ex-soldiers started to freak themselves out.

Geoff went off to tell the kids what had happened. Between then and midnight we had three more alarm activations, but even though we knew they were false alarms we still reacted. It was just the way we'd been trained. The one time you don't react is the time when you have a real enemy to deal with, and you're watching porn on your laptop when Hajji gives you the good news. I reported each activation to our Ops on the check calls, but for all I knew, the alarms might have been monitored remotely as well. That was the usual routine in the real world, so I didn't want to give anyone an excuse to criticise my team. Geoff came back in.

'They aren't happy,' he said.

'Let me guess. We're about to be overrun by zombies,' I replied.

'That's about the size of it. They also want to split into two teams, one day and one night,' he added.

That was a good idea. The only reason I'd suggested one of us on nights with the Gurkhas was so that we'd all get the most rest, but splitting the call sign in half made more tactical sense.

'Good idea. We'll keep it simple. My vehicle takes nights and yours comes on at zero seven hundred. How's that?' I said.

'Sounds good. Do you want a break; maybe have a chat with the women?' he laughed.

I nodded and went outside. The weather had settled a bit— well, the wind had dropped— but it was freezing. I made a mental note to make sure we started the vehicles up every couple of hours and let them run so they wouldn't freeze up. It was something that we used to have to do when I was mechanised infantry in Germany. We kept some antifreeze in a jar outside the guardroom and when it started to freeze, all the drivers had to start the APCs and keep them running. It didn't help that most of our vehicles were thirty years old, but it was as cold in Iraq as it had been in Germany, and I doubted that our vehicles had any antifreeze in them, making a mental note to find out if they did.

I had a quick walk around the perimeter, and again everything was as it should have been. I then went into the kitchen and made some coffee before heading over to the recreation room where I was sure everybody would still be gathered.

'Everything okay?' I asked as I walked in. As I'd suspected, they were all still there, and they all nodded and mumbled. 'What's the matter? Scared to go to sleep?' I joked.

'They're acting like scared children, scared girl children,' Ivan said, cleaning his SAW.

'Fuck that! What idiot tries to contact the dead, in a place like this that's full of them?' Paul added.

'Well, it was one of the clog-wearers,' I said, referring to the Dutch, who we mostly called cloggies or clog-wearers.

'That's not the point. You don't do shit like that,' Travis added.

'Look, all of you. This place is a bit spooky, I'll give you that, but it's just a load of pissed and bored idiots messing around. Don't let the Gurkhas spook you. They probably think that it's funny, watching you get all scared,' I said, trying to inject some sense and logic into the situation.

'But what about the other team? You saw what they looked like. Didn't their TL mention anything to you?' Patrick asked.

It was a valid point. The TL should have mentioned it, but I had no way of getting in touch with him and didn't want to mention it to our management in case it made them look bad. I didn't want to be responsible for him losing his job, but I was going to try and find out at some point in the future.

'No, they didn't say anything. They've been here twelve weeks, and that's why I think they were in such a state. But I'll get to the bottom of it, don't worry. In the meantime, I suggest the day-shift get some sleep, and Ivan and Paul are with me. We'll take it in turns in the control room and the other two can stay in here as QRF for the alarms or the zombie apocalypse, whichever comes first. It's now zero one hundred; one of you two relieve me at zero two hundred, and the day-shift come on at zero seven hundred. All clear?'

Everyone nodded and Geoff's crew began packing up their kit and getting ready to get their heads down. I went back to the control room, told Geoff about the conversation, and suggested that he also get his head down. We'd left early that morning and weren't far off being up for twenty-four hours, and I was starting to run out of energy. The human body can keep going for a long time, but once the job's done or you start to relax, that's when you feel it. Now that all the admin was done, and hopefully the excitement was over, I was fighting to stay awake. I went and checked on the Gurkhas and found that KK was getting his head down, and I quickly told those on duty what we were doing as far as manning was concerned. There was nothing near us, and apart from the stars there was just pitch-blackness, which didn't help with the atmosphere. However, it did help to defend us against mortars, as the brighter the camp, the easier it was for a mortar team to hit you. They couldn't hit what they couldn't see. Although I've already said that it was unlikely that we'd get mortared, you got suicide bombers so why not suicide mortars?

The cold night air was helping me stay awake, and I went back to the office, sent the last check call and spent the last few minutes before my relief sending personal emails. Ivan arrived on the dot, still carrying his SAW.

'You can leave that in your room if you want,' I said, knowing the answer already.

'No, is okay. I prefer to keep it close.'

'It's better than a PKM,' I said.

'Will let you know when I've killed someone with it,' he replied, not joking.

I gave him a quick handover and replaced the battery in my radio. Normally we wore our radios attached to our assault vests and used earpieces and throat mics, but as we were now in barracks routine, so to speak, we unplugged the earpieces and just wore the radios on our belts.

As I've said before, the main reason for the earpieces was so that clients couldn't hear the conversations between the vehicles on road moves. They panicked enough without hearing what was waiting for us ahead.

'Any problems, give me a call. I've done the check call. The next one is due when I come back on, so you don't need to worry about that. Any questions?' I added.

He shook his head, so I left him to it. I was starving, so went to the kitchen to make myself something to eat and then headed to the recreation room. Only one of the lights was on, but I had enough light to see. Paul was asleep in the corner on a sofa, and I got on the other one. Within minutes of finishing my snack I was out. I woke up two hours later for my shift, luckily having set my alarm before I passed out. I'd been having the weirdest dream, but that had been the norm for me since arriving in Iraq. My dreams had gone into weird, make-no-sense mode. I couldn't remember the last time I had a normal one.

I staggered into the control room just in time for another alarm activation. I'd managed to mute the audible alarms earlier, so now just the screens flashed red. I'd also told everyone that until further notice we weren't going to sweep the camp. It wasn't that big, but whoever was on duty would just have a walk around. The strange thing was that once we stopped reacting to them, the alarms became less frequent, and I also stopped reporting them. I only had two weeks until my leave and I didn't intend to go home all strung out over what was probably nothing more than some kind of electronic fault. Checking the perimeter and the bunkers, I found that everything was secure and then made the check call, and after two hours of nothing, and with the sun beginning to come up, I handed over to the next shift. That was me done until the evening. The day-shift would be taking over after Ivan, and I had nothing for them, so I had a quick shower and went to bed, leaving strict instructions not to disturb me unless it was absolutely necessary. I woke up in mid-afternoon, had another shower and headed over to the kitchen for something to eat. Geoff must have seen me because he walked in and sat down.

'We've got a problem,' he said.

'Go on,' I replied, rubbing my face and waiting for the good news.

'Travis is really fucking freaked. He did a perimeter patrol just after sun-up and is positive he saw movement by the east wall, inside the wire.'

'I need more than movement by the east wall. What was it? This place isn't that big. We aren't talking about three clicks away,' I said.

'I don't know, but when I took over from him he was scared. He said it was out of the corner of his eye, and it was daylight. He described it as a blur,' he added, not being very helpful. That was what I was scared of—someone with an over-active imagination, as fear in situations like that is totally contagious.

'We need to get a grip of this. We can't start doubling people up. We don't have the manpower. And I'm fucked if I'm going to let this team go to pieces over crap like this,' I said, starting to get annoyed. 'Where is he?' I asked.

'He's in the control room with Patrick.'

'Alright, I'll have a word with him when I've eaten. I'm sure the waves of undead that are preparing to overwhelm us can wait that long,' I said.

After I'd finished my meal I went over to the control room.

'Afternoon, how's it going?' I asked as I walked in.

'Fine,' Patrick replied. Travis was looking a bit sheepish.

'And you; I hear you've got a UFO to report,' I said, turning to Travis, trying to keep things light-hearted.

'Well, I thought I saw something, but this bastard has spent the last hour calling me a girl, and a blind one at that,' he said, pointing to Patrick.

The best therapy for the fighting man 90 per cent of the time is talking to his friends, and it's even better if there's beer involved.

'So what are you saying? That you didn't see anything?' I pressed for an answer.

'No, I saw something, but it wasn't fully light and I was tired. It could have been anything. I'm just a bit jumpy, and I believe in all this paranormal stuff.'

'Fair enough. I'm not saying that I don't believe in the paranormal. All I'm saying is that even if it exists, we can't let it affect our jobs. It can't hurt us, after all, and don't even think about telling me about your Uncle Tom who died after a séance with a look of terror on his face,' I added.

'Okay,' he laughed.

'Well, I'm glad that's settled. I'm going to send some emails. I'll be in the recreation room, and failing that I'll take over at nineteen hundred,' I said, quite pleased with my counselling skills.

I could just get an internet signal from the base station in the control room, so pulled up a chair and put my legs up on another wheelie-type office chair. I was just turning my computer on when the chair my legs were resting on shot with considerable force across the room, making me sit bolt upright as my feet hit the floor. I know what you're thinking, but trust me on this. I've already mentioned that I'm boringly level-headed, and I am. I sat there for a moment gathering my thoughts. Should I run screaming from the room like Tippi Hedren in the film *The Birds*, should I carry on, or should I check that the chair wasn't booby-trapped and a wire hadn't been attached to it as a joke? I did the latter. I thought that maybe it had been a joke, but I knew my lot were also quite sensible and, as I'd already mentioned the possible consequences of scared people with guns, doubted that any of them really would have done such a thing. Putting my laptop on the floor, I examined the chair, but it seemed completely normal and hadn't been tampered with in any way that I could see.

'Fuck this!' I said to myself, now fighting the feeling of fear usually brought about by the unknown, and went outside and looked around. I could see a Gurkha by the gate and Geoff walking around the perimeter with Travis. Everything looked normal, and although the weather was starting to act up again, that was quite usual. Whatever had just happened was a localised event, and standing outside in the daylight, with everything carrying on as normal, I felt stupid, almost as though I'd just imagined it. But I hadn't, and there was no getting away from it. Should I tell the others or not? Something might happen to one of them. Should I take the earlier sighting seriously? Fuck, this was not what I was trained for.

'Geoff, when you've done your patrol, can you meet me in the recreation room,' I said into the radio.

'Roger,' came the reply.

I went back inside and against my better judgement repeated what I'd been doing before the event. I'd been sat there for about five minutes when Geoff walked in, nearly making me jump out of my skin because I was concentrating so hard on the chair that I'd forgotten about him.

'Fuck! Don't scare me like that,' I blurted out.

'Why, what's the matter? Not getting nervous, are you?' he laughed.

I told him what had happened, even going through a demonstration including sound effects and an action replay of the flying chair. When I was finished he just looked at me.

'You're not kidding, are you?' he asked.

'Not one fucking bit. And before you ask the obvious questions— no, I wasn't asleep or imagining it, there wasn't a strong wind, and it definitely wasn't a joke. I checked the chair thoroughly.'

'So is this place haunted, then?'

'I don't know, but let's look at the evidence, shall we? I'd have to say that something is wrong here, but short of calling in a priest for an exorcism I don't know what to suggest. Any ideas will be gratefully received,' I said, completely unsure of what to do next.

'I don't know what to say. Are we telling the kids?' he asked.

'Fuck, no! Let's see what happens next.'

For the next few days everything was quiet. A few people swore that things had moved around on their own, one instance being a missing toothbrush that turned up in the kitchen, which was a bit strange, but there was nothing that we could say with any certainty was of a paranormal nature. On the third night, the weather was decent, the sky was clear and, although cold, there was no wind or snow, and at twenty one hundred, there was a very loud explosion and a flash on the horizon. I saw it quite plainly from the control room window, and judging by the sound it was a click or less away. There was nothing there, so the obvious choice was a mortar, in which case there would be more coming, but none did. Leaving Travis at the site with the Gurkhas, the rest of us crashed out on foot. If it had been an IED on the track, it could have been a come-on designed to get us out in our vehicles into an ambush. The distance was short, so on foot with night vision the plan was simple.

'Geoff— you, Patrick and Paul go right of the track and advance towards the blast. Look for an ambush or possible come-on. If it's a US call sign there, pull back because they'll engage us. Ivan and myself will go left and come in from the high ground. Stay in comms and use your night vision. All clear?'

Everyone nodded and we did a quick radio check and left the camp. I didn't really notice the cold, as the adrenalin that races through your body at these times heightens your senses but dulls the feeling of cold or pain. Well, it does for me, but I dare say that it's different for everyone. Once we'd cleared the dead ground we were higher up than the track. I was looking for something that had been blown up, but couldn't see anything on the roadway. The obvious thing would have been the Army coming to visit and being hit on the way in, but there weren't any vehicles for as far as the eye could see, and if there wasn't any wreckage it would be hard to find a crater in the dark.

'I can't see anything from the high ground,' I said into my radio mic. I'd quickly refitted my earpiece before we left.

'Nothing here either,' Geoff replied.

'Okay, we'll push on a bit further and RV at the fork in the road,' I replied. About a click from our front gate the track forked, one going to the main road that we'd taken and the other seeming to go nowhere according to the map.

As I got closer I could hear something that sounded like moaning. I signalled to Ivan, and he stopped moving and cocked his head to listen. He obviously had better hearing than me, as he pointed to our right flank which was towards the junction. Looking through the night sight (NVGs),

I could see the blinking of the infra-red beacons that we wore. I made sure that I could see three separate blinks, which was the other team.

'Geoff, stop where you are. Can you hear something? We've definitely got something near the junction,' I said over the net.

'I can hear something, but can't make it out,' he replied.

It would turn out to be the one thing I hadn't thought of, and as we got a bit closer we could definitely hear either talking or movement.

'Geoff, I can hear something. We'll put down some fire. Hold your position,' I said.

Looking through the night sight again, I could see where they were. I handed the NVGs to Ivan so he could see and signalled for him to open fire towards the sound. He put the legs down on the SAW and got down on the ground. I tapped him on the shoulder and he squeezed the trigger, and tracer rounds screamed across the terrain, smashing into the area around the junction. He fired several short bursts, and then stopped. I couldn't her anything else.

'Geoff, move forward. We'll cover you from here. If anything happens, go firm and we'll give you fire support,' I said over the net.

'Roger; moving,' he replied. I followed them as they moved forward individually, covering each other as they bounded forward. 'You better get over here,' Geoff said into the net. Ivan and I moved over to his position, and there in a crater by the side of the road was most of a Hajji. 'We've had a look around but couldn't find anything or anyone else.'

'I bet the little shitbag was digging in an IED and it went off,' I said.

I risked using my flashlight. He was a mess, and I was pretty sure that he'd survived the initial blast— that must have been the noises we heard— but when we opened up, he must have taken cover in the crater. Both his legs were missing below the knee and he was badly burnt, but I couldn't see any bullet holes. We hadn't actually hit him, because the rounds had all landed about 20 feet away and he definitely hadn't crawled that far.

'That makes sense,' Geoff said.

'Yeah, works for me. Ivan, you missed him,' I said.

'Typical,' Ivan muttered.

'We better call the Yanks. They need to know, and I'm not touching him,' I said.

'Well, he's already buried,' Paul said.

'Most of him, anyway,' Patrick added.

I marked the position on my GPS and we headed back to our location, making sure that the Gurkhas knew we were coming in. I didn't want a blue on blue. On the upside, I'd forgotten about the ghostly goings-on—

there's nothing like having a purpose to make you focus. I called the local army base and told them what had happened, giving them the grids, and they said that they'd send up a drone and get back to us. While we were waiting, I informed our Ops room, and the Army called us back two hours later, asking if we had any assets on the ground. I rechecked that they had our base location correct and told them that we didn't have anything outside our perimeter, and was then informed that they were about to engage a vehicle and foot mobiles and would call us back. Ten minutes later there was a series of explosions beyond where we'd just been, and shortly after that the Army called to tell us that they'd just engaged a target further down the track towards the main road and would send a patrol to our location first thing. They also told us to stay in our location and not venture out unless it was an emergency, but that if we had to leave, to make sure that we informed them first. I thanked them and got the team together, including the Gurkhas, to pass on the info that I'd just received and told them that we'd carry on as usual.

I still doubted that anybody would attack us directly, as we still held the high ground and anybody who tried to take us on would have their arses handed to them for sure. I knew Hajji's limit was sneaky hit-and-run tactics, and that attacking a static location defended by trained expats with a shitload of weaponry was not on his dance card. To me it looked like an IED either for us or the Army, probably with a pressure plate to activate it. That way they could just dump it off and forget about it. I doubted any local traffic came past the junction, as you'd be on that part of the road only if you were going to our location, and the locals would have been warned off anyway. Obviously it had cooked off, and there could be many reasons why— maybe unstable explosives, or he might even have hit it with a shovel. It was probably a 155-mm shell, and the vehicle further down probably contained his friends and all the ingredients for the IED. Fortunately for us, but not for them, they were spotted and taken out by a drone strike or fast air, or even artillery if they were in range. The one thing that I had learnt in Iraq was that the Army weren't slow about using their assets and didn't mess around. The last thing the insurgents probably expected was this, but if the IED hadn't detonated prematurely we wouldn't have known about it and someone would have triggered it. It was not likely to have been us because we would have been staying put until relieved, so an Army patrol or the PSD team bringing the clients back in would have been the most likely candidates. We'd had another weird night of alarms and moving items, but to be honest I'd almost forgotten about the moving chair. Considering what had happened since, a chair moving on its own seemed quite pedestrian compared to drone strikes and Hajji own goals.

The Army turned up just after first light. They had found the car, containing three bodies as well as weapons and IED ingredients, and were very happy because the vehicle was wanted in connection with several incidents and they were sure that they'd taken out a crew that had been responsible for a lot of bad things. Another unit was collecting the bodies, which would be taken to the morgue before being released to the families. They of course would accuse us of murdering a car full of farmers who were out tending their crops at night and had either found the weapons or borrowed a friend's car and didn't realise what it contained, or we had planted them there. Either way, I had that warm, fuzzy feeling that you get when you've achieved something good and worthwhile, and a few less murdering vermin on this planet suited me just fine. The Army stayed at our location for a couple of days, and it was good to have extra guns around. While they were there we had no more insurgent activity— they would give us a wide berth for a bit— and as there were no survivors, the rest of their group wouldn't have known what had happened so would assume all sorts, from Special Forces teams in waiting to round-the-clock aerial surveillance, and would bother someone else until one of them took a brave pill and tried again. Unfortunately they might have more success next time, but that was the numbers game that we played, I'm afraid.

The clients turned up at the end of the week, and by the time they arrived most of us had experienced something inexplicable. Mine was the chair, Geoff had the hard drive wiped on his laptop, Travis kept seeing things out of the corner of his eye, Ivan couldn't find his weapon-cleaning kit (and considering that he slept with it under his pillow almost, that was a very mysterious event), every time Paul had a shower the water went cold (but that was because Patrick kept turning the hot water tank off whenever he got in the shower, as he said that he didn't want him to feel left out) and Patrick said something kept pushing him out of his bed. He got so pissed off with it that he started sleeping on a sofa in the recreation room.

Five minutes after the clients arrived, I got a call from Ivan who'd pulled a very sleep-deprived and almost insane Patrick off the clog-wearing idiot who'd done the Ouija board. Ivan was now busy holding him back while he thrashed about like a drowning man, and luckily for the cloggie, Ivan was twice the size of Patrick. He threatened to complain, but I told him that I'd kill him myself if he did, and then clued him in about what had been happening and how we blamed him entirely. I'm also sure that the company would have frowned heavily upon it if we had reported the incident, and as fantastic as the story would have sounded, our company was owned by a southern Baptist religious nut job who would have accused the cloggie of devil worship and probably shit-canned him in a heartbeat.

Thankfully the following week went quickly and our relief was soon on its way. This time we gave them a proper handover, even though they looked at us like we were mental, but at least nobody could accuse my team of keeping anything to themselves. I also wanted to get the fuck out because this team had just cleared the route to the main road and I needed to get down it before anyone had a chance to leave us a present. However, we did look a lot better than the team we'd relieved a fortnight earlier, but we'd only had two weeks of it and by the end we didn't let it bother us. We passed the wrecked vehicle on the way out, which had obviously been hit by something large and was badly peppered with frag. I was really relieved to get back to Anaconda, and after unpacking our stuff and showing our faces at the office we headed to the PX. We all met up at the seating area near the fast food outlets, and most of the guys went to Burger King but I'd been craving pizza all week.

'Glad to be back?' I asked everyone.

'I never want to go through anything like that again,' Paul said, unwrapping his Whopper.

'I do not understand problem,' Ivan said, probably upset that he didn't have his weapon with him.

'Well maybe in Mother Russia, the land where the Kalashnikovs grow on trees, this kind of thing's normal,' Geoff joked.

'Kalashnikov not grow on tree; it grow underground like potato,' he replied, reminding us that he did really have a sense of humour, albeit very dry.

'Well I don't think we should ever mention it to anyone because it'll sound like we became hysterical,' I said.

'It was strange, though. The whole place had a fucking horrible feeling to it,' Travis added.

We all nodded in agreement. It hadn't been a massive hassle, but it had definitely been strange. Whether it had all been to do with the Dutch idiot and his do-it-yourself séance I don't know, but either way, something had been there and it hadn't been friendly. However, on the upside, the following day we would be on leave. We'd already organised a ride to Baghdad on a couple of Blackhawks, and then it would be the big metal freedom bird to nowhere city, in this case Dubai, for twenty-four hours of drinks, prostitutes, more drinks and five-star luxury, before getting our flights to wherever we'd come from, although Paul and Travis were going to Thailand for a spot of sex tourism.

'Okay, it's agreed then. We won't mention it to anyone,' I said. Everybody agreed, and that was the end of it. We pretended that it had never happened and moved on. That night we packed our kit, and the following morning we handed in our equipment and weapons before boarding the choppers. We were soon in Baghdad and were on the first flight to Dubai, but what followed was a blur of Russian working girls, some very strange bars and a lot of real food. I sacked it early— prostitutes aren't my style— and I wanted to enjoy the hotel for a bit. Real sheets, a bath— all the things I'd been missing. In the early days I used to spend a fortune on leave because after a couple of months of making do, all you wanted to do was spoil yourself, and I did a lot of that, but now I wanted to be sober enough to make the flight the following morning. I did find out later that when Ivan had a drink he turned into a real lady-killer and was soon fighting the girls off— a strange thought. But that was that, another rotation done. Still alive and still with no intention of quitting.

10

What's The Worst That Can Happen?

I spent my leave thinking seriously about where I was going and what was going to be next. I was becoming more and more conscious of the fact that unless I had a game plan, ten years from now I'd still be a PSD team leader. True, I'd still be earning a lot of money compared to most people, but I would have been playing the numbers too long and asking for trouble. What's more, it was a young man's game— and I wasn't young when I started. I didn't want to be like a lot of the guys that were well over 50 and still grunting around, and if I didn't have an exit strategy, that would be me. Unfortunately I didn't have a lot of mates giving me a leg-up into management, the other reality being that people rarely got promoted on merit. It was mostly knowing the right people or kissing the right arse. I'm not exaggerating. Of all the managers I ever had, maybe 10 per cent of them I had any respect for; the rest I just tried to stay alive following their orders, which is not a good figure. I've been doing this for over ten years, not counting military service, so I know what I'm talking about.

I flew back and met up with the team in Kuwait. They'd all had a great time. The sex tourists had several blanks in their memories, one of whom, I won't say which one, was fairly certain he'd had sex with a lady boy, although he said it was okay and that he wasn't gay. The other one had a strange rash that he was certain would go away on its own, but unfortunately for him it didn't and he ended up on a course of very strong antibiotics. A few weeks later, when he showed me his undercarriage in the showers one day, I pointed out that it looked like he'd been shot in the bollocks with a shotgun and ordered him to go and see the army medics at the field hospital. It was then that we found out that 27 per cent of the soldiers at that base had the clap, which made sense. You had thousands of soldiers of both sexes living in close proximity and risking their lives every day, so it doesn't take a Sigmund Freud to work out that they'll be at it all the time, and as a result, most US Army camps had a clap epidemic going on. I don't know why I was surprised, but I was.

We continued on the survey missions, and the country manager came and visited us, thanked us for doing such a good job and promised us another six years. He also banged on about how the project was sewn up and the clients were really happy, but less than a week later he was back, telling us to pack our bags as the company had lost the contract to Aegis. Yes, the clients were happy, but they would have been happier paying less, which was the way of things. Companies that undercut each other got the gig, and clients made sure that contracts were short and were always inviting bids for new suppliers. But that's business, as I soon learnt. There's no loyalty where money is involved. As a result of this we all spent the next few weeks bouncing around all over the place, filling in for teams that were on leave or undermanned. Unfortunately one of those jobs meant us going back to Mosul, at the height of the bad old days, but work is work and you don't turn it down. I warned the others about the place, which hadn't got any safer. In fact, recent intelligence reports indicated that it was rapidly descending into chaos.

'Remind me when I get there to rewrite my résumé,' Geoff said over the net. We'd only just hit the main road from Anaconda and were accelerating northwards.

'It's not that bad, surely?' I said.

'Yes it is,' Travis replied.

We were all getting a bit pissed off with the uncertainty, and teams that were on leave were being told to stay at home because they weren't needed. With contracts finishing or being lost to other companies, people were often put in a very difficult position. Should you wait it out and hope that the company would get new contracts and redeploy you quickly? Don't forget that you wouldn't be getting paid while the company expected you to wait. Should you take a chance and jump ship? That's if you could. Jobs were getting scarcer, wages were dropping, and suddenly there were a lot more ex-military types with Iraq and Afghan experience who would work for less to get their foot in the door. Bearing in mind the rubbish money a soldier was on, even a lower wage in the private sector was a massive improvement, but for those of us who had been earning those high salaries it was rapidly becoming a choice of staying and working for less or quitting while you were ahead. I'm afraid that I wasn't that smart, even though my wages had recently gone down, not by a lot, but the writing was on the wall. I had the feeling that Geoff wouldn't be the only one working on his résumé.

'Static vehicle, left,' I said over the net.

It was my job to warn the vehicle behind of any potential threats that I spotted during missions— parked vehicles, Hajji squatting in a bush having a piss, anything that looked odd. The downside was that *everything* looked odd, and on an average road move you were pretty much on the net constantly.

Two clicks in reply, then bang! The static vehicle was a VBIED (vehicle-borne IED). I remember the windscreen of my vehicle exploding and coming out of its frame, and how clear the sky looked without the thick armoured glass that I'd spent my days looking through, making it look slightly out of focus all the time. Another slow-motion moment. I tried to clear my head but couldn't. I knew this was serious. My left side was covered in blood and I could smell diesel and smoke. More worryingly, I could feel myself losing my senses and knew that I was about to lose consciousness— every operator's nightmare. In a contact you need to be awake; if you're out, you don't know what's going to happen to the rest of the team. My biggest worry was being the only survivor but not being able to defend myself, because when Hajji picks through the convoy like a vulture you're going straight into the boot of a car and away to the nearest town. If you're lucky, you'll die of your wounds or have enough of your wits left to pull the pin on the hand grenade that you keep in your assault vest for that very purpose. If you're not lucky, you'll wake up chained to a radiator in Sadr City making your YouTube debut in an orange boiler suit and having your head hacked off for the whole world to see.

The rest of this story is told from the point of view of Geoff and the rest of the team, as I lost consciousness seconds after the first IED and was out of the fight.

The front vehicle disappeared in a massive fireball as the car parked just off the road detonated. Geoff immediately began looking for targets as a second IED detonated just behind his vehicle, the force of the blast pushing him sideways and the vehicle disappearing into the thick smoke of the first IED. They narrowly missed the rear of the front vehicle as they slid past. Geoff could see that the windows were shattered and had become crazy-paved but couldn't see the crew. It was a surreal moment, like suddenly driving into a fog-bank on a dark night. Hearing AK-47 fire from the rear, they'd already decided that the priority was the front vehicle. They could use the smoke as cover and hopefully extract the crew. Geoff looked at Patrick, his driver. He was okay.

'Travis, you okay?' he asked over the radio.

'Yeah, can't see a thing. Definitely taking rounds from the rear,' Travis replied from the rear gunner's position. Geoff knew that he wouldn't return fire yet. Firstly he couldn't see anything and, most importantly, if anyone had got out of the front vehicle he could easily have hit them by accident.

'Roger; we're going to dismount and try to extract the other vehicle. When we stop, give us covering fire,' Geoff added.

'Roger,' Travis replied.

'Anyone in the front vehicle, can you hear me?' Geoff said over the net desperately. He repeated himself several times but heard nothing. 'Take the keys, leave the vehicle,' he said to Patrick.

For all they knew, all the occupants of the other vehicle were dead, and it would take everyone to extract them quickly. Travis jumped down from the bucket as Geoff and Patrick reached the rear of their truck.

'Follow me. Everything's hostile,' Geoff said as they ran back into the smoke.

It had started to clear, but the rear tyres of the damaged vehicle were on fire and giving off poisonous thick smoke that was still providing them with a bit of cover. As they reached the bonnet Geoff saw movement just off the road about 50 metres away.

'Target, front!' he screamed as he leant over the bonnet, flicked off the safety and started firing towards the threat.

Geoff heard someone shout and was sure his first round hit the target dead centre. Travis began firing short bursts at the same place, and beyond that was a car on a small parallel track. Sneaky bastards. From their position on the ground they could see it, but from the direction we had come it was hidden by dead ground. Geoff looked inside the stricken vehicle. From the angle it had stopped at he could only see the driver, but it didn't look good. There was a massive chunk missing from the headrest, and the whiteness of the foam sticking out of it drew his attention because it looked so out of place. Paul's head was back against the door, his face covered in blood, but that was all Geoff could see. There was no movement, and it was obvious that the driver's side had taken the full force of the explosion.

'Take out the vehicle, and anyone near it!' Geoff shouted.

Travis switched his fire and began engaging the car. If it was the getaway vehicle, they weren't going to be using it. If it wasn't, tough luck. Wrong place, wrong time. Patrick was kneeling by the front bumper on Geoff's right and knew that their flank was covered. If the enemy had been clever enough to put shooters on the other side of the road also, they would have had problems covering left, right and rear with only three people left, but they were lucky. Geoff needed to get inside the vehicle, but was worried about what he would find. But he knew he had to do it. Steeling himself, he opened the commander's door. It was slightly smoky but he could see clearly enough.

I was unconscious, but looked okay. My left side was covered in blood. He slung his rifle and quickly looked for injuries. I had a gash in my leg and upper arm, and Geoff could tell that the blood had come from Paul. He lifted my eyelid and saw that my pupils dilated from the light, and that I was breathing, but he needed to be fast and quickly prioritise the situation. He then looked at Paul, who looked fucked. Geoff leant over and could see straight away that most of the back of his head was missing. A large piece of frag had come through the side armour, taking out the headrest and killing Paul, and had exited through the roof. Looking at the patterns of the holes, and their size and position, he could see this quite plainly. He could also see that Paul had just landed at the bottom of the list for medical treatment. 'It must have been instantaneous,' was all that he thought to himself.

The other two were still engaging targets outside. Geoff opened the rear door and found Ivan lying across the rear seats, semi-conscious and holding the top of his thigh. There was a ragged hole in his trousers and the whole leg and groin area was soaked in blood. Geoff knew that it was another life-threatening injury. Many people think that taking a round to the leg, like in the movies, is nothing, but if the femoral artery gets compromised you can bleed to death in minutes.

'Patrick, get in here!' Geoff shouted as he backed out of the doorway, grabbing Ivan's SAW. He wouldn't be needing it and the extra firepower would be useful. Patrick ran over.

'Lew looks okay, Paul's dead and Ivan has an arterial leg wound. I'll swap with you,' Geoff said as he moved to the front of the vehicle and started to return fire with the SAW.

Patrick nodded and went to work. He was a very good medic, and Geoff knew that Ivan was in better hands with him.

'Travis, can you see anything?' Geoff said over the net.

'There's a few of them behind the car, I think.'

Geoff pulled a grenade out and threw it, but the car was just a bit too far away and it fell short. It did, however, make one of them run straight into fire from the SAW that Travis was firing. Patrick put his rifle down and climbed inside the rear of the vehicle to get better access to Ivan's leg.

'You're okay, Ivan, just a scratch,' he said, trying to reassure him.

Ivan nodded but was rapidly losing consciousness, and also loosening his grip on the wound. Using the Tuffcut scissors that he carried, Patrick cut away the trouser leg to expose the wound. It was a nasty hole halfway between the knee and waist on the inside of the thigh, exactly where the femoral artery is.

There are several methods available to the combat medic when treating this potentially fatal yet manageable wound, and most carry a tourniquet, which is effective but very painful due to the huge amount of pressure that has to be used to cut off the blood flow. A friend of mine who lost both legs and one arm when he was blown up in Afghanistan said that the most painful thing of the whole experience was having three tourniquets used on him. One of the biggest problems is that it replicates a crush injury, so under the point of pressure cells begin to break down and become toxic. When the tourniquet is released the toxins are flushed into the bloodstream, and for this reason it's generally accepted that once you put a tourniquet on, it stays in place until removed by medical professionals at a hospital.

Another method is direct pressure using one of the many field dressings available. Unfortunately with arterial bleeds, the only really effective way to stop the bleeding is by cutting off the blood supply or plugging the hole. Field dressings help, but not enough, and judging by the amount of blood that was soaked into the trousers and the rear seat, something had to be done quickly and effectively.

This leaves haemostatic treatments, which are total life-savers and became popular really quickly after the invasion of Iraq and Afghan. There are many on the market, but I used Celox, which in simple terms is a powder that forms a synthetic clot big enough to plug an arterial bleed. It works almost instantly and, unlike a tourniquet, doesn't hurt and allows blood to get to the rest of the leg through the undamaged veins. It therefore reduces the risk of tissue death, which could result in the loss of a limb, and for that reason I always used it rather than a tourniquet. I used tourniquets only for traumatic amputations. Celox was originally military issue, but now anyone can buy it from a number of online stockists. You pour the entire contents of the sachet into the hole and it clots—it's that simple. Apparently it's made from the shells of marine crustaceans, which is amazing when you think about it. At the time, a new delivery device had recently come on the market, designed specifically for this kind of penetrating femoral injury. The pre-packed syringe-type applicator was pre-loaded with the product, which allowed it to get right where it was needed. Among the best things to come out of wars are the advances in medical science, and in my opinion this is right up there with infection control.

Travis had been banging on about the applicator for weeks. He'd bought half a dozen using his own money and had given Patrick two to put in his personal med kit that he carried in his assault vest. He ripped it open, assembled it, pulled off the blue cap on the end, looked at the hole, and taking a deep breath pushed the applicator into the hole. Ivan moved slightly. It must have hurt, as he was still just about awake but not coherent. Patrick kept pushing until most of the applicator was in, pushing the plunger and then withdrawing it, making sure that all of the Celox was used. Pulling out a field dressing, he tightly wrapped the leg, using extra pressure to help the Celox do its job, and then quickly checked Ivan over for other injuries before moving on to the other casualties. Now he was in medic mode. The other two would handle the enemy, but his priority was the lives of his friends. Behind the driver's seat was most of Paul's brain, and it made Patrick stop for a second. But he knew he had to carry on, pushing it to the back of his mind, to become one of those things that you find yourself thinking about years later, usually for no reason, or after seeing something that reminds you. Then before you know it you're staring into space and someone's asking you if you're okay. It happens to me all the time.

Patrick got out of the vehicle and went to the commander's seat. He checked my breathing and pulse, but couldn't find any life-threatening injuries. There was nothing to suggest any kind of brain injury, uneven breathing or any other symptoms. TBI (traumatic brain injury) was a common injury, often fatal, and any kind of head trauma could lead to things like cerebral compression. A bang on the head today can kill you tomorrow. Essentially the brain swells and has nowhere to go because the skull's trapping it, and this requires hospitalisation and the usually surgery. Patrick knew this, so there was nothing more he could do. He'd done his job, having stopped the bleeding and stabilised Ivan, confirmed that Paul was dead, and checked that his TL was stable. Now we had to extract.

'We need to get these guys to a hospital,' Patrick shouted over to Geoff.

'Take these, call it in, get medevac and QRF,' Geoff said, handing over his GPS and satellite phone. Everyone in the team knew how to use the comms equipment and the procedure for reporting a contact or requesting support. 'We're going to kill every last one of these bastards,' he added.

Looking very pissed off, Patrick nodded and went back to the casualties, calling in the necessary support and sending a quick contact report with our location back to our Ops room, which would then co-ordinate and chase the Army, making sure that we had the help that we needed. It wasn't the fastest way of doing it, as we didn't always have direct comms with the Army, but it worked.

'Travis, move forward. We need to secure the ground for choppers,' Geoff said over the net.

They'd been on the ground for about five minutes now and needed to get control of the situation quickly or risk being engaged by opportunists in the area.

'Firing warning shots,' Patrick said over the net, followed by several shots at some locals who were showing an interest in what was going on.

He was covering our rear while Geoff and Travis prepared to push forward— all pretty textbook stuff thus far. Travis bounded forward while Geoff covered. They needed to push up to the vehicle and take out any targets along the way, as it was the only place that any fire was coming from, so the only current threat. Travis hit the dirt and started to put down heavy fire while Geoff moved forward and slightly beyond him. There were some trees on the right and he got down behind one and began covering while Travis moved forward into cover.

'Grenades,' Geoff said over the net.

There was still sporadic fire from the rear, as Patrick was busy keeping the locals' heads down. Travis pulled a grenade out and looked over to Geoff. They threw their grenades at the same time, and as soon as they'd clearly heard two explosions they charged the last 20 metres to the vehicle, intent on killing everything. On reaching the car, they found three bodies but five rifles on the ground, pissing Geoff off that at least two had escaped. Travis checked the bodies to make sure they were dead and then began changing the box of ammo on his SAW. Geoff rattled his and found it was low, but the spare ammo was still with Ivan. However, he still had his M4 slung, so even if he ran out on the SAW he was covered.

They both headed back over to the vehicles and began to secure the area as best they could. Travis didn't look inside— he couldn't deal with seeing Paul's body. We were all close, but those two were room-mates and had a lot in common. Twenty minutes later the first ground unit appeared, closely followed by the medevac choppers. The casualties and Paul's body were loaded while Geoff stripped all the kit out of the dead vehicle and burnt it. They then followed the US call sign back to Speicher, which luckily was were the casualties were going, and once in, did the necessary reporting and were told to stay firm until support arrived. However, that might not be for a couple of days, so they got some accommodation from KBR and cleaned up. Nobody wanted to talk about it. They just sat there, surrounded by all the soldiers at the food area.

'I'm done, guys. That's it for me,' Travis said.

'Me too. It's not worth it,' Patrick added.

Geoff nodded. He hadn't yet decided, but knew that he'd probably wrap as well. He didn't want to work with another team, so that would be it now. Ivan would be out for a while, although everyone suspected that he'd come back. Geoff wasn't sure about me, but nobody could blame him if he sacked it. He'd seen more than most.

'Okay, I'll tell the grown-ups. Make it official. When you get a chance, go to the MWR and send an email to HR,' Geoff said. He was the second in command, so while I was unable to do the job that made him responsible for the team.

'What about you?' Travis asked.

'I don't know. I really don't,' Geoff replied.

11

How Many Fingers Am I Holding Up?

My head was thumping. I didn't have the guts to open my eyes. I knew I was in a safe place because I could hear people speaking English and wherever I was smelt clean. I opened one eye, which didn't help the pain— in fact, it made it a lot worse— then the other, and the light increased my headache considerably. I looked around and it was obvious that I was in a hospital. I thought I was in Speicher because I'd been there before and recognised it. The first thing I did was to make sure that everything was still attached. I then felt my face, and it felt like it should have. I lay there for quite a while before I tried to move. My watch was missing, so I couldn't tell what time or even what day it was. One of the nurses saw me awake and came over.

'How are you feeling?' she asked.

'How do I look?' I replied.

'You'll be fine. Just a few stitches and cuts and bruises.'

'How many others came in with me?'

'You and a Russian guy. He's been in surgery so he's a bit out of it at the moment, but he'll be fine.'

I asked what else she knew, but she only had the details of me and Ivan. She said that she didn't know about any fatalities but would find out for me, but I remember vaguely knowing that Paul was dead. It was the last thing I remembered before everything went black. It was three o'clock in the morning, but the nurse let me get up and after an hour or so I felt strong enough to walk around. I found Ivan, who was asleep, but I could see from the bandages that he'd been hit in the leg and guessed that it must have been serious if he'd needed surgery.

It was very odd waking up in a strange place with only part of the story. I didn't have my stuff as that had all been picked up by the team earlier. I'd arrived the previous afternoon and the team had come in shortly after, grabbed my kit and made sure that Ivan and I were okay. The medics had told them to come back in the morning, which was still several hours away, so I used the time to try and decide what I was going to do. I'd suddenly lost interest, and was 90 per cent in favour of binning it and moving on. As I went past Ivan's bed at six o'clock I saw that he was half awake.

'How are you doing?' I asked.

'Okay. I get shot in leg, or maybe shrapnel. Anyway needed surgery to repair artery,' he replied.

'You were lucky. You could have bled to death.'

He nodded. I could tell that he didn't want to talk, so left him and went back to my bed. The rest of the team arrived after breakfast, and I knew as soon as I didn't see Paul that I was right and that he was dead. Part of me had hoped that I was remembering the events wrong and that maybe I'd imagined those last few moments of consciousness. Geoff told me what had happened while Travis and Patrick went to find Ivan and steal as much medical kit as they could.

'What are you going to do?' I asked.

'We've all quit. I wasn't sure, but I've thought about it and don't think I can do this any more. The other two quit straight away, so I knew the team wouldn't be the same. I think our team's the only reason I carried on so long,' Geoff said.

At that moment I knew what to do also. He'd hit the nail on the head. It had all been about the team, not the company or the country, or even the money. It was the team. Some are average and you can take it or leave it, but ours was tight and professional. Without that, we had nothing.

'Same here. I've had enough to,' I said. My mind was made up there and then.

I was allowed out the next day. Ivan was medevaced out of the country, but was back the following year and went onto a convoy contract with another company. He sacked it a year later and I lost touch with him, but at least he got out alive, which was the main thing. Over the next week the company sent us all home, but unfortunately we didn't go out together and had to say our goodbyes in Baghdad rather than on an epic bender in Dubai. I was left with a real feeling of loss after that. I wasn't depressed in the clinical sense, but it took me a few months to get my head back into it. I still keep in touch with the other three. Travis and Patrick became paramedics and deploy as medics to remote locations— less security- and more clinic-based. One works offshore on an oil rig and the other works in an oilfield in Basra. Geoff joined the police and is currently doing very well. Still in harm's way, but that's what we're used to.

I spent the next couple of years as an instructor on hostile environment courses run by one of the large PSD outfits, training people who wanted to be PSD operators. The money was good but the job was boring, and the longer I was out of the sandpit the more I felt that it was changing and that what I was teaching was out of date. Last year I redeployed, only to find out how right I was. I was offered a job as a PSD team leader. The money now is almost laughable, but that is across the industry. The one thing that all the companies agree on is keeping the wages similar, as you get a lot less jumping ship. Now everyone who's done three years in the Army has been to Afghanistan or Iraq and knows about the PSD companies because they've seen them during their deployments, and although the companies know the money is shit, they also know that these kids will work for it because it's still a lot better than what they were getting in the Army. So there's been a massive influx of 25-year-olds, all earning what for them is a good wage, which means that the wages are constantly dropping and making it more difficult to get out in the sandpit now, as there are far more operators than there are jobs. Some companies have started employing Eastern Europeans and paying them even less, but for a Romanian it's still a good wage. When I first deployed, I was on $145,000 a year, whereas the average now is $78,000 a year, give or take a few grand. That's a massive jump backwards.

I had my flight details sent to me. I flew to Istanbul and then took a connecting flight to Baghdad. Unlike the old days, several carriers now fly direct to Iraq, and now that the Yanks and British have left, the Iraqi Police and Army are most definitely in charge of the country. The old days are a distant memory, but that's fine. I'm all for evolution. When I arrived in Baghdad, I had to get a visa, which involved queuing up for a couple of hours and paying $80. This gave me a three-month visa, but I had to apply for residency within ten days, which involved a blood test for HIV and then more money until I eventually got my passport back with permission to stay. So you pay for permission to enter, then for permission to stay, and before you leave you pay for an exit stamp for permission to leave. I then took a taxi from the airport terminal to the airport car park, which can cost up to $50 for a trip of roughly 3 kilometres. PSD teams are allowed within the confines of the airport only with special permission, so most just wait at the car park and the taxis do the dropping-off and picking-up from the terminal.

There are no foreign military bases now, all the old ones having been handed back to the Iraqis to fuck up as they see fit. No more PXs, I'm afraid, but it's their country, so fair's fair. We now also had to abide by the rules of the road, and the Iraqi Police and Army had total jurisdiction over us. Baghdad could be hard to navigate purely because the traffic was a nightmare. There were many checkpoints in place in an attempt to stop all the IEDs and terrorist activity, the attention having shifted from us to sectarian violence. I've spoken to people recently in Baghdad, talking about the old days from both my perspective and theirs as Iraqis living under occupation, and found out that they all believed that we were Jews, the rumour mill of the mosque or street corner having spread that nugget of misinformation and instantly made us a righteous target in their minds.

All security companies now had to be registered with several government agencies, such as the Ministry of Interior, which issued the paperwork that allowed you to travel on the roads. Everything had to be registered— the vehicles, the weapons, the personnel— with appropriate passes for everything. I had to carry a card for my weapon, a card for me, and paperwork for the vehicles, all of which was examined at checkpoints, and if you were unlucky a zealous police officer could go through all your equipment to make sure that the serial numbers matched the paperwork. If not, you could get arrested and your equipment was confiscated. Obviously we got charged for all this by the Iraqi Government, and another favourite trick was to issue things weekly or fortnightly so that the company was constantly applying for permission to do its job and constantly paying for the privilege. I personally don't care if the Iraqi Government was making a killing, as the majority of the clients now are oil companies, which I'm sure are making a killing also. On the upside, the vehicle situation had improved, as we were now using factory armoured Land Cruisers with all the bells and whistles, which was comforting. All companies were issued with a number that the vehicles had to carry, like racing numbers, on the side, front and back, the number corresponding to the company, so if you did something wrong your company could be identified straight away.

The team structure had also changed. Before, everybody was an expat, but now the government insisted on locals being employed. In my team, for instance, there were two vehicles. I was the TL and had an Iraqi driver, and my 2ic in the other vehicle was a local, as was his driver. Don't get me wrong, I'm not complaining— I'm just pointing out the differences. I was lucky as the team that I had were good, having been trained very well, and we also did our own training all the time. They were as good as anyone I'd previously worked with, and I'd have fought with them and defended them as much as any of the people I'd worked with in the past, but I know that a lot of the old guard would point-blank refuse to work with Iraqis. Some people fear change, and the one thing I noticed quickly was how much I was in the minority. Hardly any of the other expats had been out of the Army long, and none of them had worked out there in the old days, which to be fair was probably a good thing, as they didn't know any different. The funny thing was, a lot of my local PSD guys had worked with the US Army as interpreters and were the first Iraqi PSD guys when the DOD was still operating. I was amazed how many had ended up living in the US, being entitled to a US green card (subject to security checks) because they'd worked for the US Government in Iraq. I was quite surprised and impressed that the Yanks had recognised their sacrifice. Working for the Coalition as an Iraqi wasn't the safest way to spend your time. However, while I had my Iraqi team at least two came back to Iraq and said they were disappointed with living in the US. It wasn't like they'd seen it on television, and was expensive, which is one thing that hadn't changed in Iraq. It was still cheap, and the locals were paid very well as PSD operators, so to go from that to probably working in McDonalds— well, I know where I'd rather be.

The missions are also very different now. In Baghdad at least, you're just an armoured taxi service and missions are short. A meeting here, a meeting there, pick-ups from the airport, and that's about it. You get in the vehicle at a safe location, get out at a safe location, and do the same in reverse— it's mind-numbing. I managed a year like this but found it hard to stay awake. I can't remember the last time I heard about a PSD team getting in a contact. There were a few IEDs down in Basra, but the general opinion was that it was meant for the Army and that the teams just happened to be in the wrong place at the wrong time. Fortunately there weren't any casualties. Operating down south is very different to the cities. The guys in the Basra area spend their days on the oilfields, shuttling engineers around rigs and oil refineries. Fourteen-hour days aren't unusual, and no days off. This is the majority of the PSD work available now, and you can drive around the oilfields and see nothing but PSD vehicles all day, whereas in Baghdad I was lucky if I saw another PSD team once a week on the roads. It's the shit jobs down south that the young lads leaving the Army are getting, and the few old sweats like me with a lot of experience get a cushy number in Baghdad, if lucky. However, those contracts are few and far between, and I know people as experienced as me, and who need the money, working like a dog in Basra for peanuts. But that's the nature of the game.

I lasted a year back in Iraq before I left. It didn't hold the same appeal as it had done. I dare say that if I hadn't known any different I could have stuck it out, but the soul was gone, the whole feeling had changed. The Iraqis used to say that they could leave their doors open at night because all the crooks were in the government, and it was soul-destroying to see the country being ruined from within by Iraqi bureaucrats and corruption, and to see the people killing each other, often because some politician or religious leader was winding them up to do it. Every month hundreds of civilians are killed just because they are Shia or Sunni, and all that the people in power care about is making as much money as possible.

I have to say that last year gave me a whole new respect for the Iraqis. They want the same things we do, albeit that they have some strange habits and some of them have tried to kill me, but we did invade their country and turn everything upside down. Working in Baghdad with an Iraqi team gave me a new insight that I hadn't had before, and as one of them pointed out to me, I'd given my blood for the country, I'd seen my friends die and had spent many years living there, and whatever my personal motivations had been for going to Iraq, I'd been part of its destruction and reconstruction. So it was as much my country as anyone else's, as I'd sacrificed for it and risked everything for it. As far as my team was concerned, I was as Iraqi as they were. I have to admit that it was true that part of me was at home in Baghdad. I didn't hate the country, and it did feel like my second home. Iraq to me is like that barking dog that everybody kicks, but it won't stop barking.

So that was it for me. Ten years on, I was finally done. I would like to say that it had been a pleasure, but I can't. I deployed straight from the Army, and in many ways it was exactly the same. We operated along the same lines, used the same discipline— well, some more than others— and fought in the same sand. I met a lot of interesting people, probably killed as many interesting people, and nearly died on more than one occasion. I made a good living and learnt a lot, working with people from all parts of the planet and trying to learn as much as I could about the places they were from. As a result, I'm a better, more rounded person with a lot of knowledge that I'd otherwise not have. But if you asked me what overriding feeling I came away with from my years in Iraq, I'd have to say that it was one of emptiness, with a lot of sadness. Like when you're told you have cancer or some other life-changing bad news, you go through stages— anger, denial and finally acceptance. For me, working in Iraq was like that. I've been through many stages and evolutions, and my personality and character have been changed dramatically as a result.

The average person goes through life without ever getting into a fight or having a near-fatal car crash; they just exist. But for me, and those like me, life was lived in a different world, walking a very different path. To us it was normal, and the thought of gardening and conservatories scares me as much as a complicated ambush would scare the average history teacher. I would do it again. True, it has scarred me both physically and mentally, but it has definitely made me what I am now. Some may not think that a good thing, but it works for me. I have a lot less patience with the mundane, but I don't focus on or obsess about things that aren't important. I spend my time worrying about the important things and ignoring the irrelevant, and that also includes people. I try not to talk to idiots, although that's hard to do because there are times when I feel surrounded by nothing but morons and oxygen thieves, but I don't allow them to bog me down. Unfortunately ignorant people are more common than enlightened ones.

Working in Iraq was no less honourable than fighting for my own country. Only a fool kids himself that he's defending his country. All the wars that I've fought have been doing the dirty work of politicians. I've never stood behind my country's borders ready to repel an invasion. That's what fighting for your country means. If anything, the people we invaded were the ones fighting for their way of life, and I never kidded myself that what I was doing was making the population of my country any better. However, we are soldiers; we fight for the man on our left. It's that simple. The politicians are the ones who probably have priority for boarding the hell express.

As for the locals, I feel for them, I really do. Many older people remember Saddam Hussein with fond nostalgia. Yes, he might wipe out your family if you looked at him the wrong way, but the country was safe. You could leave your windows unlocked, the Shias and the Sunnis lived together without any friction, utilities were free, and everything else was cheap, especially fuel. In the world they now occupy of constant suicide bombings and kidnappings, corrupt government and, even worse, religious leaders getting their young people to kill themselves in the name of whatever group they belong to, it's no surprise that people look back and miss the old mentally unhinged dictator.

I can understand why Iraq is now in total chaos. What is worse is the fact that the same people who were part of the old regime are still there, and are still the ones with the money. And all these foreign jihadists are crawling all over Iraq, killing the locals because they claim to know what's best for the population. The one thing that was constant when I worked there, apart from local criminals attacking convoys for their cargo, was that the majority of the insurgency were all foreigners claiming to represent the Iraqi people— and they're still doing it today. Groups like the Islamic State, who are now fighting in Syria and northern Iraq, want their own caliphate on the Iraq/Syria border and are giving the Iraqi army the runaround in Fallujah and occupying several cities, and are also the ones using IEDs against the civilian population. If the locals want to be evaporated when out shopping, then they're definitely giving them what they want, and this is the unfortunate legacy of the 'freedom' that we constantly shouted from the rooftops before and after the invasion. Having seen it for myself, the cost of that freedom was not only thousands of lives on both sides, but a massive amount of instability that will gather momentum throughout the whole region, not just Iraq, and will come back to haunt us with a vengeance. Sadly I suspect that all those PSD operators who are currently hanging around for contracts won't have to wait too long before they're being offered employment further afield than Iraq, and that what's coming will make my experiences seem like a picnic.